MICROECONOMICS
DEMYSTIFIED

DR. CRAIG A. DEPKEN, II

McGraw-Hill

New York   Chicago   San Francisco   Lisbon   London
Madrid   Mexico City   Milan   New Delhi   San Juan
Seoul   Singapore   Sydney   Toronto

The McGraw·Hill Companies

McGraw-Hill
2100 Powell Street, 10th Floor
Emeryville, California 94608
U.S.A.

To arrange bulk purchase discounts for sales promotions, premiums, or fund-raisers, please contact **McGraw-Hill** at the above address.

Microeconomics Demystified

1234567890 FGR FGR 0198765

ISBN 0-07-145911-1

Acquisitions Editor
Megg Morin

Project Editor
Samik Roy Chowdhury (Sam)

Acquisitions Coordinator
Agatha Kim

Technical Editor
Trisha Bezmen

Copy Editor
Ritu Mundra

Proofreader
Connie Blazewicz

Indexer
Broccoli Information Management

Composition
International Typesetting
and Composition

Illustration
International Typesetting
and Composition

Cover Series Design
Margaret Webster-Shapiro,
Brian Boucher

Cover Illustration
Lance Lekander

This book was composed with Adobe® InDesign® CS Mac.

This book is dedicated to Linda and Campbell; both have helped demystify my life.

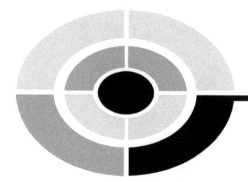

ABOUT THE AUTHOR

Dr. Craig A. Depken, II, is an associate professor of economics at the University of Texas at Arlington. Dr. Depken graduated with an undergraduate degree in economics from the University of Georgia in 1991, and with a PhD in economics from the University of Georgia in June 1996. He received a tenure-track appointment at the University of Texas at Arlington in the fall of 1996. Dr. Depken was promoted to Associate Professor with Tenure in the spring of 2002.

Dr. Depken has published extensively in peer-reviewed journals, such as *The Review of Industrial Organization, The Journal of Business, The Journal of Economic Behavior and Organization, The Journal of Sports Economics, Economics of Education Review, and Economics Letters*, focusing primarily on the economics of sports and various topics in applied microeconomics. He has also received awards for his teaching, including the inaugural *Innovation in Teaching* award in the College of Business at the University of Texas in Arlington for his integration of the then young Internet and traditional classroom teaching. He was nominated in 2004 for the National Faculty of the Year award of the National Society of College Scholars.

CONTENTS

ACKNOWLEDGMENTS

I primarily want to thank my parents, Geraldine and Craig Depken for their countless sacrifices in helping me throughout the years. Their examples of personal dedication to learning and investigation are testimony to the effect that parents have on their children.

I also owe a debt to the faculty of the economics department at the University of Georgia, especially Arthur Snow, Fred Bateman, and David Kamerschen. Without these individuals I would not have been able to complete my graduate degree program or obtained the extensive experience of teaching at the undergraduate level that ultimately provided the basis for the approach taken in this book.

For their anonymous efforts, I acknowledge the undergraduate students that took my principles of economics courses at the University of Georgia and the University of Texas at Arlington. At the University of Georgia, especially, several students made significant contributions to my approach in teaching the principles of microeconomics, many of which appear in this book.

I thank the faculty of the Department of Economics at the University of Texas at Arlington for providing one of the best environments in the country for research and collegiality. Our countless discussions about economics—always interesting and provocative—have provided some of the examples included in this text. I specifically want to thank Daniel Himarios for his personal support during my appointment as assistant professor and my promotion to associate professor. Richard Buttimer, Bill Crowder, Courtney LaFountain, Robert Sonora, Mike Ward, and Dennis Wilson are also acknowledged for their indirect contributions to this text.

Finally, I thank Trisha Bezmen for her helpful comments on an earlier version of this manuscript; her eye to fine details is greatly appreciated.

INTRODUCTION

This book provides a self-study approach to understanding the theory of microeconomics, avoiding unnecessary mathematics. The approach in this book assumes that you have not studied economics before.

What exactly is economics? You are probably familiar with economic terms from watching the nightly news or reading the daily newspaper. Economics is often discussed in terms of unemployment, the stock market, gross national product, the trade deficit, or consumer confidence. However, none of these topics really defines economics. Instead, these are elements of the broader set of questions that economics addresses.

Economics is a relatively young field of formal investigation. While individuals have made choices from the first days of consciousness, the focused investigation into the elements of human choice that would today be considered "mainstream" economics can be dated to Adam Smith's 1776 treatise *An Inquiry into the Causes of the Wealth of Nations*. As the title suggest, Smith was concerned with what influenced the general well being of nation states and the citizenry therein. After Smith's work was disseminated (in the non-Internet age!) several notable economists extended his analysis to include topics that are today considered standard elements of a principles course in economics, including Ricardo, Mill, Jevons, Edgeworth, Marshall, and Keynes.

Many of these names are unfamiliar to those who have not studies economics, but that does not indicate that their contributions are inconsequential. Like any field of study, economics has its "mighty pillars" upon which later generations base their study, philosophy, and approach to problem solving. The names of those who contributed the "principles of economics" are perhaps less important than the concepts themselves.

Over the past hundred years, the field of economics has expanded from the study of what makes a country "wealthy" to an area that investigates all sorts of human behavior. Indeed, some might point out that economics is less the study of numbers, such as unemployment, interest rates, and prices, as it is a study of human behavior—borrowing what "we" as economists want from the various social sciences such as sociology, political science, psychology, and anthropology. However, economists do like "labels" so that we can categorize things in a somewhat efficient manner, using a language that all economists can understand (even if they don't always agree!).

There are two basic approaches to economics: the intuitive and the mathematical. These approaches are not mutually exclusive, however, they do require different tools. Many economics textbooks are full of mathematical symbols and complicated statistical analyses accompanied by very little explanatory language; the language is mathematics and as long as one understands that language, everything intended is communicated. The alternative to the heavily mathematical treatment of economic concepts is the purely intuitive which relies upon long explanations, consisting of pages of text to describe in excruciating detail the same basic issues that the mathematical approach address. The purely intuitive approach is often dry, difficult to comprehend, and ultimately can prove frustrating to the student.

The alternative employed in this book is to combine the intuitive approach with "practical" mathematics, using nothing more than graphs and simple arithmetic to convey the concepts addressed in as simple a manner as possible. I wrote this book as if you and I were sitting and discussing the topics across a table with a couple of pencils and few pieces of scratch papers. So, I have tried to write in a conversational tone rather than a professorial tone. I have provided a brief mathematical review in Chapter 2 to refresh the basic concepts in arithmetic of the students. The rest of the book is structured as follows.

Chapter 1 introduces some of the unique terms that economists use to describe human behavior and which will be utilized throughout the rest of the book. Chapter 3 discusses production and economic growth and introduces the concept of comparative advantage, which is one of the fundamental reasons for trade. Chapter 4 develops the basic demand and supply model, a very powerful tool with which to address just about any problem in economics. Chapter 5 extends the simple supply and demand model to include the concepts of elasticity. The use of these concepts is a common-place in economics and for that reason alone warrants the focus it receives. Chapter 6 extends the simple supply and demand model in a different dimension, to include the concepts of consumer surplus and producer surplus. Chapter 7 develops the theory of household decision making, that is, how individuals decide how much to consume of the variety of products available. In my opinion, although this chapter is not unimportant, but it be considered the "most expendable." Chapter 8 derives the theory of the firm, specifically how firms decide what combinations of inputs to hire and also introduces the concept of cost. The next few chapters rely heavily upon the basic idea of why firms exist and help explain why firms do what they do. So, based on Chapter 8 and all the basic concepts developed in the previous chapters, Chapters 9, 10, and 11 outline various market models including perfect competition, perfect monopoly, and monopolistic competition. These models are examples of the exceptions to the basic supply and demand model. Chapter 12 considers the markets for the various factors of production, including labor, capital, and land. In this chapter, the basic supply and demand model is applied to perhaps the most important aspect of everyday life—where does one work and how much does one get paid? The astute reader might recognize that the role of government is essentially limited throughout the text. This is not necessarily an indication of my political leanings. Rather, the role of government in markets is a complication that can only be addressed *after* the operation of unfettered, so-called free market is understood. Hence, Chapter 13 discusses these aspects of economics.

Scattered throughout the chapters, albeit not uniformly, I have included small "insets" which take one or more of the concepts in a particular chapter and apply them to an "everyday problem." In some of these insets, there is reliance upon what is called *econometrics*, which is the statistical analysis of economic data. Econometrics is a powerful tool but also requires significant investment of time and effort to fully comprehend the underlying methodologies. Nevertheless, I have included econometric "results" for the sake of completion, although your full under-standing of the techniques is neither required nor expected.

To assist you in the learning process, and to provide a diagnostic with which you can gauge your understanding of the concepts discussed, at the end of each chapter is a short ten to fifteen question multiple choice quiz. The questions range in difficulty from basic concepts and definitions to more advanced concepts including extending the relatively simple discussion in the text to more advanced reasoning and application of the topics discussed. The end-of-chapter quizzes are supplemented by a 140 question "final exam" which is intended to be a comprehensive test of your understanding of the material discussed in the text. It is anticipated that after reading this text and successfully completing the end-of-chapter quizzes and the final exam that you should have a basic understanding of microeconomics consistent with a freshman-level introductory course.

1

The Language of Economics

Welcome to the study of microeconomics. To many people, economics is as confusing as physics. Just as we use physics every day even if we don't know its technical aspects, we all use economics on a daily basis even if we don't know its technical aspects. Yet, unlike physics, introductory economics is not as difficult as it might appear at first. However, it is true that economists speak a different "language" in the sense that we often use terms that are not common in everyday conversation.

For example, economists use terms such as the natural rate of unemployment, the elasticity of demand, opportunity cost, and comparative advantage. These terms are nothing more than a shorthand way of conveying a general concept that all economists understand, even if they don't necessarily agree with each others conclusions. While specific terms will be introduced throughout the text, this introductory discussion will focus on some general terms and concepts.

What exactly is economics? You are probably familiar with economic terms from watching the nightly news or reading the daily newspaper. Economics is often discussed in terms of unemployment, the stock market, gross national product, the trade deficit, or consumer confidence. However, none of these topics really defines economics. Instead, these are elements of the broader set of questions that economics addresses.

Economics is often thought of as a boring, dry field populated with nerdy professors who have spent too much time indoors looking at tables of numbers and discussing how things *might* work in the real world while ignoring what *actually* happens in the real world. Such stereotypes are embodied in terms such as "dismal science" and clichés such as "economists know the price of everything but the value of nothing." However, these terms are used by those who do not understand economics and its connection to everyday life. Believe it or not, the vast majority of economists are *not* concerned (in their professional or academic lives) with the intricacies of the unemployment rate. As in other fields of investigation, such as medicine, engineering, or chemistry, economists often specialize in one or more subfields of investigation. These subfields have many underlying similarities even though they demand specific concepts. Economics, broadly defined, includes the analysis of education, sports, international trade, public policy, strategy, politics, marriage, family development, transportation networks, military conflict, and pollution, as well as the intricacies of the unemployment rate and trade balances. However, even listing these subfields fails to convey what economics is truly about.

There are many definitions of economics. Even famous and brilliant economists have often disagreed amongst themselves about a simple, one-sentence definition of economics. One easy definition of economics is the study of choice, or how individuals make choices in everyday life. This definition does not induce cartwheels of excitement in most people. However, an alternative definition seems a bit more interesting: Economics is the study of how to allocate limited resources to unlimited wants. This definition implies the study of choice, or allocation of scarce resources, but conveys the important point that economics is grounded in the hard reality that most things that are desirable are unfortunately scarce.

For the most part, we all desire more of one thing or another and, for many reasons, it is likely that we are not able to satisfy all of these desires. For instance, you might want a new car but are unable to afford one; you face scarcity in your disposable income. Another person may easily afford a new car, but wants to spend more time with her family. Still another person might want a job as a taxidermist in Ames, Iowa, when there is no job to be had. This person would face a scarcity in the job market, perhaps not of their own volition, but a scarcity nonetheless.

The point is, choice without scarcity is rather uninteresting. What proves interesting, to economists at least, is how individuals, whether they be parents, employees, or business owners, make choices when they are limited in their ability to satisfy all their wants and desires. Everybody knows that some choices are easy and other choices can prove very painful. However, for the most part economics does not focus on the "difficulties" in reaching decisions. Rather, economics focuses on the process and consequences of making decisions.

When a choice is made, certain other options are necessarily not chosen—if there weren't, there would be no scarcity. Of all these possibilities involved in a choice, the most valuable option foregone in that choice is considered the opportunity cost. For example, consider your choice to spend one hour studying economics. There are countless other things you could do in that same hour, say, sit under a tree and contemplate life, watch television, or read a book. Each of these countless other things you could do can, at least conceptually, be assigned a dollar value, say, $10 per hour for sitting under a tree, $6 an hour for watching television, and $3 an hour for reading a book. Assuming these are the only three things you might do instead of studying economics, the opportunity cost of studying economics would be sitting under a tree contemplating life.

The simple example of opportunity cost given above is arguably silly; however, it is often through seemingly "silly" thought exercises that economic concepts are most easily understood (at least initially). Economics is not as abstract as you might be led to believe by watching the nightly news. In reality, economists are often most interested in understanding how actual people and organizations reach their decisions. Economists delineate different types of decision makers into three types of economic agents. An economic agent is any individual, group of individuals, or organization that participates in the allocation of scarce resources to unlimited desires. The three types of agents that economists analyze are households, firms, and governments.

A household is a person or group of people that acts as a single decision-making unit, typically in the area of consumption. For example, you and your roommates buying groceries or paying the power bill would be considered a household. However, individuals can also be considered a household; for example, a hitchhiker, a homeless person, or an individual shopping for clothes.

A firm is an organized entity that produces goods or services for households and other firms. Examples include the corporations that many of us would recognize, such as General Motors. However, the neighborhood boy who mows lawns would also be considered a firm in economics. Firms are organized and managed by households.

A government is an organization that provides goods and services to households and firms, provides redistribution of income, and provides a structure of laws in which firms and households can operate with some level of certainty. Governments are organized, manned, and managed by households.

Agents interact in an economy. An economy is an overarching mechanism that facilitates the allocation of scarce resources to competing uses. An economy decides three things: (a) what goods are produced and in what quantities, (b) how goods are produced, and (c) the distribution of the goods produced.

There are different types of economies in today's world. A pure market economy (also known as *laissez-faire* capitalism) is an economy in which individual households and firms determine the allocation of resources and the government plays an extremely limited role, primarily in enforcing property rights through a legal system and providing for a common defense. A centrally planned economy (also known as a command economy) is one in which a single individual or small group of individuals determines the allocation of resources, and individual firms and households have little say over what is produced, how goods are produced, and the distribution of these goods. A mixed economy is one in which government plays a more active role in the market process, including regulation, standardization, taxation, and income redistribution. Households and firms still have some control over what is produced, how goods are produced, and the distribution of those goods; however, the government also influences these decisions.

A market is a mechanism that facilitates the exchange of specific scarce resources amongst competing agents. There are two major types of markets: (a) goods markets in which services and finished goods are exchanged and (b) factor markets in which factors of production, that is, the things used to produce other goods and services, are exchanged. A good is anything deemed desirable by the agents in the economy, e.g., soda, pizza, Porsches, running water, or a lack of pollution. Factors of production are items used to produce goods and services. There are three major factors of production:

- *Land*. All natural resources: gold, coal, plutonium, etc and the like
- *Labor*. Effort, mental and physical, of human beings
- *Capital*. All equipment, tools, factories, and goods used in production

Thus far, the terms introduced are part of the basic language of economics. Once these and similar definitions are understood, economists can talk to each other with little difficulty. However, it is valuable to also delineate general areas of focus within the overall field of economics. In general, there are two major branches of economics. *Microeconomics* is the study of individual markets, how individual agents interact within those markets, and how individual economic agents make decisions. *Macroeconomics* is the study of national and global economic activity. To many, this distinction seems relatively semantic; after all, you can't have the macro economy (that is a national economy) without the micro economy (that is individual economic agents). While this is true, the areas of focus are somewhat exclusive to each field (although many economists would argue this point).

Macroeconomists focus on general time trends at the national or perhaps regional level. These issues would include the overall unemployment rate, overall interest rates, and whether the national income of a country is increasing or decreasing, although this list is by no means exhaustive. On the other hand, microeconomists would perhaps investigate the unemployment rate in a particular industry, or the number of employees hired by a particular firm, or whether a firm will purchase new technology at prevailing interest rates. Notice the subtle difference in the level of focus between the two areas. Macroeconomics is akin to astronomy, or the study of the universe as a whole, whereas microeconomics is akin to molecular chemistry, or the understanding of how the basic building blocks of the universe operate. In a similar way, macroeconomics addresses the overall operation of the economic "universe," whereas microeconomics focuses on the operations of the building blocks of that universe.

To be clear, this book focuses on microeconomics and the tools that have been developed over the past 150 years. While the tools of the trade can often be considered "dry," just like the tools of any trade, I would like to take exception to the stereotype that portrays economists as lacking compassion and being too factual, embodied in the cliché that economists know the prices of everything and the value of nothing. This is not the case, and some of the most heated and interesting debates in economics center on our concern over value rather than price. Economists are humans and enjoy the same range of emotion as others, even if economists are quick to point out "on the other hand." The perception that economists are too factual is the consequence of confusion between positive economics, which is the study of *what is*, and normative economics, which is the study of *what should be*.

Positive economics addresses questions such as "what is unemployment?" whereas normative economics addresses questions such as "what should the government do about unemployment?" The first question is in the spirit of "just the facts, ma'am," whereas the second question is more philosophical and, usually, controversial. Again, the distinction might seem semantic to many people but it gets to the heart of economic analysis. Economists are deeply concerned with many things, including how to foster economic development in third world countries, how to reduce criminal activity in the inner city, and how best to fund public goods such as national defense and road construction. However, before the question of what should be done about a particular problem, it is first necessary to understand the facts of the problem. Hence, economists often focus first on the positive and then on the normative.

Both positive and normative statements are tested using economic theories, which are generally based on an economic model. An economic model is a simplified view of reality. Because it is very difficult to capture all of the aspects of reality in a model, we simplify our view of reality to focus on the particular question being asked.

An economic model is comprised of two parts: assumptions and implications. The assumptions are simplifications of reality and are valid only within the context

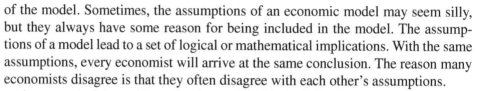

of the model. Sometimes, the assumptions of an economic model may seem silly, but they always have some reason for being included in the model. The assumptions of a model lead to a set of logical or mathematical implications. With the same assumptions, every economist will arrive at the same conclusion. The reason many economists disagree is that they often disagree with each other's assumptions.

As an example, consider a simple model with the following assumptions:

- A new car costs $20,000.
- You earn $1000 a week (legally).
- You require $600 a week for living expenses.
- You want a new car.

Given these assumptions, what is one implication of the model? If the assumptions reflect all of the aspects of your choice, you will work 50 weeks in order to be able to buy a new car. If one or more of the assumptions change, the implications of the model will change. Assume that, for whatever reason, you require $800 per week for living expenses. Now, the assumptions of the model imply that you will work 100 weeks to save for a new car.

In this book, we will analyze several different models, each investigating a different choice and using different assumptions. While each model will have its own set of assumptions, all of the models discussed have the following three basic assumptions:

- *Rationality*: Agents do what is in their best interest given the information they have at the time of their decision.
- *Preference*: Given Choice A and Choice B, agents prefer Choice A to Choice B, prefer Choice B to Choice A, or are indifferent between Choice A and Choice B.
- *Local nonsatiation*: Within a certain range, agents prefer more of a good to less of a good.

These three assumptions are relatively easy to understand. The most confusing, perhaps, is the assumption of rationality. Do people always behave rationally? In economics, we define rationality differently than in psychology. In economics, rationality only requires that people do what they think is in their best interest given the information they have. This means that people can make decisions that, after the fact, turn out to be bad decisions. For example, an individual who uses drugs is not acting rationally according to many people. However, given the information the drug user has at the time, continuing to abuse drugs might actually be a rational, even if bad, choice.

However, local nonsatiation can also be confusing. What local nonsatiation implies is that people generally desire more of the goods they consume rather than less. To some this might sound materialistic, but this is not necessarily so. Goods are items that consumers are willing to pay for but the items need not be material objects. For example, a father might want to spend more time with his children rather than working more hours at his job. On the margin, that is within a certain range or locally, the father wants more of what he deems a good, that is, spending time with his children. Whether the father actually does spend more time with his children is a question that economics is capable of answering.

Another example of local nonsatiation is finding money on the ground. Many times you see pennies, nickels, and sometimes even dimes and quarters lying on the ground. Depending on your level of nonsatiation, you might or might not bend over to pick the penny off the ground. Many people with lower income levels might be quick to pick up a penny or a quarter, whereas a multimillionaire might not bend over to pick up a $50 bill. Local nonsatiation implies that individuals prefer more of a good to less, but recognizes that each individual has his own point at which he will actually pursue more of the good in question.

Summary

This chapter has provided a brief introduction to the role of economics and some of the terms that are common to all fields of economics. Of particular focus was the delineation between microeconomics and macroeconomics. Finally, the concept of an economic model was introduced with a simple example. Three basic assumptions of economic analysis were introduced: rationality, preference, and local nonsatiation. With these basic definitions in hand, we will introduce additional terms in future chapters.

Quiz

1. Economics is the study of
    a. how to read the *Wall Street Journal*.
    b. how to allocate unlimited resources to limited wants.
    c. the back of my eyelids.
    d. how to allocate limited resources to unlimited wants.

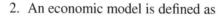

2. An economic model is defined as
    a. a waste of time.
    b. a set of assumptions that lead to a specific set of implications.
    c. a set of implications that lead to a specific set of assumptions.
    d. a normative argument as to the meaning of mankind.
3. Preference states that
    a. consumers always have an opinion between two bundles of goods.
    b. consumers never have an opinion between two bundles of goods.
    c. consumers always prefer less of a good to more of a good.
    d. none of the above
4. "The President should lower taxes."
    a. This is a positive statement.
    b. This is a negative statement.
    c. This is a normative statement.
    d. This is a silly statement.
5. An economy facilitates which of the following?
    a. What is produced
    b. How much is produced
    c. Who gets what is produced
    d. All of the above
6. Which of the following is not a factor of production?
    a. A computer
    b. A gold mine
    c. An economics teacher
    d. A $100 bill
7. The United States is most accurately described as (an)
    a. centrally planned economy.
    b. *laissez-faire* economy.
    c. unfair economy.
    d. mixed economy.

8. Which of the following is not a standard assumption in economics?

    a. Local non-satiation

    b. The profit motive is the only motive that is important.

    c. Preference

    d. Rationality

9. Microeconomics is concerned with

    a. the specific parts that make up an economic system, while macroeconomics is concerned with the economy as a whole.

    b. the economy as a whole, while macroeconomics is concerned with the specific parts that make up an economic system.

    c. the way governments raise and spend money, the changing level of prices, and the nation's total output of goods and services.

    d. explaining the "forest," while macroeconomics attempts to explain the "trees."

10. The Brady Bunch would be considered a household because

    a. they had a lot of kids.

    b. they had a dog.

    c. they acted as a single economic agent most of the time.

    d. they acted as individual economic agents most of the time.

11. If the assumptions of an economic model are not complete, then

    a. there is only one implication of the model.

    b. there are likely to be many possible implications of the model.

    c. there is likely to be no implication of the model.

    d. there are likely to be only two implications of the model.

12. If a person prefers Green to Blue and prefers Blue to Red, then

    a. the person clearly prefers Yellow to Red.

    b. the person must prefer Red to Green.

    c. the person must prefer Green to Red.

    d. the person must prefer Purple to Yellow.

13. If a person walks past a quarter without picking it up,

    a. the person clearly isn't behaving rationally.

    b. the person is locally satiated up to a quarter.

    c. the person is locally satiated only up to a dime.

    d. the person does not have consistent preferences.

14. If the government decides that it wishes to produce automobiles, it will do so

    a. within the structure of a market.

    b. without regard to markets.

    c. without regard to households.

    d. without regard to firms.

    e. none of the above

15. If an individual runs a law firm, purchases food, and is also a local city councilwoman, this person would be considered which of the following:

    a. A firm

    b. A household

    c. A government agent

    d. All of the above

    e. None of the above

2

Math Review

Economics is a mixture of history, philosophy, ethics, psychology, sociology, and other fields—the proverbial melting pot of the social sciences. However, economics often relies upon mathematics to convey concepts. Mathematics is convenient because it provides a universal language with which we can relate our economic theories and models. Advanced economics uses highly advanced mathematics and statistics; however, in this book the majority of the math will be embodied in graphs. This chapter outlines how to use and read graphs.

A graph depicts the relationship between two or more variables. A two-dimensional graph depicts the relationship between two variables, as depicted in Figure 2-1.

It is a common convention to call the variable on the horizontal or X axis the independent variable and the variable on the vertical or Y axis the dependent variable. The intuition behind this terminology is that the variable on the horizontal axis is an action variable, whereas the variable on the vertical axis is a reaction variable.

The reaction of one variable to changes in another variable can be positive, negative, or zero. For instance, if the price of gasoline increases, you may purchase less gasoline, which is an example of a negative or "inverse" relationship. On the other hand, if your income increases by $1000 per month, you might purchase a new car, which would be an example of a positive relationship. Finally, if the price of cuscus

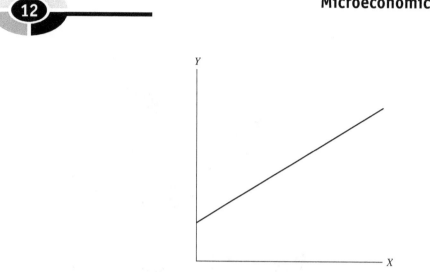

Figure 2-1   A graph of two variables.

increases in Argentina, it is unlikely that an individual in San Francisco, California, will purchase more or less chewing gum, which is an example of an independent relationship.

Knowing whether two variables are positively or negatively related to each other is important, and can be determined in a graph by measuring the slope of the relationship. The slope is the amount of units the dependent variable changes after a unit change in the independent variable. For example, it is useful to know that if the price of gasoline increases you will purchase less, but the slope of the relationship indicates exactly how much you will reduce your consumption of gasoline after a $1 increase in the price of gasoline. Slopes can be constant, which is the case for a line, or can change, which is the case for a curve. Slopes can be positive, indicating a positive relationship, or negative, indicating an inverse relationship.

The concept of the slope is relatively easy, but how is the slope used in practice? The slope of a relationship is written as $\Delta Y/\Delta X$. The Greek letter Δ indicates "change in." Therefore, the equation for the slope of a relationship can be interpreted in words as "the change in variable Y caused by a change in the variable X."

The term ΔY can be written mathematically as $(Y_1 - Y_0)$, where Y_1 is the ending value of Y, and Y_0 is the starting value of Y. Likewise, the mathematical term ΔX equals $(X_1 - X_0)$, where X_1 is the ending value of X, and X_0 is the original value of X.

Combining these two definitions, the slope of a relationship can be written as

$$\frac{\Delta Y}{\Delta X} = \frac{Y_1 - Y_0}{X_1 - X_0}$$

(2-1)

The relationship in Figure 2-1 is a linear relationship with a constant slope. Linear relationships can be described by equations in which the dependent variable's value is determined by a function of the independent variable. For example, $Y = 2 + 3X$ is an equation for a line. The right side of the equation indicates that for a given value of X, the corresponding value for Y is 2 plus 3 times the value of X. For example, if $X = 4$, then $Y = 2 + (3 \times 4) = 2 + 12 = 14$, and if $X = 8$, then $Y = 2 + (3 \times 8) = 2 + 24 = 26$. The equation for a line can be plotted on a two-dimensional graph with the variable Y on the vertical axis and the variable X on the horizontal axis, as in Figure 2-2.

From Figure 2-2, it is relatively simple to determine the slope of the relationship. Take two different values of X (X_0 and X_1) and determine the corresponding values of Y (Y_0 and Y_1) and use the equation for the slope. From the numbers calculated in the previous paragraph, if $X_0 = 2$, then $Y_0 = 8$, Point A in Figure 2-2, and if $X_1 = 4$, then $Y_1 = 14$, Point B in Figure 2-2. Using the equation for the slope, the difference in X would be $2(4 - 2 = 2)$ and the difference in Y would be $6(14 - 8 = 6)$. Therefore, the slope of the line would be $6/2$. The slope of the line is positive, indicating a positive relationship between X and Y, and the vertical intercept, which is where the line intersects the vertical axis, is $Y = 2$, which occurs when $X = 0$.

In general, a linear relationship between two variables can be written as $Y = b + mX$, where b is the vertical intercept and m is the slope of the relationship. An alternative formulation of a line, which will be used in future chapters, is when there is a constant term on the left-hand side of the equation and a "weighted" sum of X and Y on the right-hand side, for example, $20 = 4X + 2Y$. This is the equation of a line, although it doesn't look like it at first. In its current format, the equation relates X

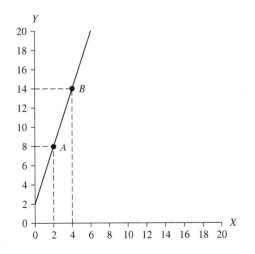

Figure 2-2   A graph of the line $Y = 2 + 3X$.

and Y to the number 20. Inspection of the right-hand side indicates that if X increases, Y will have to decrease in order to maintain the equality with twenty. Likewise, if Y were to increase, then X would have to decrease to maintain the equality with 20. It is possible to rearrange the equation so that Y is "isolated' on the left-hand side (that is, it has a coefficient of one) and the resultant equation has the form $Y = mX + b$. In the example, subtract $4X$ from both sides to obtain $20 - 4X = 2Y$. Divide both sides by two to obtain $10 - 2X = Y$. For clarity, we can flip the two sides of the equation so that it reads $Y = 10 - 2X$.

Our rearrangement of the equation $20 = 4X + 2Y$ to the equation $Y = 10 - 2X$ has not changed anything. Both equations represent the same relationship, yet the latter is more clearly the equation of a line. The relationship indicates a positive vertical intercept of $Y = 10$ when $X = 0$ and a slope of -2. For every unit that X increases, Y will decrease by two units, indicating an inverse linear relationship between X and Y.

Not all relationships in economics (or in other fields) are linear. Although many times linear relationships are used for illustrative purposes, often nonlinear relationships are more appropriate. A nonlinear relationship is one where the slope changes depending on the value of the independent variable. In other words, as the independent variable increases, the dependent variable responds at a varying rate. Figure 2-3 provides an example of a nonlinear relationship.

How do we find the slope of a nonlinear relationship if the slope is constantly changing? We can find the slope of a curve at a given point by finding the slope of a line tangent to the particular point on the curve. A tangent line is a line that shares the point of interest with the curve but does not intersect the curve. Figure 2-4 provides an example of a tangent line. Notice that the line segment between Points a and b shares only one point with the curve, Point A, but does not intersect the curve.

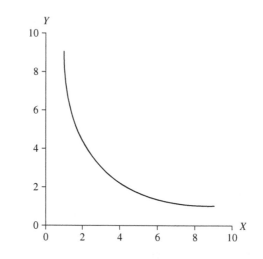

Figure 2-3 A graph of a nonlinear relationship.

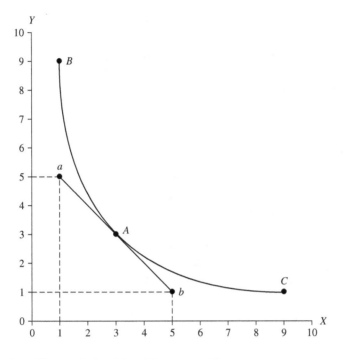

Figure 2-4   A nonlinear relationship with a tangent line.

   To determine the slope at Point A, take the slope of the tangent line between points a and b. At Point a, $Y = 5$ and $X = 1$ and at Point b, $Y = 1$ and $X = 5$. Therefore, the slope of the tangent line is $-4/4 = -1$. The slope of the curve at point A is therefore -1, indicating an inverse relationship between variable X and variable Y. At Point B, the slope of a tangent line is -9, at Point A, the slope is -1, and at Point C, the slope of a tangent line is $-1/9$. How these slopes were actually determined is the work of differential calculus, and is beyond the scope of this book. However, notice that at point B the slope of the curve is large at -9, which is interpreted as the variable Y declines by nine units when the variable X increases by one unit. However, by the time the variable X has reached a value of 3, the reaction of variable Y is not as dramatic. At Point A, the slope is -1, indicating that if the variable X increases by one unit, the variable Y declines by one unit. At Point C, the slope of $-1/9$ indicates that if the variable X increases by one unit, the variable Y will only decline by 1/9 of a unit. As the curve gets flatter, the slope becomes less (in absolute value).

   This book is written assuming only a cursory knowledge of basic arithmetic and does not require knowledge of advanced mathematics. The concept of the slope, the concept of the tangency line, and simple arithmetic (such as how to evaluate a fraction) is all the math you will need to read and understand the economic concepts in this book. Because economics provides guidance in how to make decisions, regardless of the mathematical prowess of the individual, it is not necessary to involve complex formulas and mathematics in order to convey the principles of economics.

Summary

This chapter has provided a very brief review of a simple mathematical concept: the slope. Typically remembered as "rise over the run," the slope of a line or curve indicates the direction and magnitude of the relationship between the variable on the vertical axis of a graph (the dependent variable) and the variable on the horizontal axis (the independent variable). Slopes will prove important in our graphical analysis of economic phenomena, and therefore it is worthwhile to dedicate sufficient time to become comfortable with how slopes are calculated.

Quiz

1. The vertical intercept of the relationship $Y = 15 - 2.5X$ is
    a. 37.5
    b. 6
    c. −2.5
    d. 15

2. The slope of the relationship $Y = 15 - 2.5X$ is
    a. 37.5
    b. 6
    c. −2.5
    d. 15

3. The equation $50 = 5X - 10Y$ indicates
    a. an inverse relationship between X and Y.
    b. a positive relationship between X and Y.
    c. a nonlinear relationship between X and Y.
    d. an indeterminate relationship between X and Y.

4. The equation $50 = 5X + 10Y$ is equivalent to

   a. $Y = 500 - 50X$

   b. $Y = 500 + 50X$

   c. $Y = 5 - 0.5X$

   d. $Y = 5 + 0.5X$

5. The difference between a linear and a nonlinear relationship is

   a. a linear relationship has a changing slope.

   b. a nonlinear relationship has a constant slope.

   c. a linear relationship has no vertical intercept.

   d. a nonlinear relationship has a changing slope.

Use Figure 2-5 for the next five questions:

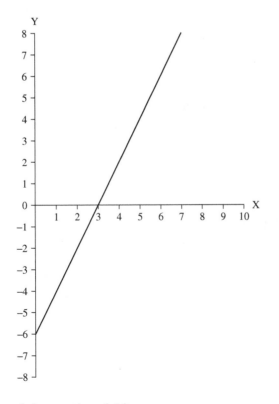

Figure 2-5   The graph for questions 6–10.

6. What kind of relationship does Figure 2-5 represent?

   a. a negative linear relationship

   b. a positive linear relationship

   c. a negative nonlinear relationship

   d. a positive nonlinear relationship

7. What is the vertical intercept of the relationship?

   a. 4

   b. 10

   c. −6

   d. 14

   e. Indeterminate

8. What is the slope of the relationship?

   a. −1.5

   b. +2

   c. −2.5

   d. +1.5

   e. Indeterminate

9. What is the equation for this line?

   a. $Y = -6 - 2X$

   b. $Y = 12 + 2X$

   c. $Y = -2.5 + 2X$

   d. $Y = -6 + 2X$

   e. Indeterminate

10. If $X = 100$, what is the value of Y?

   a. 2560

   b. 250

   c. 150

   d. 194

   e. Indeterminate

3

Production and Growth

Production

The topic of production is the closest we will come in this book to discussing macroeconomics, which is the study of national economies. Production is defined as the conversion of factors of production into goods and services. The three major factors of production are:

- *Land*: Natural resources, such as timber or oil
- *Labor*: Brain and muscle power of humans
- *Capital*: Goods and services used to produce other goods and services

Unfortunately, the total amount of goods and services that can be produced at any given time is limited by the knowledge and inputs available. The production possibilities frontier (PPF) depicts the limit between what can and cannot be produced.

In an economy with millions of products, it is almost impossible to visualize the PPF for all goods. However, it is easier to visualize a PPF for an economy producing only two goods. For our purposes, we will assume the economy produces only soda and pizza. It might sound silly to investigate an economy that produces only two goods. After all, what economy in the world satisfies that assumption? Analysis of a two-good economy provides insights equally applicable to economies that produce millions of goods.

For many people, it is difficult to visualize the PPF for an entire country. However, each individual also has their own PPF, and for many people it is easier to think of the PPF at the level of the individual. We have all heard the expression "there is only so much I can do." Taken literally, the statement indicates a limit between what can and cannot be done. In other words, everybody has his or her own PPF.

To understand how the PPF is useful in microeconomic analysis, we will derive the PPF of a model economy. This will be our first economic model and is intentionally simplistic. However, the beauty of economic modeling is that very simple models can help us understand the more complicated reality around us.

Production in a Robinson Crusoe Economy

As discussed in Chapter 1, a model is a set of assumptions that lead to a specific set of implications. Every economic model has three basic assumptions: rationality, preference, and local nonsatiation. Local nonsatiation implies that individuals always prefer more of a good to less. The Robinson Crusoe model is loosely based on William DeFoe's book in which Robinson is stranded on a deserted island and must make everything he will consume. The Robinson Crusoe model does not involve trade between individuals—this is an extension we apply later.

The Robinson Crusoe model includes our three basic assumptions and:

- All that is produced is consumed.
- Two goods are produced: soda and pizza.
- Robinson works 12 hours a day.
- The only input to producing soda and pizza is Robinson's labor effort.

To be honest, in many ways this model's assumptions are not very realistic. If Robinson were really going to make pizza and soda he would likely need more inputs than his own labor; he might also need some physical capital. However, valuable insights can be gleaned from an analysis of Robinson's PPF which do not require any more assumptions than what we have here.

Hours Worked	Pizzas	Sodas
0	0	0
2	5	5
4	10	10
6	15	15
8	20	20
10	25	25
12	30	30

Table 3-1   Production Schedule in a Robinson Crusoe Economy

To determine Robinson's PPF, we need to know how much pizza and soda Robinson can produce given different amounts of effort dedicated to each product. A production schedule as shown in Table 3-1 lists the maximum amount that can be produced with different amounts of labor effort dedicated to each product, where labor effort is measured in hours.

The production schedule tells us that if Robinson dedicates no hours to work, then zero pizzas or zero sodas will be produced. As Robinson works more hours, the amount of pizza or soda he can produce increases.

The information in the production schedule can be used to generate a PPF for Robinson. It is assumed that Robinson works 12 hours a day, but he can choose how to split his time between producing soda and producing pizza. All of the possible combinations of pizza and soda where Robinson works 12 hours a day define his PPF. For example, if Robinson spends 2 hours making soda and 10 hours making pizza, Robinson can make 5 sodas and 25 pizzas. An alternative is that Robinson spends six hours making soda and six hours making pizza. In this case, he could make 15 sodas and 15 pizzas. The entire production possibilities schedule for Robinson is depicted in Table 3-2.

Pizzas	Sodas
0	30
5	25
10	20
15	15
20	10
25	5
30	0

Table 3-2   Production Possibilities in a Robinson Crusoe Economy (12 hours worked)

The different combinations of soda and pizza that Robinson can produce in twelve hours define his PPF. We can plot these different combinations in a two-dimensional space with pizza plotted on the horizontal axis and soda plotted on the vertical axis as in Figure 3-1.

All points within and on the PPF are technologically attainable; those outside of it are not. Point *A* corresponds to 10 pizzas and 10 sodas and is inside the PPF. Robinson could produce at Point *A*, however it is unlikely that he will be satisfied there. Because Robinson likes both soda and pizza, and he has local nonsatiation, he wants more of both goods. Moreover, by definition Point *A* lies within the PPF and therefore Robinson can produce more of *both* goods. Robinson will continue to produce more of soda or pizza or both until the combination of soda and pizza that Robinson produces lies *on the* PPF. Robinson will produce on his PPF. Where on his PPF Robinson actually produces depends upon his preferences.

For example, from Point *A*, Robinson could move to Point *C* and produce more soda without producing less pizza. He could move to Point *D* and produce more pizza without producing less soda, or he could move to Point *E* and produce more of both goods. Remember that all that is produced is consumed, so as Robinson produces more he is able to consume more. Given rationality, preference, and local

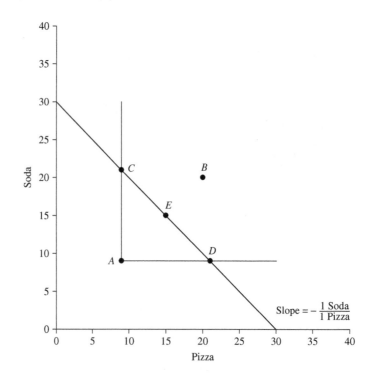

Figure 3-1 Robinson's production possibilities frontier.

nonsatiation, Robinson prefers Point C, Point D, and Point E to Point A. How does Robinson choose between Point C, Point D, or Point E? His choice depends upon his preferences (which is a problem addressed in Chapter 7).

On the other hand, Point B is outside of Robinson's PPF. Regardless of how much he desires to produce (and consume) at Point B, given the number of hours he chooses to work and the technology he employs to produce soda and pizza, Point B is not possible. How does Robinson get to a point such as Point B? Robinson must work more hours in the day (increase his labor) or create a better way to produce soda and pizzas, that is, improve his technology. Either of these would cause the PPF to expand and potentially make Point B possible.

Looking at Figure 3-1, if Robinson makes 30 sodas, he can make no pizzas because he has dedicated all his working hours to making soda. However, if Robinson decides to dedicate two hours to producing pizza, he will necessarily have less time to make soda. The opportunity cost of the two hours dedicated to pizza is the amount of soda he gives up in the process. From Table 3-1, if Robinson dedicated two hours to making pizza, he would make five pizzas. In the process, Robinson would give up five sodas. The opportunity cost is calculated as the loss divided by the gains. Therefore, the first five pizzas incurred a loss of five sodas or 1 soda for every pizza.

What if Robinson decided that he wanted to spend an additional two hours producing pizza? To do this, Robinson would have to take more time away from producing soda. From Table 3-1, if Robinson spends another two hours on pizza he can produce another five pizzas, but he gives up another five sodas. The opportunity cost of the additional two hours is also 1 soda for every pizza.

An easier way to calculate the opportunity cost of the good on the horizontal axis of the PPF is to calculate the slope of the PPF. The slope is defined as the "rise over the run," which in the case of the PPF will measure the cost of producing an additional unit of the good measured on the horizontal axis. The opportunity cost of the good on the vertical axis is the inverse of the slope of the PPF, or one divided by the slope.

Looking at Figure 3-1, the slope of the PPF can easily be determined. The two endpoints can be used to calculate the slope of the PPF and, because the PPF is linear, we know the slope is constant. The slope of Robinson's PPF is –5 sodas/5 pizzas, which implies an opportunity cost of one soda for every pizza, exactly the opportunity cost calculated from the production schedule.

Economic Growth

Politicians often claim that it is important to "grow" the economy. These claims make good political slogans and sound bites, but what does it mean to "grow the economy?" In a simple sense, economic growth is an expansion of the PPF.

However, to increase the production possibilities, it is often necessary to sacrifice current consumption. Two different activities can generate economic growth: factor accumulation and technological progress.

Factor accumulation is the increase of one or more factors of production. For example, labor can increase if people work more hours per day (or week) or the population increases, either through birthrates or immigration. Land (natural resources) accumulation can occur through geographic expansion of a country or through exploration. Capital accumulation is an increase in the machinery or other products used in production. Capital accumulation, unlike labor accumulation, requires a sacrifice of current day consumption. This is an important distinction. If an economy produces more capital goods today so as to produce more consumption goods in the future, it is necessary to sacrifice current production of consumption goods. The reduction in the amount of consumption goods in the short run is offset by an increase in the PPF in the long run.

In the context of the Robinson Crusoe model, if Robinson devoted a portion of his labor time to producing a brick oven in which to produce pizzas, he would sacrifice some of his current consumption in pizza and soda but would be able to produce more pizzas in the future.

Another way to expand the PPF without changing the amount of inputs available is to improve the technology used to produce goods and services. Technology is defined as the methodology used to create goods, and an improvement in technology is defined as being able to produce a given amount of product with fewer inputs. If a country has a fixed amount of inputs and technology improves so that the inputs can produce more, then the PPF necessarily shifts to the right as depicted in Figure 3-2.

Gains from Trade

Production possibilities frontiers differ across individuals and countries. These differences reflect different capabilities, types of inputs, and technologies of individuals or groups of individuals. These differences cause some people or countries to be better at certain things than other individuals or countries. For example, Columbia makes better coffee than Iceland, France makes better wine than Saudi Arabia, and doctors are better at surgery than economics professors. Economists define comparative advantage as the ability to produce a good or service at a lower opportunity cost than someone else. Comparative advantage is determined by comparing the opportunity cost for agent A to the opportunity cost for agent B. This is easily done by comparing the slope of agent A's and agent B's PPF. Agents tend to

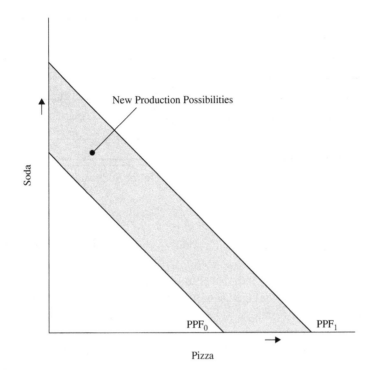

Figure 3-2   Growth in an economy.

specialize in those activities in which they hold a comparative advantage. By doing so, the economy is able to produce more than if agents focused on producing goods in which they do not hold a comparative advantage.

Assume that Robinson meets Sandy, who lives on a nearby island. Sandy also produces pizza and soda, but Sandy has a comparative advantage in producing pizza. How is comparative advantage measured? Assume Sandy's production possibilities schedule is as shown in Table 3-3.

From Table 3-3, Sandy's opportunity cost of producing soda is $^{10}/_3$ of a pizza whereas her opportunity cost of producing a pizza is $^3/_{10}$ of a soda. Sandy's PPF is depicted in Figure 3-3, and both Sandy and Robinson's PPFs are depicted in Figure 3-4.

Sandy has a comparative advantage in producing pizza because the slope of her PPF is less than the slope of Robinson's PPF. Even though Sandy has the comparative advantage in producing pizza, it is the case that Robinson has the comparative advantage in producing soda. The opportunity cost of soda is calculated as the inverse of the slope of each PPF. For Robinson, his opportunity cost of soda is $1/(1\,\text{soda}/1\,\text{pizza}) = 1$ pizza for each soda. On the other hand, Sandy's opportunity

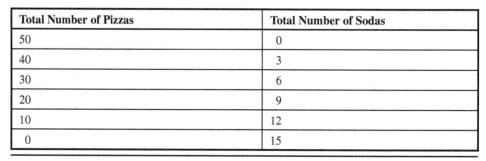

Total Number of Pizzas	Total Number of Sodas
50	0
40	3
30	6
20	9
10	12
0	15

Table 3-3   Sandy's Production Possibilities Schedule for Soda and Pizzas

cost for soda is $10/3$ of a pizza for each soda. In the case of soda, Robinson has the comparative advantage.

This is a general result: No individual or country has a comparative advantage in all goods. Comparative advantage is an important and powerful concept in economics, but is one of the least understood outside of the field of economics.

Suppose Robinson and Sandy choose not to trade and decide to produce their soda and pizza separately. They will only be able to produce and consume on their own PPF. However, if they each specialize in their respective comparative advantage, they can produce more pizza *and* soda than they could alone. Specialization occurs when Sandy and Robinson spend *all* of their working time producing the product in which they have a comparative advantage.

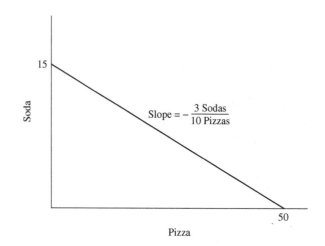

Figure 3-3   Sandy's production possibilities frontier.

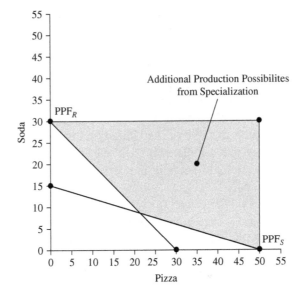

Figure 3-4   Specialization and potential gains from trade.

Referring to Figure 3-4, if Sandy specializes in producing pizza, she can produce 50 pizzas. If Sandy specializes in soda, she can only make 15 sodas. On the other hand, if Robinson specializes in producing soda, he can produce 30 sodas, whereas if he specializes in pizza he can make 30 pizzas. If they both specialize in their comparative advantage, the amount of soda and pizza available to both of them is greater than if they each produced both soda and pizza. If Sandy and Robinson agree on how much soda to trade for one pizza, that is, the price of pizza in terms of soda, it is possible for both Sandy and Robinson to consume outside of their individual PPF. Working together, Robinson and Sandy can produce 50 pizzas and 30 sodas and can split this combination of pizza and sodas in a mutually beneficial way so that each of them can consume more pizza and soda than they would if they tried to produce both pizza and soda on their own. The shaded area of Figure 3-4 represents the combinations of soda and pizza which Robinson and Sandy can consume if they specialize in their respective comparative advantage.

This too is a general result. Trade and specialization allow individuals and countries to consume beyond their individual PPF. For example, the Middle East has a comparative advantage in producing crude oil, whereas the United States has a comparative advantage in growing wheat. If the United States consumed only the crude oil it could produce domestically, there would be much less crude oil consumed in the United States. While environmentalists might consider this desirable, the reduction in crude oil would cause dramatic impacts on the U.S. economy by reducing its production possibilities while at the same time moving the U.S. economy to a different point on its PPF. For example, the United States would have to dedicate more of its resources to extracting crude oil from Texas, Oklahoma, or Alaska, and would have fewer resources to dedicate to making automobiles and computers. Moreover, there would likely be less crude oil in the United States which would reduce the ability to harvest wheat with tractors and numerous other activities. This would cause the PPF of the United States to contract. This, in turn, would reduce the amount that people in the United States could consume, reduce the number of people employed in certain industries, and possibly have additional macroeconomic consequences.

Trade between the United States and the Middle East is mutually beneficial. This is because The Middle East is very good at producing crude oil but not at producing wheat. Therefore, if the Middle Eastern countries did not specialize in their comparative advantage and instead tried to grow all the wheat they were going to consume, they wouldn't have a lot of wheat to consume. Trade allows agents to take advantage of their comparative advantage and consume more through cooperation.

There is no money in the simple Robinson Crusoe model. Rather, Robinson and Sandy would engage in barter exchange, where each trade requires negotiation and involves goods rather than money. In most modern economies, barter exchange is replaced with money-based exchange. This is because barter exchange can become very tedious and inefficient, especially when it involves thousands if not millions of people. Money-based exchange is a less costly way to trade one person's output for another person's output.

Assume you are a certified public accountant (CPA) and want to trade your accounting services for a steak dinner. In a barter economy, you have to find someone with a steak dinner to trade with you, perhaps a restaurant. In barter exchange, the restaurant will only trade with you if it needs accounting services. Because not every restaurant needs accounting services, it might be difficult for you as an accountant to find a steak dinner. However, with money-based exchange, you can sell your accounting services, say, to a local engineering firm, for money and then pay the restaurant for a steak dinner. In this way, you trade your accounting services for dinner, but you do it indirectly with money-based exchange, rather than directly, as in barter exchange.

The Robinson Crusoe model is equally applicable in an economy with or without money. In either case, the slope of the PPF should be set equal to the relative price of the good on the horizontal axis. The slope of the PPF is the opportunity cost of the product on the horizontal axis. The relative price of the product on the horizontal axis is in terms of the product on the vertical axis, rather than in dollars and cents. Thus, if the price of Good A is $4 per unit and the price of Good B is $8 per unit, the price of Good A in terms of Good B would be $4 per Good A divided by $8 per Good B, or half of a unit of Good B for a unit of Good A. On the other hand, the relative price of Good B would be $8 per Good B divided by $4 per Good A or 2 units of Good A per unit of Good B.

This idea can be expanded to introduce the concept of trade. If the relative price of Good A is one unit of Good B and the relative price of Good B is one unit of Good A, then comparative advantage indicates what each person should produce. If Robinson has an opportunity cost of one half a unit of Good B for every unit of Good A he produces, then Robinson is better off producing Good A and selling his production of Good A for a price of one unit of Good B, which is greater than what it cost Robinson to produce each unit of Good A (one half of a unit of Good B). Likewise, if it costs Sally only three-fourths of a unit of Good A to produce a unit of Good B and she can sell each unit of Good B for a whole unit of Good A, it makes sense for Sally to produce Good B and trade for Good A.

When the relative price of a product is greater than the opportunity cost of the product, the individual is better off producing the product and selling it for a profit. If the relative price is less than the opportunity cost, then the individual is better-off not producing the product because doing so will incur a loss or a negative profit.

This can be extended from trade between individuals to trade between countries. If the relative price of wheat to oil is, say, four barrels of oil per bushel of wheat, then the countries that have an opportunity cost of wheat less than four barrels of oil are better off producing wheat and selling it to the oil producing countries for a profit. Likewise, those countries with an opportunity cost of a barrel of oil less than one-fourth of a bushel of wheat are better off producing oil and trading with wheat producing countries. In this case, both the wheat producing country and the oil producing country are able to profit when they exploit their comparative advantage.

Whether prices are measured in relative or nominal terms, comparative advantage is one of the strongest forces for determining who will produce what and who will trade with whom. The area of international trade, which is the study of how and why countries trade with each other, is fundamentally rooted in the concept of comparative advantage. While it is possible in some cases for trade to occur in the opposite direction to that predicted by comparative advantage, these possibilities are very unique and require special circumstances. For the most part, comparative advantage determines trade patterns, whether between individuals or between countries.

This is not to imply that there are no consequences to following comparative advantage. In the case of U.S. textiles and steel production, the period during which the United States held a comparative advantage in these products seems to have passed. Other countries now hold a comparative advantage in textile and steel production. This implies, however, that the United States might hold a comparative advantage, say, in computers, which did not exist forty years ago. Unfortunately, not every person whose job is displaced when a textile mill relocates to another country, or simply goes out of business because of foreign competition, is able to get a job in the computer industry. Those who are rendered unemployed because of changes in comparative advantage are one of the costs of allowing the free market to determine who should produce what. However, as we will see in future chapters, protecting the jobs of a select few from the unrelenting pressure of comparative advantage is unlikely to be a good policy in the long run.

Trade and Comparative Advantage over Time

The concept of comparative advantage is one of the hardest concepts for students of economics to grasp. Thus, it is unfortunate that comparative advantage is one of the first concepts that students are presented in an introductory course. Nevertheless, the idea of comparative advantage can provide a very valuable tool to understand changes in today's global economy.

After World War II, the United States stood alone as the only developed country that had not suffered dramatic reductions in manufacturing capacity. Every other developed country, including the United Kingdom, Germany, France, Italy, the Soviet Union, and Japan, had sustained catastrophic damage to their manufacturing capabilities. As a result, in the period immediately following World War II until the mid 1970s, the United States was a net exporter of just about everything it produced, including automobiles, toys, steel, and oil. This was a clear case of comparative advantage: The United States held a comparative advantage in just about all the products it produced, and as a result it was cheaper for the rest of the world to purchase U.S.-made products rather than produce them domestically.

Until the 1980s, the United States was a net exporter of just about all that it produced, save crude oil. After the mid 1980s, however, the United States began to run a significant trade deficit (as depicted in Figure 3-5). However, this does not imply that the United States is not capable of producing for export. Quite the contrary, as the United States remains *the single largest exporter in the world*, even though the United States is also the largest single importer in the world. Figure 3-6 depicts the annual value of imports and exports for the United States.

In 2004 the United States exported $1.15 trillion dollars of goods and services and imported $1.76 billion dollars of goods and services (a substantial portion of the imports is crude oil). To put the trade of the United States in perspective, the amount of goods and services the United States exported in 2004 was greater than the *entire gross national product* of Canada (estimated to be $1.023 trillion in 2004).

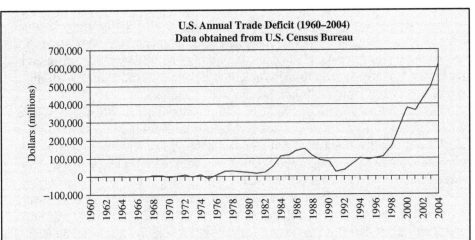

Figure 3-5   U.S. trade deficit over time.

Many people blame the U.S. trade deficit for larger unemployment levels, especially in the manufacturing sector. The thinking is that other countries might hold a comparative advantage today in some products in which the United States held a comparative advantage in the past. Those who are displaced because their employer went out of business or moved to another country in the face of foreign com-petition are often frustrated at what seems to be a lack of competitiveness on the part of the United States.

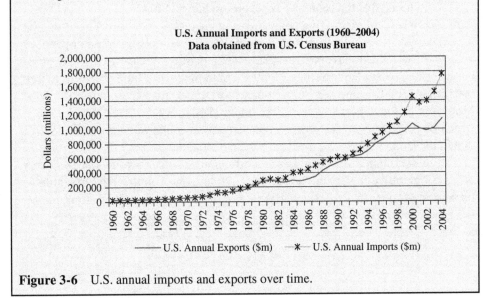

Figure 3-6   U.S. annual imports and exports over time.

However, generally economists do not interpret all jobs heading to other countries as a negative. This is not because economists lack compassion for those whose jobs relocate, but because economists believe in the power of comparative advantage to lead to the efficient allocation of production possibilities not only between individuals but also between countries.

Over the post-war period, countries such as Japan and South Korea, for example, invested in new steel-making technology whereas the steel companies in the United States did not invest in new technology. The United States now imports a lot of steel from Japan and South Korea because it is cheaper to buy from there than to produce in the United States.

Why is this the case? It is not because Japanese or South Korean workers work for less than their American counterparts, but because new technology in Japan and South Korea has flipped the comparative advantage in steel from the United States to the other countries. This, in turn, implies that the United States holds a comparative advantage in another product, which is possibly one for which steel workers are not trained to produce. For example, the United States might export more wheat or chicken to Japan and South Korea even as we import more steel from these two countries. The United States has continued to export more goods and services even while it has supposedly suffered a drastic reduction in manufacturing jobs. Figure 3-6 suggests that even while some are displaced after their job relocates to another country, there are plenty of opportunities where the United States is competitive in the world market; otherwise, the United States would not export as much as it does!

It is often said that the economy is becoming more "global" and that the United States has a harder time staying competitive in the global economy. This is not the way economists think about global competition. Being globally competitive does not imply that the United States must have a comparative advantage in every product it makes, otherwise the United States would have very little coffee. It is true that some countries are producing much more today than they did in the past. Moreover, this new production is often undertaken using the latest in technology, which might reduce the opportunity cost in another country to a lower value than that in the United States and the rest of the developed world.

The lesson here is that comparative advantage is not a static concept. Over time, comparative advantage can change. Today, one country might be able to produce a product that is less costly than in other countries. This might not be the case tomorrow.

Summary

This chapter discusses the concept of production and growth in the context of a simple model with, initially, only one person and two goods. The model is useful because it specifically recognizes that there is a limit to what can be produced, and hence what can be consumed, via the PPF. Economic growth is defined as an expansion of the PPF. The model was extended to include two people and two goods, which allows for differences in opportunity cost in producing the two goods. Comparative advantage is defined as having a lower opportunity cost in an activity compared to something else, and when individuals (or countries) recognize and specialize in their comparative advantage, the total product available to the society increases. The question of how this increased production is allocated requires a market—either barter or money-based.

Quiz

1. If Jim cannot increase production of Good X without decreasing the production of any other good, then Jim

    a. is producing on his production possibility frontier (PPF).

    b. is producing outside his PPF.

    c. is producing inside his PPF.

    d. must prefer Good X to any other good.

2. If a nation has unemployment it must be the case that it is operating

    a. on its production possibility frontier (PPF).

    b. outside its PPF.

    c. inside its PPF.

    d. without a PPF.

3. Trade, coupled with comparative advantage, allows you to

    a. produce outside your production possibilities frontier (PPF).

    b. produce within your PPF.

    c. not worry about your PPF.

    d. consume outside your PPF.

4. Assume Country A can produce 10 million bushels of corn or 10 million automobiles and Country B can produce 20 million bushels of corn or 1 million automobiles. Which country has a comparative advantage in corn?

   a. Country A

   b. Country B

   c. Both Country A and Country B

   d. Neither Country A nor Country B

5. Many developed countries are experiencing a decline in new births, to the extent that the number of workers in the future might decline considerably. Which of the following is a possible implication?

   a. These countries will have no comparative advantage.

   b. These countries will have more production possibilities.

   c. These countries might maintain their current production possibilities but will require improvements in technology or increase in other inputs.

   d. The lesser-developed countries will have all the comparative advantage.

6. If a country's production possibilities frontier (PPF) gets steeper, the implication is

   a. that the opportunity cost of the good on the vertical axis has increased.

   b. that the opportunity cost of the good on the horizontal axis has increased.

   c. that the opportunity cost of the good on the horizontal axis has decreased.

   d. that the opportunity cost of both goods has increased.

7. Rationality, preference, and local nonsatiation imply that individuals

   a. want to produce on their production possibilities frontier (PPF).

   b. want to produce within their PPF.

   c. want to produce outside their PPF.

   d. none of the above

8. What might explain a country not producing as many consumption goods as possible?

   a. The country is dedicating some of its resources to taxation.

   b. The country's citizens do not like consumption goods.

   c. The country is dedicating some of its current resources to investment.

   d. The country is running a trade deficit.

9. If the United States decided to stop importing oil from the Middle East, which of the following would be true?

   a. There would be an increase in the U.S. production possibilities frontier (PPF).

   b. There would be a decrease in the U.S. PPF.

   c. The United States would spend much more on petroleum products because of taxation.

   d. The United States would produce less of other goods.

10. If Craig can produce 3 widgets for every 2 gadgets, and Linda can produce 8 widgets for every 4 gadgets, then Linda has a comparative advantage in widgets.

    a. True

    b. False

    c. It is impossible to determine who has the comparative advantage.

Use Figure 3-7 for the next five questions:

11. Using Figure 3-7 what is Gregoria's opportunity cost of clams?

    a. 1 orange for every 2 clams

    b. $1/2$ of an orange for every 2 clams

    c. 2 oranges for every 1 clam

    d. 1 clam for every 2 oranges

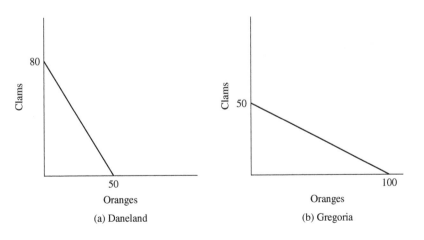

Figure 3-7   The production possibilities frontiers of Daneland and Gregoria.

12. Using Figure 3-7, what is Daneland's opportunity cost of oranges?

    a. $8/5$ clams for every orange

    b. 1 clam for every orange

    c. $5/8$ of a clam for every orange

    d. 2 clams for every orange

13. Given your answers in the previous two questions, which country has a comparative advantage in clams?

    a. Gregoria

    b. Daneland

    c. Both

    d. Neither

14. If Gregoria and Daneland specialized in their comparative advantage, what would their total production be?

    a. 60 oranges, 100 clams

    b. 100 clams, 60 oranges

    c. 100 clams, 80 oranges

    d. 80 clams, 100 oranges

15. Given the opportunity cost of clams in Daneland and Gregoria, which of the following would be a relative price at which Gregoria and Daneland would trade oranges for clams?

    a. $3/4$ of a clam for every orange

    b. 4 oranges for every clam

    c. 2 clams for every orange

    d. 1 clam for every 3 oranges

4

Demand and Supply

Most of us consume products that we have purchased in a market. While some of us might knit our own sweaters or grow our own vegetables, most of us depend on markets to provide the goods we consume. Markets for goods and services can take different forms, including formal "brick and mortar" buildings or on-line markets, and informal markets such as trading baseball cards with your friends. This chapter outlines the mechanics underlying the basic supply and demand model, a powerful tool with which to analyze the world. For example, the supply and demand model is helpful in explaining why the price of plywood increases dramatically before a hurricane hits South Florida or why the price of Christmas ornaments drops steeply after the New Year.

Markets are comprised of agents who wish to allocate a scarce resource. The market itself is the mechanism for the allocation of the scarce resource. Consider the market for luxury import automobiles. There are obviously not enough automobiles produced for everyone to have a luxury car for free. Even if the price of a luxury car were $10 there would not be enough cars to go around. The limited number of luxury cars is allocated in a market comprised of demanders, or households willing and able to pay for luxury cars, and suppliers, or firms willing and able to produce luxury cars.

The analysis of supply and demand is simply the analysis of how demanders and suppliers interact with one another in *voluntary* and *mutually beneficial* trade. Initially, demand and supply are discussed separately, and then demand and supply are combined to analyze how markets allocate scarce resources. Finally, various government interventions in the demand and supply model are discussed.

Demand

The *demand* for a product comes from consumers and is defined as the relationship between the price of the good and the quantity demanded at each price. The *quantity demanded* is the quantity of a good or service that a consumer or group of consumers plans to buy at a certain price and time.

To analyze demand (and other aspects of the economy), economists assume that everything in the economy is held fixed. In reality, very few things in the economy are truly fixed. In the time it will take you to read this sentence, many things will have happened, including people dying, babies being born, new inventions being created, and countless other things. However, it is very difficult to analyze a particular aspect of the economy when so many other things are changing. To make analysis easier, economists invoke the assumption of *ceteris paribus*, which means "all else remaining the same."

Demand is the relationship between the price of a good and the quantity of the good demanded at each price. The various combinations of price and quantity demanded can be reported in a demand schedule. Each individual in a market has a demand schedule, which reflects the quantity of a product that he will actually purchase at each possible price. For example, suppose there are four people in the market for chewing gum and that there are six possible prices for chewing gum: $0.01, $0.10, $0.20, $0.30, $0.40, or $0.50.

Each individual has a different demand for chewing gum because each person has different preference for chewing gum. However, for each person, the quantity demanded declines as the price increases. This is a general result called the *law of demand*, which states that the greater the price the lower the quantity demanded. The law of demand holds for individuals and the overall market.

The total quantity demanded in the market equals the sum of the quantities demanded by each person in the market at a given price. For example, at a price of $0.01 for a pack of gum, the total market quantity demanded is equal to

$10 + 17 + 13 + 20 = 60$. At a price of $0.10, the total market quantity demanded is equal to $7 + 16 + 10 + 17 = 50$. Notice how the total quantity demanded declines as price increases. This hypothetical market is, of course, a simplified view of reality, but the markets for automobiles, computers, houses, and other goods and services behave in the same general way. Although the actual prices and quantities demanded change depending on the good, after all cars rarely sell for $0.50, the concept of demand is the same for all goods.

The market demand schedule can be cumbersome to work with, especially in a large market with thousands, if not millions, of consumers. To make things easier, economists plot the different price-quantity combinations from the demand schedule to create a demand curve. For simplicity, we will work with linear demand curves although demand curves might be nonlinear. Demand curves are typically drawn with the price of the good on the vertical axis and quantity on the horizontal axis.

The graph in Figure 4-1 reflects the demand schedule in Table 4-1. Notice that the demand curve is downward sloping, which reflects the law of demand. The demand curve is drawn assuming *ceteris paribus*, that is, all other variables remaining the same. If something changes in the economy, it is possible that the demand schedule in Table 4-1 and the associated demand curve in Figure 4-1 are no longer valid because one or more of the quantities demanded can change.

It is important to remember the distinction between the quantity demanded and demand. Demand is the overall relationship between price and quantity demanded. The quantity demanded is the amount that would be purchased at a given price, which is the quantity in a particular cell in the demand schedule. Even professional economists often get sloppy and use the word "demand" when they really mean "quantity demanded."

A change in demand is not the same as a change in the quantity demanded. A change in demand indicates a shift of the demand curve, whereas a change in price will cause a change in the quantity demanded, represented by a movement *along* the demand curve. This distinction is depicted in Figure 4-2. If demand does

	Quantity Demanded by				Total Quantity Demanded
Price	Person 1	Person 2	Person 3	Person 4	
$0.01	10	17	13	20	60
$0.10	7	16	10	17	50
$0.20	5	15	5	15	40
$0.30	4	8	4	14	30
$0.40	2	6	3	9	20
$0.50	1	3	1	5	10

Table 4-1   Demand Schedules in the Market for Chewing Gum

Microeconomics Demystified

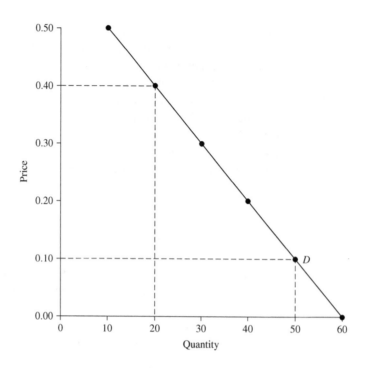

Figure 4-1 A simple demand curve.

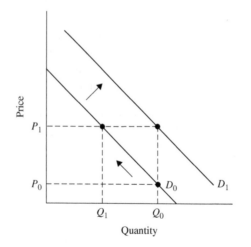

Figure 4-2 A change in the quantity demanded versus a change in demand.

not change and price increases from P_0 to P_1, then the quantity demanded will fall from Q_0 to Q_1. On the other hand, if the demand increases from D_0 to D_1, then the price people are willing to pay for quantity Q_0 has increased from P_0 to P_1.

What causes demand to change? Demand changes when one or more people change the quantity they demand at one or more prices. But how do people decide if they will change the quantity they demand? The influences on demand are rather straightforward:

1. Changes in the prices of other goods: The demand for a good might change when the prices of other goods change. However, it depends on the relationship between the good we are looking at and the other good whose price changes. There are two types of relationships between consumption goods:

   • Substitutes are goods that can replace each other in consumption, for example, Swiss cheese and American cheese, or a bus and a train. When the price of a substitute increases, ceteris paribus, the demand for the good in focus will increase. Consider two types of tennis balls: Ball A and Ball B. If the price of Ball A increases, the demand for Ball B will increase. This is because consumers will switch away from Ball A and into Ball B. In other words, a new demand schedule is generated at the new price of the substitute.

   • Complements are goods that are used in conjunction with each other, for example, DVD players and DVDs, or cars and gasoline. If the price of a complement increases, the demand for the product in focus will decline. For example, if the price of sugar increases, the quantity of coffee demanded at each price will decline.

2. The disposable income of consumers: If demand increases after an increase in income, then the good is considered a normal good. If demand decreases after an increase in income, the good is considered an inferior good.

3. Expected future prices: If a sufficient number of demanders expect the price of the good to increase in the future, these people will increase their demand for the product today in order to stock up on the good and avoid the higher price in the future. If a sufficient number of demanders think the price will decline tomorrow, the demand today will decrease.

4. The number of demanders in the market: As the number of demanders in the market or population increases, the demand for the good increases. To illustrate, consider adding a fifth person to the demand schedules in Table 4-1. In Table 4-2, it is easy to see how the total quantity demanded at each price increases.

Price	Quantity Demanded by Person 5	New Total Quantity Demanded
$0.01	10	70
$0.10	8	58
$0.20	6	46
$0.30	4	34
$0.40	2	22
$0.50	1	11

Table 4-2   The Impact of Additional Demanders in the Market

5. Preferences for the product: If the preference for a product increases, then the demand for that product will increase, and vice versa. Economists tend to think that preferences change slowly over time and therefore this influence on demand is relatively minor.

An increase in demand is represented by an increase in the quantity demanded at one or more prices, in other words, the demand curve shifts to the right, as depicted in Figure 4-3. The original demand indicates that at price P_0, the quantity demanded was Q_0. However, after demand increases to D_1, the quantity demanded at price P_0 increases to Q_1. An alternative interpretation of an increase in demand is that consumers are willing to pay more for each level of consumption. In Figure 4-3, at quantity Q_0, the original demand indicated the highest price consumers were willing to pay was P_0, however after demand increases to D_1, the most consumers are willing to pay for the same Q_0 units is now P_1. Either interpretation is correct.

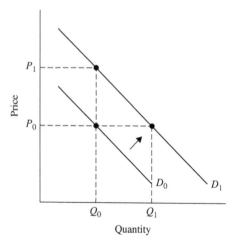

Figure 4-3   An increase in demand.

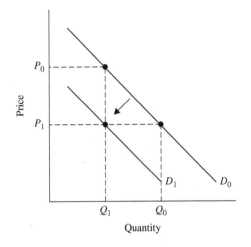

Figure 4-4   A decrease in demand.

What might have caused this? An increase in demand can be caused by an increase in the price of a substitute, a decrease in the price of a complement, an increase in consumer income (for a normal good), a decrease in consumer income (for an inferior good), an increase in the number of demanders in the market, or a shift in consumer preferences over time.

A decrease in demand is represented by the exact opposite of an increase in demand (as shown in Figure 4-4). When demand decreases, the demand curve shifts left. This indicates that at each price, there is less quantity demanded. An alternative interpretation is that the willingness to pay for every level of output declines. Either interpretation is correct. A decrease in demand can be caused by a reduction in a substitute's price, an increase in the price of a complement, a reduction in consumer income (for a normal good), an increase in consumer income (for an inferior good), a reduction in the number of demanders in the market, or a shift in consumer preferences over time.

Supply

Supply is the relationship between the price of a good and the quantity supplied by producers. In many ways, supply is similar to demand: A market supply is found by adding up individual producer supply schedules. We can generate a supply schedule as we did for demand.

The market supply schedule can be cumbersome to work with, especially in a large market with hundreds, if not thousands, of producers. To make things easier, economists plot the different price-quantity combinations from the supply schedule on a supply curve. A supply curve is simply a graph of a supply schedule. For simplicity, we will work with linear supply curves although supply curves might be nonlinear. Supply curves are typically drawn like demand curves, with the price of the good on the vertical axis and quantity on the horizontal axis.

The graph in Figure 4-5 reflects the supply schedule in Table 4-3. The supply curve is upward sloping, which reflects the law of supply: *Ceteris paribus*, the higher the price of a good, the greater the quantity supplied. The supply curve in Figure 4-5 is drawn assuming *ceteris paribus*. If something changes in the economy, it is possible that the supply schedule in Table 4-3 and the associated supply curve in Figure 4-5 are no longer valid because one or more of the quantities supplied can change.

What can cause a change in supply? Several of the influences on supply are similar to the influences on demand and others are unique to the supply-side of a market.

1. The prices of factors of production: As the prices of factors increase, the cost of production increases, and supply decreases (shifts left). If factor prices decline, then it is cheaper to produce and supply will increase (shift right).

2. The price of related goods: Prices of other goods influence the choice of what to produce.

   - Substitutes in production are goods that have similar production processes. Assume Good A and Good B are substitutes in production. As the price of Good B increases, the supply of Good A will decrease as suppliers shift production into Good B. Car manufacturers often use the same assembly line (method of production) to produce sports cars or sport utility vehicles. If the price of sports cars increases, the quantity of sports cars produced

Price	Quantity Supplied by			Total Quantity Supplied
	Firm 1	Firm 2	Firm 3	
$0.01	10	15	0	25
$0.10	20	25	5	50
$0.20	30	35	10	75
$0.30	40	45	15	100
$0.40	50	55	20	125
$0.50	60	65	25	150

Table 4-3 Supply Schedules in the Market for Chewing Gum

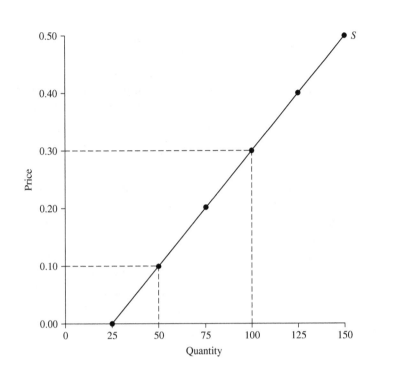

Figure 4-5   A simple supply curve.

will increase (an increase in the quantity supplied). However, because there is a limit to the total number of cars that can be produced on the assembly line, the production of the sport utility vehicle will necessarily decrease (a reduction in the supply of SUVs).

- Complements in production are goods produced together using, for example, regular unleaded gasoline and premium unleaded gasoline. Assume Good A and Good B are complements in production. If the price of Good B increases, the supply of Good A will increase. When the price of Good B increases, the quantity of Good B supplied also increases, but this in turn increases the supply of Good A.

3. Expected future prices: If a sufficient number of suppliers expect the price of the good to increase in the future, suppliers will hold off producing today and, instead, produce more tomorrow. For example, consider the production of chocolate Easter bunnies. The supply of bunnies is low during Halloween because suppliers anticipate that the price of bunnies will be relatively low at that time. However, suppliers are confident that the

price of bunnies will increase during the Easter season, and therefore the supply of bunnies is greater during the Easter season.

If a sufficient number of suppliers think the price will decline tomorrow, supply today will increase. This is because suppliers would rather produce and sell today, when they can get a higher price, than to wait until tomorrow when prices will have already dropped.

4. Number of producers: As the number of producers increases, *ceteris paribus*, the supply of the good will increase.

5. Technology: An improvement in technology reduces the amount of factors of production required to produce a given amount of output. Therefore, an improvement in technology will reduce the cost of production and lead to an increase in supply.

A decrease in supply indicates that less of the good will be produced at each price. For example, in Figure 4-6, the shift of supply from S_0 to S_1 is a decrease in supply. On the other hand, an increase in supply indicates a greater quantity supplied at each price, as in a shift from S_0 to S_2 in Figure 4-6.

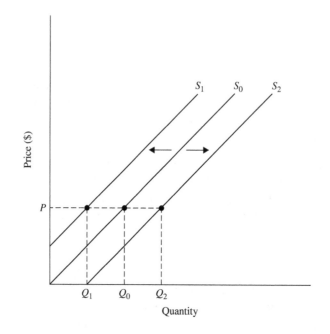

Figure 4-6   Changes in supply.

Price as a Regulator in the Market

Supply and demand are interesting on their own, but they are most useful in analyzing how consumers and firms interact via supply and demand. Drawing the supply curve and the demand curve on the same graph, in what is commonly called a Supply and Demand diagram or a Marshallian diagram, depicts this interaction.

In Figure 4-7, at price P_0 the quantity supplied (indicated at Point B) is greater than the quantity demanded (indicated at Point A). Suppliers are willing to supply more than the demanders are willing to buy at the price of P_0, that is, there is excess supply. How can suppliers reduce excess supply? They can lower the price to entice more demanders to buy. By lowering price, the quantity supplied will decline and at the same time the quantity demanded increases, thereby reducing excess supply.

At P_1, the quantity supplied (indicated at Point C) is less than the quantity demanded (indicated at Point D). Here, consumers demand more of the good than suppliers are willing to provide at the price of P_1, that is, there is a shortage in the market. Consumers will bid up the price of the good to encourage suppliers to make more of the product.

As price changes in response to surpluses or shortages in the market, the market naturally approaches a state of equilibrium. An equilibrium is a state that once obtained tends to be maintained, *ceteris paribus*. In the supply and demand model, the equilibrium occurs when there is neither a shortage nor a surplus in the market. At this point, suppliers do not wish to reduce their price to remove a surplus nor do consumers wish to bid the price up to remove a shortage.

The equilibrium price occurs where the price paid by consumers equals the price received by suppliers. The equilibrium quantity occurs where the quantity demanded exactly equals the quantity supplied.

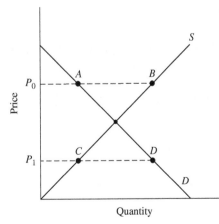

Figure 4-7   Supply and demand diagram.

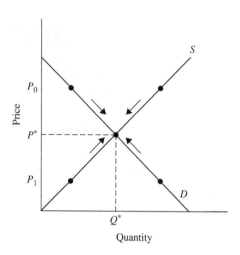

Figure 4-8 Market equilibrium.

At price P_0 in Figure 4-8, the quantity demanded is less than the quantity supplied. If suppliers lower their price, they will sell more than at P_0. At price P_1, suppliers produce too little. Suppliers can increase their price and sell more. Only at price P^* are suppliers not motivated to produce more and consumers are not motivated to bid up the price.

The equilibrium depicted in Figure 4-8 is only valid as long as the assumption of *ceteris paribus* holds. If something happens to change supply or demand, or both, the equilibrium price and quantity will likely change. The power of the supply and demand model is its ability to predict the directional change of price and quantity when something happens in a market. What happens to equilibrium price and quantity if supply, or demand, or both change?

The Supply and Demand for Crude Oil

After the U.S. invasion of Iraq in 2003, there was a considerable run-up in the price of crude oil. Some analysts blamed the threat of terrorist activity, either in the United States or in the Middle East, for the increase in price. Still others pointed to standard demand and supply influences to explain the increase in crude oil prices.

On the demand side, while the United States is the single largest consumer of crude oil in the world, since 2000 China has quickly become the second largest demander of crude oil in the world. The increase in demand can cause an increase in price. On the supply side, the United States has not dramatically increased its production of crude oil over the past few decades while the rest of the world's output of crude oil has remained stable or has slightly declined (mainly because of supply interruptions in Iraq).

The combination of supply and demand influences, coupled with uncertainty about the future of oil supply and demand conditions, are the main contributors to the increase in crude oil prices over the past few years.

Figure 4-9 shows how precariously close the interaction between supply and demand is for crude oil on the world market. From 1997 through 2004, and estimated for 2005, the world supply of crude oil has barely been more than the world demand for crude oil. Thus, any shock to the supply or the demand for crude oil, for example, a dramatic decrease in oil production from the Middle East or Venezuela could reduce the amount of crude oil available to the world market, leading to a shortage, and demanders would bid the price of oil up. On the other hand, the demand for oil could increase dramatically, say from China or India, and likewise bid up the price of oil.

Given the supply and demand model, there is very little that can be done to reduce the price of crude oil in the world market. The only way prices will fall

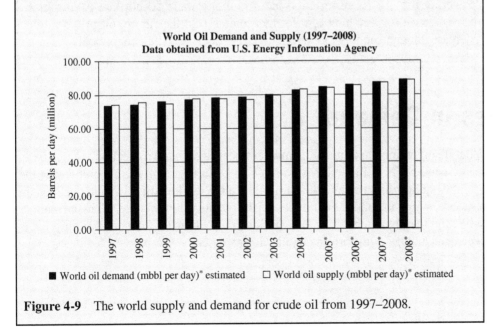

World Oil Demand and Supply (1997–2008)
Data obtained from U.S. Energy Information Agency

■ World oil demand (mbbl per day)* estimated   □ World oil supply (mbbl per day)* estimated

Figure 4-9 The world supply and demand for crude oil from 1997–2008.

in the future is if supply increases or demand decreases. It is unlikely that the demand for crude oil will decrease over the next century. As the developing and lesser-developed countries continue to produce more and their populations consume more, the demand for petroleum-based products (including, but not limited to, gasoline) will continue to increase. On the other hand, is it likely that the supply of oil will increase dramatically in the near to medium future? That is an important question for the world oil market. The supply of oil in the Caspian Sea area and the untapped reserves in Alaska and the Middle East and Africa might lead to an increase in the amount of oil supplied in the market, which might pose some downward pressure on the price of crude oil. However, the demand for crude oil in the future is likely to outpace supply, suggesting that the price of crude oil will likely increase.

An interesting possibility is an alternative fuel, which could reduce the demand for crude oil considerably. This is the stated goal of the United States, the European Union, and the United Nations. However desirable it is to reduce the amount of crude oil consumed, it is dangerous to assume that a replacement fuel would necessarily reduce the costs of transportation and other petroleum based products. Indeed, it is entirely possible that alternatives to oil will be more expensive, because if they were cheaper than oil, they would have already been introduced to the market place. Notwithstanding conspiracy theories about the big oil companies controlling the oil market and squashing alternative means of powering the U.S. transportation industry, consumers do not like paying high prices for oil (or anything else for that matter!). In the future, oil prices might increase enough such that an alternative fuel does become economical.

Changes in Demand

What if something happens in the market to cause demand to decline? In this case, the demand shifts to the left, say from D_0 to D_1 in Figure 4-10. If Point E was the original equilibrium, there will be a surplus in the market after demand declines. In response, suppliers reduce their price and the quantity they wish to sell in the market. When the market reaches its new equilibrium at Point E', the equilibrium price is decreased and the equilibrium quantity is decreased.

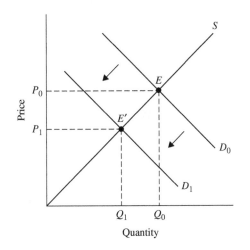

Figure 4-10   Changes in demand.

If something occurs in the market to cause an increase in demand, the demand curve shifts to the right. If supply does not change, what happens to equilibrium price and quantity? In Figure 4-10, if the original equilibrium was at Point E', an increase in demand would cause a shortage at the original equilibrium price. In response, consumers would bid up the price and encourage suppliers to offer more quantity in the market. The result is that at the new equilibrium, Point E, the equilibrium price and quantity will have both increased which is the exact opposite of what happened when demand decreased.

Changes in Supply

An increase in supply corresponds with the supply curve shifting right. If demand does not change, what happens to equilibrium price and quantity? In Figure 4-11, supply increases from S_0 to S_1. After supply increases, there is a surplus in the market at the original equilibrium price. In response, suppliers cut price, which increases the quantity demanded. At the new equilibrium, Point E', the equilibrium quantity has increased and the equilibrium price has decreased. If supply decreases, say from S_1 to S_0, the impact on equilibrium price and quantity is exactly the opposite: equilibrium price P^* increases and equilibrium quantity Q^* declines.

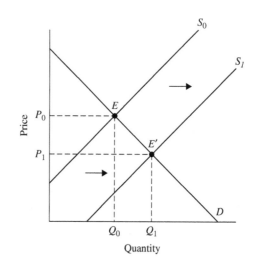

Figure 4-11   Changes in supply.

Changes in Supply and Demand

What happens to the equilibrium price and quantity if both supply and demand change simultaneously? The answer depends on the relative changes in supply and demand. If both supply and demand increase, then the equilibrium quantity Q^* will increase (quantity increases after both an increase in supply and an increase in demand). However, it is not clear what will happen to equilibrium price (price increases after an increase in demand but decreases after an increase in supply). If supply shifts more than demand, the equilibrium price will decrease. On the other hand, if demand increases more than supply, the equilibrium price will increase. In Figure 4-12, both demand and supply have increased from an original equilibrium at Point E to a new equilibrium at Point E'. In Figure 4-12, supply increases more than demand and therefore equilibrium price falls from P_0 to P_1.

If both supply and demand decline simultaneously then equilibrium quantity Q^* will decrease (quantity decreases with a decrease in supply and also with a decrease in demand). However, once again it is not clear what will happen to equilibrium price (price tends to drop if demand declines but tends to increase if supply decreases). If demand decreases more than supply, then equilibrium price will decline. On the other hand, if supply declines more than demand, then equilibrium price will increase. If S_1 and D_1 represented an original equilibrium at Point E', a decrease in both supply and demand to Point E would cause an increase in price because supply decreased more than demand.

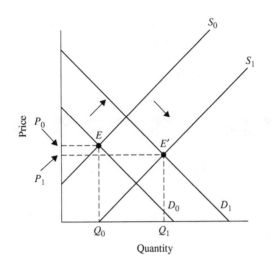

Figure 4-12   Increase in both demand and supply.

Additional combinations of supply and demand changes can be investigated. Consider an increase in supply and a decrease in demand. In this case, equilibrium price is guaranteed to decline (price decreases with an increase in supply and price decreases with a drop in demand). However, it is not clear if equilibrium quantity will increase or decrease (the equilibrium quantity declines after a decrease in demand but increases after an increase in supply). In Figure 4-13, the original

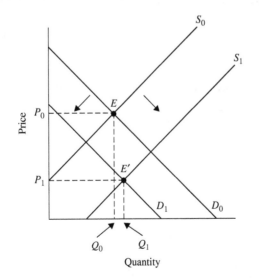

Figure 4-13   Increase in supply and a decrease in demand.

equilibrium condition is at Point E. Supply increases from S_0 to S_1, whereas demand decreases from D_0 to D_1. After the market moves to the new equilibrium at Point E', the equilibrium price declines from P_0 to P_1. Because the decrease in demand is less than the increase in supply, quantity increases from Q_0 to Q_1.

Seasonal Demand for Convertibles

The demand for convertible automobiles in December is likely to be different compared to June, at least for most places in the United States. Driving a convertible is only fun during the warm months when having the top down is enjoyable. When the weather is warmer, the demand for convertible automobiles is likely to be high, and when the weather turns cold and dreary the demand for convertible automobiles drops.

Automobile manufacturers understand that the demand for convertibles is seasonal and therefore target their promotional material to coincide with the time when convertible demand is greatest. As an example, consider the graph in Figure 4-14, which depicts the average monthly sales of Mazda Miata convertibles from 1998 through 2003.

It is readily apparent that sales for Mazda Miatas peak in May, hold relatively steady through the summer months, and then fall off dramatically during the fall and winter months. Thus, if you were in the market for a Mazda Miata, you might find a better price during the winter months when the equilibrium number of Miatas sold is relatively lower than during the summer months when the equilibrium number of Miatas sold is relatively high.

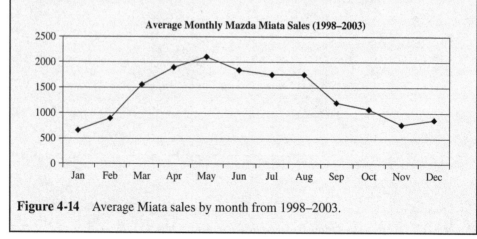

Figure 4-14   Average Miata sales by month from 1998–2003.

The last possibility is that supply decreases while demand increases. In this case, P^0 will increase (price increases when supply drops and price increases when demand increases), yet it is not clear if equilibrium quantity will increase or decrease. If the decrease in supply is more than the increase in demand, then equilibrium quantity will decrease. If the increase in demand is more than the decrease in supply, then equilibrium quantity will increase.

Government Interventions in the Market

Markets are surprisingly resilient mechanisms. When left to their own devices, suppliers and demanders interact with each other through price and quantity to reach equilibrium. If price is allowed to freely fluctuate, a change in either supply or demand that leads to a shortage causes price to increase, whereas a change in either supply or demand that leads to a surplus causes price to decrease. Both of these reactions allow a market to reobtain equilibrium after something has changed.

However, many times the response by the market is not what people desire. For instance, when a hurricane warning is in effect in Florida, it is likely that the demand for plywood will increase and the supply of plywood will not increase dramatically in the immediate short run. Given our knowledge of supply and demand, we would expect the price of plywood to increase in the short run. This is the market's response to the increase in demand and is rather intuitive. Unfortunately, people often do not like the market's response and accuse suppliers of price-gouging or charging exorbitant prices. Legislation in many states makes it illegal for suppliers to increase their prices dramatically, even if demand increases dramatically in the short run.

In the case of plywood, if price is not allowed to increase after an increase in demand, the quantity demanded will be greater than the quantity supplied and there will be a shortage in the market. In a free market, prices would increase and some people would be priced out of the market for plywood. These individuals would (hopefully) find some alternative to plywood with which to protect their property. However, if the price is not allowed to increase, then people who would normally be priced out of the market stick around, hoping for plywood and, perhaps, being lucky enough to obtain some. In cases like this, individuals who obtain the product have, in essence, won a lottery instead of participating in a market in which price reveals the value that people place on the product.

The only agent that has the means and power to intervene in markets of reasonable size is the government. Governments intervene in many, if not most, markets in various ways, including regulation, taxation, standardization, liability, and other

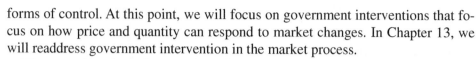
forms of control. At this point, we will focus on government interventions that focus on how price and quantity can respond to market changes. In Chapter 13, we will readdress government intervention in the market process.

There are three basic interventions that governments can undertake in a market. Price floors, or policies that limit how low prices can fall, price ceilings, or policies that limit how high prices can rise, and quantity quotas, or limits on how much quantity can be sold in the market.

Price Floors and Ceilings

A *price floor* is a policy that limits, by law, how low a price can fall in a market. Usually the limit is chosen arbitrarily, but if the law is to be binding, it must set the price floor above the free market equilibrium price.

If the price is frozen above the equilibrium level, say at P^F in Figure 4-15, the quantity supplied (indicated at Point B) is greater than it would be at the free market equilibrium (Point E). Also the quantity demanded (indicated at Point A) is less than it would be in a free-market equilibrium. Why would the government want to impose a price floor? Price floors usually arise when suppliers want to be "protected" from lower prices and therefore pressure the government to pass legislation that will raise price above its natural equilibrium price.

Price floors lead to surpluses because the price is higher than it would be in equilibrium. Suppliers who would not supply the good at the lower free-market equilibrium price are encouraged to produce at the artificially high price. Likewise,

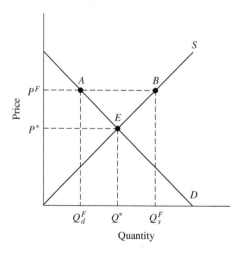

Figure 4-15   The impact of a price floor.

consumers who would purchase the good at the lower equilibrium price will not buy at the artificially high price.

Because a price floor prevents prices from falling, excess inventories for the good develops and free-market price movements cannot remedy the surplus in the market. Often the government purchases the excess supply. An additional negative effect of a price floor is that resources are diverted away from activities in which they have a comparative advantage. If the price of the good were allowed to drop to the market equilibrium, then some resources would move to other markets where they have a comparative advantage.

A *price ceiling* is a legal limit on how high a market price can increase. For the law to be binding, it must restrict price to be *lower* than the free-market equilibrium price. Why would such a policy be chosen? Often, government officials claim they want to make the good affordable to more people. However, this is a false promise. Goods with price ceilings tend to have long lines associated with them, such as concert tickets. Therefore, the real cost of purchasing a product with a price ceiling is often just as great as it would be without the price ceiling. For example, assume the equilibrium price is $15 and a price ceiling keeps the price at $5. This sounds like a good deal. However, if you have a job that pays $10 per hour and you have to wait in line for one hour to purchase the product at $5, then the real cost of the good is $15—exactly what the free-market equilibrium price would be.

Why do lines develop for goods with price ceilings? Consider Figure 4-16, where the free-market equilibrium price and quantity are indicated by P^* and Q^*, respectively. At the equilibrium price level, the quantity supplied equals the quantity demanded.

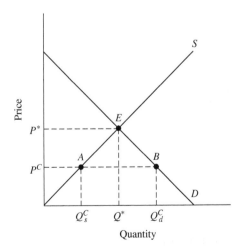

Figure 4-16 The impact of a price ceiling.

When the price of the good is restricted to be no higher than P^C, there is an artificial shortage in the market. The quantity demanded, indicated at Point B, is much greater than the quantity supplied, indicated at Point A. Even if the price ceiling were intended to make it easier for people to afford the good, the artificial shortage leads to individuals waiting in line or otherwise not being able to obtain the product when they want it.

If the price could increase, then those consumers who value the product more would bid up the price and the line (or wait time) would diminish. This is because some consumers will leave the market as the price increases.

Quantity Controls

Sometimes, governments intervene in a free market through a quantity quota. A quota is a legal limit placed on the quantity that can be sold in the market. To be binding, a quota must be set below the free-market equilibrium quantity. Normally quotas are placed upon imported goods.

In the market depicted in Figure 4-17, the free-market equilibrium quantity is at Q^*, however the government restricts quantity in the market to be less than Q^*, say Q_q. The quantity quota creates a shortage in the market relative to the free-market equilibrium quantity. In response, consumers bid up the price of the limited amount of product on the market. Suppliers increase the price until the quantity demanded is equal to the quantity quota, at price P_q in Figure 4-17. The price of the product

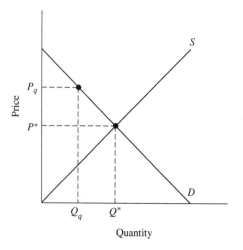

Figure 4-17   The impact of a quantity quota.

with a quantity quota is greater than the free-market equilibrium price P^*. In response, the demand for the product's substitutes will increase. For example, if a quota is placed on Hondas being imported from Japan, the price of Hondas will increase and the demand for substitutes to Hondas, such as Pontiacs or Fords, will also increase.

Taxation in the Supply and Demand Model

The vast majority of products sold in the United States are subject to either a sales tax or a per-unit tax. For example, when you purchase a compact disc you pay the sticker price, but you also pay sales tax, say 5%. Thus, if the sticker price of the compact disc is $15, the total price, you, as the consumer will pay is $15 + ($15 × 0.05) = $15 + $0.75 = $15.75. It may seem that you as a consumer pay the entire tax or that suppliers simply "pass along" the tax to consumers. However, this is not the case. The analysis of taxation using the supply and demand model leads to insights that most people do not naturally obtain without using economics. A sales or per-unit tax is yet another case where economic reasoning provides tools with which to analyze the world and to obtain a deeper understanding of what is happening around us.

There are several types of taxes that local, state, and federal governments place in markets. Some of these taxes are fairly obvious, such as sales taxes and vehicle registration taxes. Other taxes are less obvious. For example, each year lawyers in most states must pay a fee in order to practice law in their state. Other examples of licensing fees include drivers' licenses, business licenses, fire-arms licenses, and hunting licenses, to name a few.

Licensing fees are an example of a per-unit tax, which is a fixed fee charged on each unit. An alternative is the *ad valorem* tax, which is a tax based upon the value of the good involved. A sales tax is an example. If the sales tax is 5%, then the total tax paid on a $15 compact disc is $0.75, but the total tax on a $15,000 automobile is $750. While the percentage stays the same, the total tax paid varies by the value of the good being taxed. Most governments use a combination of per-unit and *ad valorem* taxes, the choice of which to use is sometimes common sense and other times determined by political considerations.

Nevertheless, the imposition of a tax in a market is likely to alter the equilibrium from its natural price and quantity combination; if it didn't, then there would be no "cost" to a government imposing a tax and we would see a lot more taxation than we do today. The questions to ask when analyzing the impact of a tax is what happens to the quantity sold in the market, what happens to the price consumers pay, what happens to the price producers receive, and how much revenue is generated by the tax (there are actually a few more questions, but we will address those in Chapters 5 and 6).

It is natural to assume that the imposition of a tax will raise the price that consumers will spend on a product, but it is not so obvious what will happen to the price producers receive, nor how much quantity will be sold in the market. It might seem that there would be no impact on the equilibrium quantity sold in the market, but this would seem to violate the law of demand, which claims that as price increases, the quantity demanded decreases. Notice that the law of demand does not specify *why* price increased—it can happen because of changes in demand, supply, or because the government intervenes in the market.

It is easiest to depict the impact of a tax by using a per-unit tax (things do not change very much if we analyze an *ad valorem* tax, but the graph is a little more messy). Consider the demand for gasoline in the state of Montana. The state government knows that there is a supply and demand for gasoline. The greater the price, the fewer the gallons of gasoline demanded and the more the gallons of gasoline supplied. Assume that the state of Montana decides to place a $0.30 per-gallon tax on gasoline; what will happen in the market for gasoline?

Let us consider the impact of the tax by looking at the original equilibrium condition, as depicted in Figure 4-18. There, the equilibrium price for a gallon of gasoline is $1.45 and the equilibrium gallons of gasoline sold each day is 250,000. What will happen when the state decides to impose a tax on gasoline? First, the price that consumers pay no longer equals the price those producers keep. This is because someone has to pay the tax to the state government. Indeed, the difference between what consumers pay and producers keep is the per-unit tax: $t = P^d - P^s$. This is different than the free market in which $P^d = P^s$.

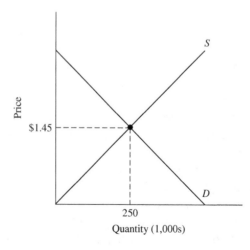

Figure 4-18 The market for gasoline without a per-unit tax.

At this point, all we are interested in is what will happen to the market price and quantity of gasoline sold in Montana. Let us take a generic approach first and then return to our specific example of gasoline in Montana. Figure 4-19 shows the impact of a per-unit tax in a generic supply and demand model.

The per-unit tax increases the effective price for every unit sold in the market. Therefore, it is convenient to interpret the per-unit tax as shifting the supply curve "up" (actually to the left), such that at every possible quantity the effective price is t more than what the suppliers require, P^s. The "shift" in the supply curve is depicted by what is called a "shadow supply curve," which is the supply curve the *market* will use to reach equilibrium. The original demand curve, original supply curve, and shadow supply curve are all depicted in Figure 4-19.

The market equilibrium quantity is obtained when the quantity demanded is equal to the quantity supplied, which occurs at Q_t in Figure 4-19. Notice that the quantity sold in equilibrium is less than Q^*, which was the amount of output sold in the free market. The price consumers pay is P^d, but the price producers keep is P^s. In general, the price of a good tends not to increase by the full amount of the tax, although it might seem that way when you pay the tax at the checkout counter. What happens in most markets is that when taxes are imposed on the market, the equilibrium price that consumers pay is not simply the free-market price plus the tax.

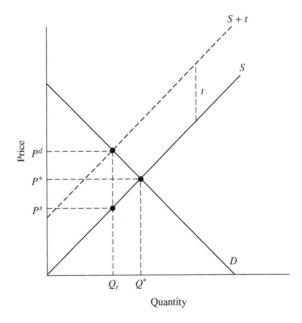

Figure 4-19 The impact of a per-unit tax in generic supply and demand model.

Rather, consumers pay a portion of the tax (the difference between P^d and P^* in Figure 4-19), and producers pay a portion of the tax (the difference between P^* and P^s in Figure 4-19).

Now, we can turn back to our hypothetical example of imposing a $0.30 per-gallon tax on gasoline in Montana. Figure 4-18 depicts the hypothetical market and provides numbers for discussion purposes. The original supply and demand curve intersected to provide a market-clearing price of $1.450 per gallon and a market clearing quantity of 250,000 gallons per day. After the tax is imposed, the supply curve will shift "up" to the shadow supply curve $S + t$, depicted by the dashed line in Figure 4-20. The new equilibrium occurs at 200,000 gallons of gasoline sold, consumers pay $1.60 per gallon and suppliers keep $1.30 per gallon. The difference between the price paid and the price kept by suppliers is the per-gallon tax of $0.30.

A common mistake made by politicians and the general public is to suspect that changing tax rates (whether per unit or *ad valorem*) will have no impact on the purchasing behavior of individuals. Unless the product is very unique in that prices do not affect the quantity demanded, it must be the case that raising taxes will reduce the quantity demanded. In many cases, taxes are used for this very purpose, that is, to dissuade consumption. For example, cigarette and liquor excise taxes are commonly justified on the grounds that the public would like to discourage smoking. However, it is important to remember that if the taxes are raised sufficiently

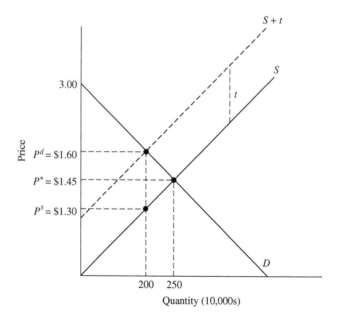

Figure 4-20   Demand, supply and shadow supply with a per-unit tax.

high, the tax revenue can be driven to zero. This is because sufficiently high tax can drive consumption to zero. If there is no quantity sold in the market, there is no tax revenue generated in the market.

A proper analysis of tax changes considers the "dynamics" of the market, that is, how will people respond *after* the tax has been increased or imposed on the market. It is incorrect to base projected tax revenue assuming that the original equilibrium quantity Q^* will be sold after the tax is imposed in the market.

Genetic Manipulation of Children

As medical science continues to improve, there is one area of bioethics that has concerned many: the potential to genetically engineer children to predetermined specifications. For instance, it might one day be possible to manipulate the genetic contribution of mother and father to ensure that the child has blue eyes, blonde hair, or is seven feet tall. The general concern is that income might determine the ability for parents to genetically alter their children, and this might further exacerbate income inequality or otherwise favor the "haves" over the "have-nots."

While it is possible that a certain proportion of parents might want to ensure that their children have blue eyes and blonde hair, the supply and demand model can provide some guidance as to how prevalent the practice is likely to be and whether it is necessary to pass legislation to prevent such manipulation in the future.

Consider the demand and supply of seven-foot-tall basketball players. The demand for seven-foot-tall basketball players is basically limited to the professional basketball leagues around the world, most notably the National Basketball Association (NBA) in North America. While there are other jobs for which seven-foot-tall people have a comparative advantage, such as changing lightbulbs without a ladder, these are not the jobs that those concerned about the ethics of genetic manipulation point to. The tremendous amount of money available to today's seven-foot-tall basketball players who are good enough to play in the professional leagues might provide sufficient temptation for a set of parents to predispose their children to be seven feet tall and therefore have at least one of the conditions necessary to be seven-foot-tall basketball player.

Simply making a person seven-foot-tall does not guarantee that the individual will be a good basketball player, nor does it guarantee that they will be good enough to earn a spot on a NBA roster. However, given the current supply and demand conditions, the payoff to a seven-foot-tall basketball player can be substantial, as depicted in Figure 4-21. The supply of seven-feet-tall basketball

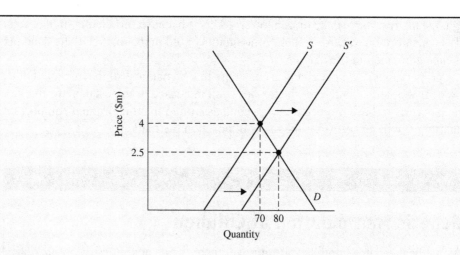

Figure 4-21 The demand and supply of seven-foot-tall basketball players.

players is relatively fixed, and hence the supply curve is relatively steep. On the other side of the market, the demand for seven-foot-tall basketball players is likewise relatively steep because of the limited number of teams who demand tall basketball players.

The equilibrium price and quantity of tall basketball players indicates that there will be 70 basketball players hired at a salary of $4 million per year. What is likely to happen if individuals can genetically alter their children?

Assume that every couple that could genetically alter their children to be seven feet tall did so. This would dramatically increase the supply of seven-foot-tall basketball players. If the demand for tall basketball players did not change, the equilibrium price for these players would drop, but the number of tall basketball players hired would not change much. Therefore, a lot of parents would make their children seven feet tall, but not many of these children would be likely to get a job playing in the NBA.

Unfortunately for the child, if the parents manipulate their genes such that they do become seven feet tall, this alteration is not reversible. Perhaps being seven feet tall and *not* playing in the NBA would be a detriment to the child as an adult. Economists would predict that rational parents would foresee these demand and supply conditions, as well as the potential for additional costs to be imposed on their genetically altered children. Thus, the fears that all parents would make their children seven feet tall might be misplaced.

However, what if parents instead changed something less drastic, say hair color or eye color. Would the bioethicists be justified in voicing concern that, if children could be genetically altered, those parents who could afford, would make their children blue eyed and blonde haired, thereby leading us to a world of homogenous children? The first thing to question is why the parents would choose these attributes in their genetic alteration. Perhaps the parents would choose these attributes because they perceive them as having some higher value in society.

However, the parents' perceptions would be based upon the society they live in, not the society their children will live in. Perhaps the society in which the parents live places a larger premium on blue eyes or blonde hair, and less on red hair and green eyes, and thus parents might want to ensure their children the advantages of blue eyes and blonde hair. However, these parents are actually undermining the premium with which they hope to endow their children with. As the supply of blonde-haired, blue-eyed people increases, the value placed on these attributes will decrease, as depicted in Figure 4-22. However, as the supply of red-haired, green-eyed individuals declines (as some of these people would now be genetically altered to have blonde hair and blue eyes), society would place a greater value on red hair and green eyes, as depicted in Figure 4-22.

Thus, the genetic manipulation of children in certain characteristics would be expected to reduce the differences between the values placed on the very attributes the parents are trying to change. While there might be legitimate concerns

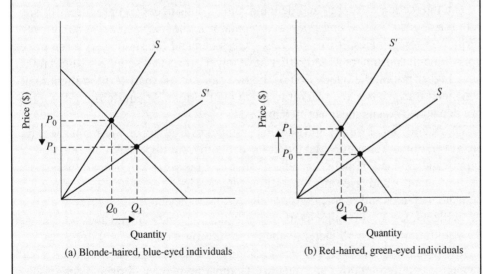

(a) Blonde-haired, blue-eyed individuals   (b) Red-haired, green-eyed individuals

Figure 4-22 Changes in the supply of blonde-haired, blue-eyed individuals and the supply of red-haired, green-eyed individuals.

on the part of bioethicists about genetically altered children, the concepts of supply and demand would suggest that the high benefits that accrue to some attributes today might not be so high in the future, and some attributes which do not seem to be highly valued today might become more valuable in the future. This suggests that concerns about genetically altering children might be overstated. This is because rational parents will recognize that the attributes they find so desirable are also the traits that other parents find desirable. In the end, perhaps the reasons to choose one trait over another would not be dollars and cents but aesthetics or the personal preferences of parents, neither of which are in the direct purview of ethics.

Summary

This chapter develops the model of supply and demand. Demand is the relationship between price and the quantity of a product that consumers wish to purchase. Supply is the relationship between price and the quantity of a product that suppliers are willing to sell. The law of demand states that consumers will purchase more when prices are lower, and vice versa. The law of supply states producers will make more when prices are higher, and vice versa.

The interaction of supply and demand allows consumers and producers to allocate scarce resources. Using price as a regulator in the market, excess supplies (or surpluses) force prices down, whereas excess demand (or shortages) force prices up. Although consumers would rather have lower prices and suppliers would rather have higher prices, the interaction of the two sides of the market through mutually beneficial trade causes the market to reach equilibrium. At equilibrium, the quantity demanded equals the quantity supplied.

The interaction of supply and demand assumes everything else remains the same. However, things constantly change in the economy. An important question that the supply and demand model is capable of answering is what will happen to the equilibrium quantity and price after something changes in the economy. For example, if demand increases and supply does not change, both the equilibrium price and quantity will increase. On the other hand, if supply declines and demand does not change, the equilibrium price will increase and the equilibrium quantity will decrease.

It is possible to combine changes in supply and demand to determine what will happen to equilibrium price and quantity. Comparing two equlibria and determining whether price or quantity increases or decreases is called comparative statics. Comparative statics is a powerful tool with which to predict the impact on price and quantity.

The chapter concluded by analyzing the impacts on equilibrium price and quantity after government intervention in the free-market: including price floors, price ceilings, quantity quotas, and per-unit taxation.

Quiz

1. If demand decreases and supply decreases, then in the short-run

   a. both equilibrium price and quantity increase.

   b. both equilibrium price and quantity decrease.

   c. equilibrium price increases and equilibrium quantity decreases.

   d. equilibrium quantity decreases and equilibrium price can either increase or decrease.

2. The law of supply states that

   a. as price increases supply decreases.

   b. as price increases quantity supplied increases.

   c. as price increases quantity supplied decreases.

   d. as price increases quantity demanded decreases.

3. A normal good is one where

   a. demand does not change after an increase in income.

   b. demand increases after an increase in income.

   c. demand decreases after an increase in income.

   d. demand decreases after an increase in supply.

4. Which of the following would not permanently affect demand?

   a. Weather

   b. Expected future prices

   c. Income

   d. Prices of substitutes and complements in consumption

5. Suppose we observe a decrease in the price of oranges. Which of the following is *not* a possible cause?

   a. A decrease in the price of apples

   b. A freeze in Florida

   c. An increase in the number of orange growers

   d. An increase in the price of furniture made from orange trees

6. If congress debates a ban on flip-flops, what would one expect to see happen?

   a. An increase in the demand for flip-flops and a decrease in the supply of flip-flops

   b. A decrease in the demand for flip-flops and an increase in the supply of flip-flops

   c. An increase in the demand for flip-flops and an increase in the supply of flip-flops

   d. A decrease in the demand for flip-flops and a decrease in the supply of flip-flops

   e. None of the above

7. If population increases and the number of firms decreases, what would one expect to see happening to equilibrium price and quantity?

   a. Price increases and quantity decreases

   b. Price increases and quantity increases

   c. Quantity increases and the price change is ambiguous

   d. Price increases and the quantity change is ambiguous

   e. None of the above

8. Price floors are typically favored by

   a. suppliers.

   b. demanders.

   c. the government.

   d. foreign investors.

   e. none of the above.

9. Which of the following is a result of a price ceiling?

   a. Excess supply

   b. Long lines or wait times for consumers

   c. The cost of removal of excess supply

   d. The cost of shifting resources away from their comparative advantage

   e. Producers sell their products at higher prices

10. Minimum wage laws are an example of what kind of market control?

   a. Quota

   b. Price floor

   c. Price ceiling

   d. Cruise control

   e. None of the above

11. Figure 4-23 depicts two market equilibria. Equilibrium *A* is the original equilibrium, and Equilibrium *B* is the new equilibrium. Which of the following is a possible explanation for the change?

   a. An increase in the price of a complement

   b. An increase in the price of a substitute in consumption

   c. An increase in the income of the consumers

   d. An increase in the price of a vital component to the good

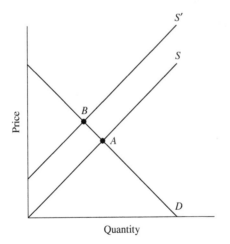

Figure 4-23

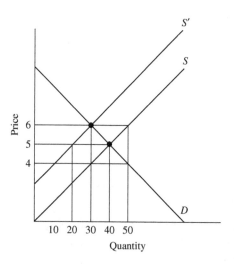

Figure 4-24

12. Use Figure 4-24. Suppose the government proposes to impose a $2.00 per-unit tax. What will be the impact on the quantity sold in the market?

   a. It increases by 10.

   b. It decreases by 20.

   c. It decreases by 10.

   d. It decreases by 30.

   e. It does not change.

13. In the market depicted in Figure 4-24, what is the total tax revenue generated by the $2.00 tax?

   a. 80

   b. 40

   c. 45

   d. 60

   e. 30

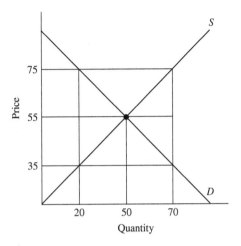

Figure 4-25

14. Use Figure 4-25. Suppose the government proposes to impose a price floor. What price is most likely to be chosen?

    a. 75

    b. 55

    c. 35

    d. 0

15. Use Figure 4-25. If the government proposes to impose a price ceiling, which price is most likely to be chosen?

    a. 75

    b. 55

    c. 35

    d. 0

5

Elasticity

The previous chapter described the mechanics of the supply and demand model and how changes in supply and demand influence equilibrium price and quantity. For instance, a decrease in supply, *ceteris paribus*, causes a decrease in the equilibrium quantity sold and an increase in the equilibrium price.

Suppose a supply change occurs that causes an increase in the equilibrium price and a decrease in the equilibrium quantity. For example, a cold snap wipes out half of the orange crop in Florida. We know that the price will increase and the quantity sold will decrease. However, what will happen to the total revenue in the orange market? Total revenue is defined as the product of price and quantity. While it might seem that revenues are guaranteed to increase because price increased, this is not the case. In fact, the change in industry revenue depends on the change in equilibrium quantity relative to the change in price.

To help clarify the ambiguity, economists use a measure called elasticity. Elasticity measures the relative change in one variable in response to a relative change in another variable. There are numerous elasticities used in microeconomics, but this chapter will discuss the most popular.

Price Elasticity of Demand

One of the most common elasticities used in microeconomics is the price elasticity of demand, which is defined as the relative change in quantity demanded due to a relative change in price. The elasticity of demand is measured between two points on the demand curve, which correspond to two different price-quantity combinations. These two combinations provide the numbers required to calculate the price elasticity of demand (see below). The price elasticity of demand is formally defined by the following formula:

$$\varepsilon_D^P = -\frac{\%\Delta Q^d}{\%\Delta P^d}$$

which comprises three elements. First is the percentage change in the quantity demanded, calculated as

$$\%\Delta Q^d = \frac{Q_1 - Q_0}{\bar{Q}}$$

where Q_0 is the original quantity demanded and Q_1 is the new quantity demanded, and $\bar{Q}$ is the average quantity in the two price-quantity combinations. The second element is the relative change in the price, calculated as

$$\%\Delta P^d = \frac{P_1 - P_0}{\bar{P}}$$

where P_0 is the original price and P_1 is the new price, and $\bar{P}$ is the average price in the two price-quantity combinations. The third element is the minus sign at the front of the equation for the price elasticity of demand. The law of demand states that there is an inverse relationship between price and quantity demanded. Therefore, if price increases, the quantity demanded will decrease, and if the price decreases, then the quantity demanded will increase. Either way, the price elasticity of demand is naturally negative because the numerator and denominator of the equation for price elasticity will have opposite signs. For convenience, economists convert the negative number into a positive number by multiplying it by –1.

If we substitute the two equations for $\%\Delta Q^d$ and $\%\Delta P^d$ into the original equation for the price elasticity of demand we obtain:

$$\varepsilon_D^P = -\frac{\%\Delta Q^d}{\%\Delta P^d} = -\frac{\dfrac{Q_1 - Q_0}{\bar{Q}}}{\dfrac{P_1 - P_0}{\bar{P}}} = -\frac{Q_1 - Q_0}{P_1 - P_0} \times \frac{\bar{P}}{\bar{Q}}$$

This equation looks complicated, but it is actually very simple to use. Consider three examples. First, assume $Q_0 = 10$, $P_0 = 3$ and $Q_1 = 6$, $P_1 = 5$. The change in quantity is from 10 to 6 or –4. The change in price is from 3 to 5 or +2. The average quantity is 8 and the average price is 4. The price elasticity of demand is then calculated as

$$\varepsilon_D^P = -\left(\frac{6-10}{5-3}\right)\left(\frac{8/2}{16/2}\right) = -\left(\frac{-4}{2}\right)\left(\frac{4}{8}\right) = 1$$

A second example: Assume $Q_0 = 10$, $P_0 = 2$ and $Q_1 = 6$, $P_1 = 5$. Here, the quantity change is –4, the price change is +3, the average quantity is 8, and the average price is $7/2$. The price elasticity of demand is then calculated as

$$\varepsilon_D^P = -\left(\frac{6-10}{5-2}\right)\left(\frac{7/2}{16/2}\right) = -\left(\frac{-4}{3}\right)\left(\frac{7}{16}\right) = \frac{7}{12}$$

A final example: Assume $Q_0 = 10$, $P_0 = 4$ and $Q_1 = 6$, $P_1 = 5$. Here, the quantity change is –4, the price change is +1, the average quantity is 8, and the average price is $7/2$. The price elasticity of demand is then calculated as

$$\varepsilon_D^P = -\left(\frac{6-10}{5-4}\right)\left(\frac{9/2}{8}\right) = -\left(\frac{-4}{1}\right)\left(\frac{9}{16}\right) = \frac{9}{4} = 2\frac{1}{4}$$

We use average price and average quantity because if we didn't, there would be two different elasticities between the same two points on the demand curve. This would not make sense and is avoided by using the average price and average quantity.

The concept of elasticity is valuable because elasticities are "unitless." The measure does not depend on the goods being measured or how prices are measured. The price elasticity of demand can fall anywhere on the range of zero to infinity, but most markets have demand elasticities in the neighborhood of one.

The following conventions are used in economics: perfect inelasticity (elasticity equal to zero), relative inelasticity (elasticity between zero and one), unitary elasticity (elasticity equal to one), relative elasticity (elasticity greater than one and less than infinity), and perfect elasticity (elasticity equal to infinity). Above, we had three different price elasticities equal to 1, $7/12$, and $9/4$. The first is unitary elastic (that is equal to one), the second is relatively inelastic (that is less than one), and the last is relatively elastic (that is greater than one).

Perfect inelasticity corresponds with price elasticity equal to zero; perfectly vertical demand curves are perfectly inelastic. On the other hand, perfect elasticity corresponds to a price elasticity that is equal to infinity; perfectly horizontal demand curves are perfectly elastic. Most demand curves fall between the extremes of perfectly vertical or perfectly horizontal and therefore tend to have elasticities

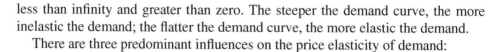

less than infinity and greater than zero. The steeper the demand curve, the more inelastic the demand; the flatter the demand curve, the more elastic the demand.

There are three predominant influences on the price elasticity of demand:

1. *The number of substitutes for the good.* Recall that substitutes are goods used in place of each other. If a product has several substitutes, then an increase in price will lead to a relatively large decrease in quantity demanded as consumers switch to substitutes, implying a relatively elastic demand. On the other hand, if a good does not have many substitutes, a price change does not change quantity demanded very much, implying a relatively inelastic demand. For example, apples have a relatively large number of substitutes, including oranges, grapefruit, and grapes, to name a few. An increase in the price of the apples will likely cause a relatively large decrease in quantity demanded, i.e., the demand for apples is relatively elastic. On the other hand, doctors do not have easy-to-find substitutes. Therefore, if the price of visiting your doctor increases, it is unlikely that you will choose not to visit her when you are sick. The demand for doctors is relatively inelastic.

2. *The amount of disposable income spent on the good.* The greater the share of your income spent on a good, the more elastic the demand. This is because a small percentage increase in price can take a big bite out of a household's discretionary income and cause the household to reconsider how they will spend their money, i.e., look for substitutes. For example, if the price of chewing gum increased in price from $0.30 to $0.40, this would represent a 33% increase in price, and yet you would likely not purchase dramatically fewer packs of chewing gum. On the other hand, if the price of a $20,000 car increases by the same percentage ($6,600), it is likely that the quantity demanded for cars will decline dramatically.

3. *The duration of the price change.* Generally, the longer a price change is in place, the more elastic demand is. As time passes, it is more likely that a substitute can be found for the good. For example, if the price of gasoline increased by $0.10 a gallon for a single week, it is unlikely that you will purchase a more fuel-efficient car; you will likely pay the higher price in the short run. In other words, the short-run demand for gasoline is extremely inelastic. However, if the price of gasoline were to increase by $2.00 per gallon for the next year, most of us would try to substitute out of gasoline either through carpooling or by buying more fuel-efficient cars; the quantity of gasoline purchased would decline dramatically. In other words, the long-run demand for gasoline is more elastic.

It is possible to qualify the elasticity as relatively elastic or relatively inelastic. However, what do these conventions imply? If demand is elastic, a price increase will correlate with a decrease in industry revenue. On the other hand, if demand is inelastic a price increase will correlate with an increase in industry revenue.

Total revenue in a market equals the equilibrium price times the equilibrium quantity, i.e., $TR = P^* \times Q^*$. How much quantity drops relative to the price increase determines what will happen to industry revenue. If a one percent change in price causes less than a one percent decline in quantity demanded, then demand is relatively inelastic and the price change will cause an increase in the industry's total revenue. For example, assume that $P_0 = \$10$ and $Q_0 = 100$, and $P_1 = \$15$ and $Q_1 = 80$. What is the price elasticity of demand? The original equilibrium corresponded to a total revenue of $TR = \$10 \times 100 = \$1000$, and the new equilibrium corresponds to a total revenue of $TR = \$15 \times 80 = \$1200$. Therefore, even though price increased and quantity decreased, total revenue increased.

If a one percent change in price corresponds with a greater than one percent change in quantity demanded, then demand is relatively elastic and the price change will cause a decrease in industry total revenues. For example, assume that $P_0 = \$10$ and $Q_0 = 100$, and $P_1 = \$15$ and $Q_1 = 60$. What is the price elasticity of demand? The original equilibrium corresponds to a total revenue of $TR = \$10 \times 100 = \$1000$, but the new equilibrium corresponds to a total revenue of $TR = \$15 \times 60 = \$900$. When demand is relatively elastic, price increases lead to a decrease in total revenue.

A final example is, a one percent increase in price corresponds to a one percent decrease in quantity demanded, in which case demand is unitary elastic and a price change does not change total revenue. For example, assume that $P_0 = \$10$ and $Q_0 = 100$, and $P_1 = \$20$ and $Q_1 = 50$. What is the price elasticity of demand? The original equilibrium corresponds to a total revenue of $TR = \$10 \times 100 = \$1000$, and the new equilibrium corresponds to a total revenue of $TR = \$20 \times 50 = \$1000$. When demand is unitary elastic price increases do not cause changes in total revenue.

Returning to the question asked at the beginning of this chapter, if a cold snap destroyed half of the orange crop in Florida, we know that price will increase and the quantity sold will decrease. However, the price elasticity of demand for oranges will ultimately determine whether industry revenue will increase or not. It is entirely possible that the demand for oranges is inelastic, in which case industry revenues will actually increase after the natural disaster. On the other hand, if demand is relatively elastic, then industry revenues will decline. It is common to assume that industry revenues are guaranteed to decline after a natural disaster of this kind; after all, there is less in the market to sell. However, as long as market prices are allowed to fluctuate and individual demanders are free to purchase or not purchase the product as they see fit, the price elasticity of demand ultimately determines whether revenues increase or not.

Income Elasticity of Demand

Elasticity can be measured between any two variables of interest. Another popular elasticity of demand is the income elasticity of demand. This elasticity relates the percentage change in quantity demanded due to a percentage change in consumer income and is calculated as

$$\varepsilon_D^I = \frac{\%\Delta Q^d}{\%\Delta I}$$

where the numerator is calculated exactly as it was for the price elasticity of demand

$$\%\Delta Q^d = \frac{Q_1 - Q_0}{\overline{Q}}$$

and the denominator is calculated similar to that of the price elasticity of demand, substituting income for price

$$\%\Delta I = \frac{I_1 - I_0}{\overline{I}}$$

Using these two equations, it is possible to rewrite the equation for the income elasticity of demand as

$$\varepsilon_D^I = \frac{\%\Delta Q^d}{\%\Delta I} = -\frac{\dfrac{Q_1 - Q_0}{\overline{Q}}}{\dfrac{I_1 - I_0}{\overline{I}}} = -\frac{Q_1 - Q_0}{I_1 - I_0} \times \frac{\overline{I}}{\overline{Q}}$$

Unlike the price elasticity of demand, which is always negative because of the law of demand, the income elasticity of demand can be positive or negative, depending upon whether the product is normal or inferior. The demand for a normal good increases after income increases whereas the demand for an inferior good decreases after income increases. If the income elasticity of demand is positive, the good is normal. If the income elasticity of demand is negative, the good is inferior. Examples of normal goods include automobiles, jewelry, steak, and imported beer. Examples of inferior goods include hamburger, bus rides, and used cars.

Cross Elasticity of Demand

Another popular elasticity measures the relative change in the quantity demanded of Good A due to a relative price change in Good B. The elasticity measure is calculated in the same fashion as the price elasticity of demand. In Chapter 4, goods were related to each other as complements or substitutes; complements are goods consumed together and substitutes are goods consumed in place of one another. One way to determine whether goods are complements or substitutes is to see what happens to the demand for Good A when the price of Good B changes using the cross elasticity of demand. The cross elasticity of demand is calculated using the following equation:

$$\varepsilon_D^X = \frac{\%\Delta Q^d}{\%\Delta P^X}$$

where P^X is the price of the "other good." If the cross-price elasticity is positive the two goods are substitutes. On the other hand, if the cross-price elasticity is less than zero then the two goods are complements.

Elasticity of Supply

When discussing the price elasticity of demand, we looked at how a change in supply would cause a movement along the demand curve. Now, consider a change in demand that causes a shift along the supply curve. To know how price and quantity are affected by a change in demand, we need to know the elasticity of supply. The price elasticity of supply is calculated in the same basic manner as other elasticities.

$$\varepsilon_S^P = \frac{\%\Delta Q^S}{\%\Delta P^s} = \frac{\Delta Q^s}{\Delta P^S} \times \frac{\overline{P}}{\overline{Q^S}}$$

The price elasticity of supply is positive because the law of supply implies a positive relationship between price and quantity supplied. If the price elasticity of supply is zero, supply is perfectly inelastic. If the elasticity of supply falls between zero and one, supply is relatively inelastic. If the elasticity of supply equals one, then supply is unitary elastic. If the elasticity of supply is greater than one, supply is considered relatively elastic. Finally, if elasticity of supply is infinite, supply is perfectly elastic.

Two things affect the price elasticity of supply: the technology used to produce the good and the length of time during which the price change is in place. Consider first the technology to produce the good. Some goods have a technology that is impossible to replicate. For example, given its location and history, The Chrysler Building in New York City is a one-of-a-kind building. Because it would be impossible to replicate the building, its elasticity of supply is zero. Other products, such as gravel or tomatoes, have easy-to-replicate technologies and therefore have more elastic supplies.

The amount of time during which the price change is in effect will also influence the price elasticity of supply. Momentary supply reflects the immediate response by suppliers to a price change. Momentary supply is typically extremely inelastic as producers often have a hard time dramatically increasing production overnight. Short-run supply pertains to the time during which only part of the technological process can change. Easy adjustments might include the amount of labor a firm hires or the amount of short-term capital a firm uses, such as rental equipment. The short-run supply is relatively more elastic than momentary supply but less elastic than long-run supply. Long-run supply pertains to the time it takes for all aspects of a technology to adjust. This would include new factories, assembly plants, and research and development processes. These changes can take years. Thus, while long-run supply is the most elastic, it only applies to long time periods.

Applications of Elasticity

The price elasticities of demand and supply have practical implications for the supply and demand model developed in the previous chapter. If the demand is perfectly elastic, that is, the price elasticity is infinity in absolute value, the demand is perfectly horizontal at the market price. As depicted in Figure 5-1, if demand is perfectly elastic, then any change in supply has only an impact on the quantity sold in equilibrium—the equilibrium price does not change.

The alternative extreme is that the price elasticity of demand is zero, which would correspond with a perfectly inelastic demand curve. A perfectly inelastic demand curve is perfectly vertical, and the quantity demanded does not change with price. As depicted in Figure 5-2, any change in supply is therefore reflected in changes in price—there is no change in the quantity sold.

There are similar effects when supply is either perfectly elastic or perfectly inelastic. A perfectly elastic supply curve is perfectly horizontal at the market price, and changes in demand are only reflected in changes in the quantity sold—prices do not change, as depicted in Figure 5-3.

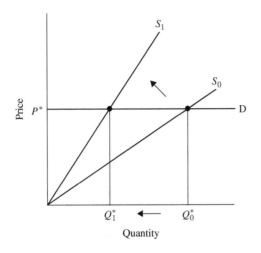

Figure 5-1 Change in supply with perfectly elastic demand.

If the supply curve is perfectly inelastic, then the quantity supplied is the same regardless of what price prevails in the market. Changes in demand only influence the market-clearing price, as depicted in Figure 5-4.

Why does any of this matter? In the previous chapter, changes in supply and demand were analyzed, and it was shown that a change in demand, *ceteris paribus*, would cause a change in *both* the equilibrium quantity and price. On the other hand,

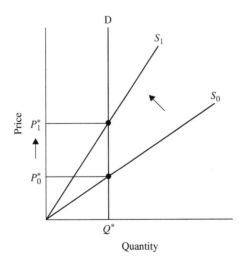

Figure 5-2 Change in supply with perfectly inelastic demand.

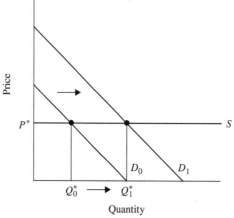

Figure 5-3 Change in demand with perfectly elastic supply.

if supply is perfectly elastic, then any change in demand is *only* reflected in a change in quantity. Therefore, only one of two possible variables is allowed to change in order to accommodate the market adjustment process.

In this case, both price and quantity can be thought of as pressure valves that can both share part of the burden of adjusting the market back to equilibrium when a

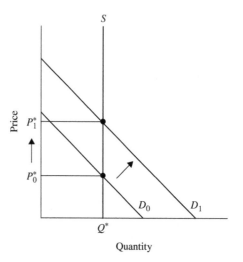

Figure 5-4 Change in demand with perfectly inelastic supply.

demand or supply shock occurs. The only way both price and quantity can both help the market adjust to a new equilibrium is if demand and the supply are not in the extremes of elasticity. Consider Figure 5-5 as an example.

In Figure 5-5, the demand curve labeled D_0 is relatively elastic, whereas the demand curve labeled D_1 is perfectly inelastic. Assume the supply of this product decreases from S_0 to S_1. In the case of D_0, it is evident that the new equilibrium corresponds to a higher price and a lower quantity than the original equilibrium. However, if the demand were perfectly inelastic as in D_1, then after the decrease in supply from S_0 to S_1 the market would only have one way to adjust, through price; the equilibrium quantity would not change. As is evident from Figure 5-5, the price increase that would occur with a perfectly inelastic demand curve is greater than that which would prevail when demand is relatively elastic.

Figure 5-5 shows the value of having relatively elastic demand and supply curves. A change in either supply or demand leads to both price and quantity changing in equilibrium, which reduces the amount that either price or quantity have to change to accommodate a new equilibrium.

It is relatively rare for demand or supply to be perfectly inelastic. Academic research suggests that the demand for gasoline, for certain medications (such as insulin), and for certain life-saving medical procedures (such as heart bypass surgery) are almost perfectly inelastic, at least in the short run. However, most products have a demand that is close to unitary elastic, give or take a little. The same empirical findings seem to hold for supply: Most products have a price elasticity of supply close to one.

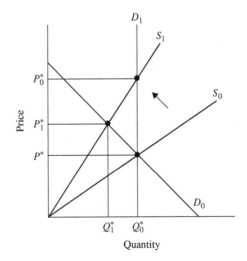

Figure 5-5 Market adjustment with different elasticities of demand.

The Population Elasticity of Lottery Sales

This chapter discusses the more prominent elasticities in microeconomics. However, it is possible to derive the elasticity between any two variables of interest. In general, the ranges of elasticity are consistent regardless of what is being measured, an elasticity measure less than one is considered relatively inelastic, an elasticity equal to one is considered unitary elastic, and elasticity greater than one is considered relatively elastic.

An example of how elasticities can be used beyond the traditional response of quantity demanded or supplied to price changes is in the case of lottery sales and state population. As of 2002, 38 states had instituted a state lottery. State lotteries are often controversial because many think that lottery tickets are inferior goods: The demand for tickets increases as income decreases. This, in turn, suggests that lottery sales might represent a regressive tax as those who have lower income spend a greater proportion of their income on lottery tickets than those with greater income.

Lottery sales are often put into the state's general treasury, but some states dedicate lottery sales to special items, including education and environmental protection. However, as the population of a state increases, the demands placed on the state government tend to increase as well. Therefore, the elasticity of lottery sales with respect to population changes might be of interest to policy makers. Why?

Consider a state where lottery proceeds are dedicated to education spending. If the population elasticity of education spending is greater than one, this would imply that a one percent increase in the state's population causes more than a one percent increase in education spending. If the one percent increase in population does not cause a more than one percent increase in lottery sales, then the state would have to find tax revenue from some other source to fund education.

It is possible to calculate the population elasticity of lottery sales in the same fashion as we calculate price elasticity or income elasticity. In this case, we will use the point elasticity, which is defined as

$$\varepsilon_{sales}^{population} = \frac{\%\Delta \text{ sales}}{\%\Delta \text{ population}} = \frac{\Delta \text{ sales}}{\Delta \text{ population}} \times \frac{\overline{\text{population}}}{\overline{\text{sales}}}$$

To actually calculate the population elasticity of lottery sales, it is necessary to estimate the change in lottery sales due to a change in population. This can be done using the tools of econometrics, which is the statistical analysis of economic data. The techniques used in econometrics are taught in many upper division undergraduate classes and are an integral part of most graduate economics curricula.

Using data from the 38 states that had state lotteries in 2000, as reported by the North American Association of State and Provincial Lotteries and the U.S. Bureau of the Census, it is possible to estimate the average change in lottery sales due to a change in a state's population. On an average, a one-person increase in a state's population corresponds with an additional $111 per year of lottery sales. While this might seem high to those who do not play the lottery on a regular basis, this value corresponds to approximately one lottery ticket per drawing (assuming two lottery drawings per week). The states with lotteries averaged approximately $986.15 million in annual lottery sales and had a state population of 6.395 million people.

Combining the information provided in the previous paragraph, it is possible to calculate the population elasticity of lottery sales as

$$\varepsilon_{sales}^{population} = \frac{\$111}{1 \text{ person}} \times \frac{6.395 \text{ million persons}}{\$986.15 \text{ million}} = 111 \times 0.0064 = 0.72$$

The first ratio in the calculation of the elasticity is the change in lottery sales due to a one-person change in the state population. The second ratio is that of the average state population (of the states with lotteries) to average lottery sales. The units in the denominator of the first ratio cancel with the units of the numerator of the second ratio. Likewise the units of the numerator of the first ratio cancel with the units of the denominator of the second ratio. In the end, the population elasticity of lottery sales is a unitless measure. The estimated population elasticity of lottery sales is 0.72, which is less than one. Therefore, lottery sales are relatively inelastic with respect to population growth.

The next page provides the data used to estimate the population elasticity of lottery sales. The state population data were obtained from the Bureau of the Census and ticket sales data were obtained from the North American Association of State and Provincial Lotteries available at *http://www.naspl.org.*

State	2000 Population (Millions)	Ticket Sales (Millions)
Arizona	5.131	255.55
California	33.872	2598.38
Colorado	4.301	370.96
Connecticut	3.406	837.51
Delaware	0.784	556.45
District of Columbia	0.572	215.51
Florida	15.982	2324.39
Georgia	8.186	2313.55
Idaho	1.294	86.51
Illinois	12.419	1503.86
Indiana	6.08	582.63
Iowa	2.926	178.21
Kansas	2.688	192.56
Kentucky	4.042	583.68
Louisiana	4.469	276.38
Maine	1.275	147.91
Maryland	5.296	1175.14
Massachusetts	6.349	3697.97
Michigan	9.938	1694.75
Minnesota	4.919	397.29
Missouri	5.595	508.02
Montana	0.902	29.9
Nebraska	1.711	68.17
New Hampshire	1.236	190.81
New Jersey	8.414	1839.8
New Mexico	1.819	110.61
New York	18.976	3629.26
Ohio	11.353	2209.1
Oregon	3.421	760.01
Pennsylvania	12.281	1679.86
Rhode Island	1.048	864.32

Table 5-1 2000 State Lottery and Population Data

State	2000 Population (Millions)	Ticket Sales (Millions)
South Dakota	0.755	581.05
Texas	20.852	2657.29
Vermont	0.609	75.92
Virginia	7.079	973
Washington	5.894	452.81
West Virginia	1.808	447.97
Wisconsin	5.364	406.7
Averages	6.395	986.152

Table 5-1   2000 State Lottery and Population Data *(Continued)*

Price Elasticity of Supply and Demand and the Burden of a Sales Tax

The previous chapter described the influence of a per-unit tax on the equilibrium price and quantity in a market. Armed with the concept of the price elasticity of demand and the price elasticity of supply, it is possible to take a closer look at how the burden of a sales tax is shared between demanders and suppliers.

Consider Figure 5-6 in which a per-unit tax of t has been placed in the market. The original equilibrium is depicted at Point E and the new equilibrium is depicted at Point E'. When both supply and demand are relatively elastic, both consumers and suppliers share the burden of the tax. This is because the price paid by consumers is greater than they paid at the original equilibrium, and the price received by producers is less than they received at the original equilibrium.

However, if the supply of the product is perfectly elastic, then the tax will increase the price paid by consumers but not change the price received by producers. To see this, consider Figure 5-7, in which demand is relatively elastic and supply is perfectly elastic. When a tax of t is imposed on the market, the shadow supply curve shifts upward to $S + t$, which corresponds with a new equilibrium price P_1 and equilibrium quantity Q_1. However, unlike the case when both supply and demand are relatively elastic, in Figure 5-6, the entire burden of the tax falls on consumers. The price suppliers receive is P_0, regardless of whether the tax is in place or not. Only consumers pay more than they would without the tax.

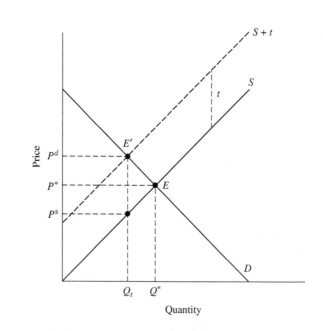

Figure 5-6 Burden of a sales tax when both supply and demand are relatively elastic.

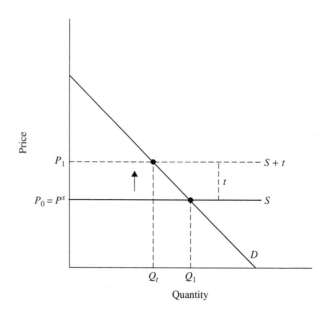

Figure 5-7 Burden of a sales tax when supply is perfectly elastic.

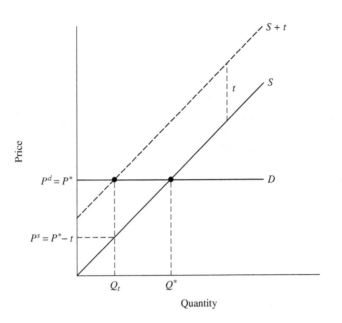

Figure 5-8   Burden of a sales tax when demand is perfectly elastic.

It is also possible that the entire burden of a tax falls on suppliers. This occurs when the demand for a product is perfectly elastic, as depicted in Figure 5-8. In this case, the imposition of a per-unit sales tax t shifts the shadow supply curve to the left to $S + t$, but the only change is in the quantity sold at equilibrium. Consumers pay the same price they did before the tax was imposed, and producers keep the difference between the price consumers pay and the tax, i.e., $P^s = P^d - t$.

Summary

This chapter has expanded the supply and demand model to include the concept of elasticity or the relative change in one variable caused by a relative change in another variable. The elasticity is similar to a slope except the units of the two variables involved have been normalized out of the measure. Thus, elasticity measures are "unitless" and can be compared across different markets. For example, the price elasticity of demand for oranges can be compared to the price elasticity of demand for luxury automobiles, although the two products are clearly very different.

Several elasticity measures were discussed although they share a common form. On the demand side, three elasticity measures were discussed. First, the price elasticity of demand indicates the percentage decline in quantity demanded after a one percent increase in price. If the elasticity is less than one, demand is called relatively inelastic. In markets such as health care, demand is likely very steep, which would indicate that price can increase dramatically and the quantity demanded will not decline very much. On the other hand, the price elasticity of demand could be greater than one, in which case the demand is said to be relatively elastic. In elastic demand, a small increase in price will lead to a large decrease in the quantity demanded. The various influences on the price elasticity of demand were discussed. The other two demand elasticities discussed were the income elasticity of demand, with which it is possible to determine if a good is normal or inferior, and the cross-price elasticity of demand, with which it is possible to determine if goods are substitutes or complements.

The elasticity of supply was also developed and momentary supply was differentiated from short run and long run supply. In the immediate short run, both demand and supply are often very inelastic. If prices change for a considerable amount of time, both consumers and suppliers have time to respond to the price changes (either consuming less or producing more) and supply and demand are much more elastic.

Quiz

1. If an increase in price causes a decrease in total revenue, then the industry is
   a. operating on the unitary elastic portion of its demand curve.
   b. operating on the upward sloping portion of its demand curve.
   c. operating on the elastic portion of its demand curve.
   d. operating on the inelastic portion of its demand curve.

2. If a good has a population elasticity of demand of 0.23, then the good is
   a. Perfectly Population Elastic.
   b. Normal Population Elastic.
   c. Relatively Population Elastic.
   d. Relatively Population Inelastic.

3. The price elasticity of demand relies upon

   a. the relative share of a consumer's income spent on the good.

   b. the time involved in the price change.

   c. the number of substitutes.

   d. all of the above.

4. The demand for health care is relatively inelastic because a one percent change in price results in

   a. more than one percent decrease in quantity demanded.

   b. no change in quantity demanded.

   c. less than a one percent decrease in quantity demanded.

   d. a one percent decrease in the quantity demanded.

5. If a good has a price elasticity of demand of 10 and a 1% tax is placed on the good, what will happen to the quantity demanded?

   a. The quantity demanded would increase by 10%.

   b. The quantity demanded would decrease by a 10%.

   c. The quantity demanded would decrease by a 1%.

   d. The quantity demanded would not change at all.

   e. None of the above.

6. If the supply for a product is perfectly elastic, what happens to price when demand increases?

   a. It increases.

   b. It decreases.

   c. It does not change.

   d. It depends upon the magnitude of the demand change.

7. If the demand for a product is perfectly inelastic, what happens to price when supply increases?

   a. It increases.

   b. It decreases.

   c. It does not change.

   d. It depends upon the magnitude of the supply change.

8. What might explain an increased demand for clean air in the United States?

    a: The price elasticity of clean air is positive.

    b. The income elasticity of clean air is positive and large.

    c. The income elasticity of clear air is negative and small.

    d. The price elasticity of clean air is nearly zero.

9. Consider a price change from $200 to $250 causes the quantity demanded to drop from 4000 to 3500. What is the price elasticity of demand?

    a. 0.60

    b. 1.5

    c. 0.5

    d. 1.0

10. Gerry receives a raise from $10 per hour to $12.50 per hour. After the raise, Gerry increases the number of channels in her cable subscription from 50 to 75. What is Gerry's income elasticity of cable demand?

    a. 3.5

    b. 1.8

    c. 2.0

    d. –1.5

Consumer and Producer Surplus

In Chapter 4, the basic demand and supply model was developed. In Chapter 5, the demand and supply model was extended to the measure of elasticity. In this chapter, we take a closer look at demand and supply.

Consumer Surplus

How do we measure the value that consumers place on the equilibrium quantity sold in the market depicted in Figure 6-1? We know that each unit is sold at the same price, and therefore the total expenditure at equilibrium equals $P^* \times Q^* = TE^*$ However, is the total amount spent on the good the same as the total value demanders place on the good? In general, the value placed on a product is greater than or equal to the price paid. This follows from the assumptions of rationality, preference, and local nonsatiation. If the product is desirable, then a consumer will only

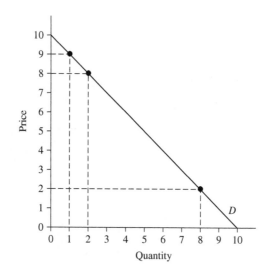

Figure 6-1   Demand as a willingness-to-pay curve.

purchase it if they value it at least as much as the price. Otherwise, the consumer would be trading, say, $10 for a product they only value at $8, which would violate the assumption of local nonsatiation and preference.

It is useful to consider the demand curve as a willingness-to-pay curve, in which individuals have been ranked from highest to lowest by their willingness to pay. In Figure 6-1, the most any individual is willing to pay for a single unit of the good is $9. The second highest willingness-to-pay is $8, and so forth. The demand curve can be interpreted as reflecting the highest value (willingness-to-pay) for each marginal unit. However, Chapter 4 described how price, not value, is obtained in the market. At the equilibrium price and quantity, all units are sold for the same price regardless of how much the individual customer values the product.

Figure 6-2 depicts a hypothetical market. For units less than the equilibrium quantity (five in this case), the value placed on each unit is greater than the price paid for the unit. The price paid for each unit is P^* (five in this case) but the value placed on the unit is determined by the demand curve. The difference between the value received and the price paid is consumer surplus. In mathematical terms, consumer surplus is defined as the difference between total value and total expenditure or $CS = TV - TE$.

In Figure 6-2, the equilibrium price is five and the equilibrium quantity is five. For the first unit, the difference between its value and the price paid is $9 – $5 = $4. The individual who purchases the first unit receives $9 of total value from the good, pays only $5 for the unit, and the $4 is considered consumer surplus.

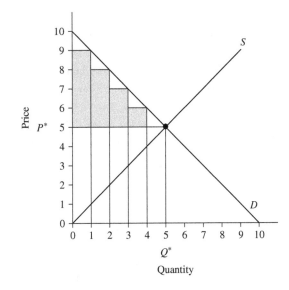

Figure 6-2 Consumer surplus in a market with nondivisible goods.

Figure 6-2 shows the consumer surplus for each of the first five units sold in the market. For the first unit, the consumer surplus was $4. For the second unit of the good, the consumer would be willing to spend $8, but only has to spend $5, thus the consumer surplus is $3. For the third unit of the good, the consumer would have been willing to spend $7 on it, but only has to spend $5, thus the consumer surplus is $2. For the fourth unit of the good, the consumer would have been willing to spend $6 but only spends $5, thus the consumer surplus is $1.

The fifth unit of the good has zero consumer surplus associated with it. The consumer values the good at $5 and only pays $5. The person who purchases the fifth unit receives five dollars of value but no surplus (or extra value). The people who purchase the first five units actually get *more than their money's worth*, whereas the person who purchases the last unit gets *just his money's worth*. Notice that beyond the fifth unit, the consumer surplus would actually be negative.

To calculate total consumer surplus in the market, simply total the consumer surplus obtained from each unit sold. From Figure 6-2, the total consumer surplus would equal $4 + $3 + $2 + $1 + $0 = $10.

A closer look at Figure 6-2 reveals that for every unit of the good sold, there is a small, unshaded triangle at the top of the shaded rectangle. This triangle is potential consumer surplus not received by consumers because the goods are being sold on a unit basis. For example, the product might be a case of soda, comprised of 24 cans. When it is possible to divide a good into fractional units, more consumer surplus can be extracted from the market. For example, a product might be divided into halves, quarters, or eighths. Each time the product is divided in half, another portion of the empty triangles in Figure 6-2 is converted into consumer surplus.

This is an important result. Many times consumers like products to be divisible. For example, at times consumers find it advantageous to purchase an entire case of soda, but at other times the consumer might only want a twelve-pack (one half of a case), a six-pack (one fourth of a case), or a single soda. The reason consumers like divisibility is because they are able to gain more consumer surplus from their purchases.

If it is possible to divide a good into very small fractions, then each of the empty triangles in Figure 6-2 is converted to consumer surplus. In this case, the total consumer surplus in the market can easily be calculated as the area below the demand curve and above the "price line." Figure 6-3 depicts consumer surplus in the case of an infinitely divisible good. If demand is linear, consumer surplus is actually a triangle with area $1/2$(base) × (height). In Figure 6-3, the base of the consumer surplus triangle is the equilibrium quantity, $Q^* = 5$, and the height of the consumer surplus triangle is the difference between the vertical intercept of the demand curve ($10) and the equilibrium price, P^* ($5).

From Figure 6-2, if the good is not divisible, the consumer surplus was calculated to equal $10. If the good is divisible, consumer surplus increases to $1/2 \times \$10 \times \$5 = \$12.50$. The proper way to calculate consumer surplus depends on how the good is sold, and whether it is divisible or not. If it is not possible to purchase fractional

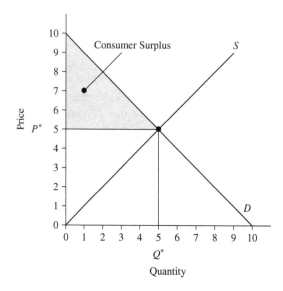

Figure 6-3 Consumer surplus in a market with a divisible good.

units of a good, then it is not appropriate to calculate consumer surplus as the area below the demand curve and above the "price line."

Producer Surplus

The previous section outlined how to measure consumer surplus in the supply and demand model. In this section, producer surplus is discussed. Producer surplus is the supply-side analogue to consumer surplus and reflects the value received by producers from selling a product above and beyond that required to produce and market the product. The intuition is easier to grasp if the supply curve is interpreted as a need-to-be-paid curve.

For each unit produced and sold, suppliers incur cost. As more is produced, more inputs have to be hired away from alternative endeavors, and therefore the cost of production increases. Suppliers are willing to produce and sell additional units of their product but only if they are able to cover the extra cost they incur. Therefore, the supply curve is upward sloping because the only way to entice suppliers to produce more is to offer them a higher price for their product.

Figure 6-4 reproduces the market depicted in Figure 6-2, but this time the focus is on the supply side of the market. For each of the five units sold in the market, the price is $5. Consumer surplus focused on the difference between the value of each

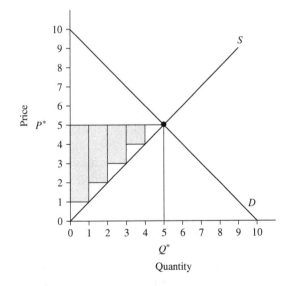

Figure 6-4   Producer surplus in a market with nondivisible goods.

unit and the price paid for each unit. Producer surplus focuses on the difference between the price received for each unit sold and the amount of money required by producers to offer the product on the market.

For unit divisible goods, the shaded rectangle below the "price line" reflects the producer surplus for each unit. In the market depicted in Figure 6-4, the producer surplus for the first unit is the difference between the $5 received from selling the first unit and the amount of money required to produce the first unit of the good, $1. The producer surplus for the first unit is then $5 – $1 = $4. For the second unit of the good, producers require $2 to produce the unit and still receive $5 for selling it, yielding a producer surplus of $5 – $2 = $3. Each unit sold up to the equilibrium quantity has a positive producer surplus although the producer surplus declines. The fifth unit of the good has zero producer surplus associated with it. The fifth unit cost $5 to produce and was sold for $5, therefore the producer broke even on the last unit.

Given the standard assumptions of rationality, preference, and local nonsatiation, no producer will want to sell units beyond the equilibrium quantity Q^* because to do so would lead to negative producer surplus. In Figure 6-4, the cost of the sixth unit will exceed the $5 price, and the producer would be irrational to sell beyond the equilibrium quantity Q^*.

In Figure 6-4, the total producer surplus in the market is the sum of each unit's producer surplus, that is, $4 + $3 + $2 + $1 + $0 = $10. In this case, the total producer surplus is equal to the consumer surplus calculated in the previous section. However, this is not true in general. Consumer surplus almost always exceeds producer surplus.

Figure 6-4 has empty triangles similar to those discussed in Figure 6-2 and their source is exactly the same. If goods cannot be divided, then the small triangles represent lost producer surplus. Therefore, producers are motivated to divide their products and will do so, when feasible, without government coercion. Soda companies are more than happy to provide consumers with cases of soda, twelve packs, six packs, and individual cans because doing so increases their producer surplus, as depicted in Figure 6-5.

An important implication from the supply and demand model is that the free-market equilibrium maximizes *combined* producer and consumer surplus, as depicted in Figure 6-6. To increase consumer surplus, perhaps through a price ceiling, is only possible by reducing producer surplus. Likewise, increasing producer surplus, through a quota or a price floor, can only occur by reducing consumer surplus.

Government intervention in a market is essentially a normative decision. Positive analysis helps indicate whether a price floor will reduce consumer surplus and increase producer surplus, but makes no judgment about the appropriateness of the policy. Normative analysis considers whether any gain in consumer surplus *is worth* any loss in producer surplus, and vice versa. Such discussions are more philosophical and political than factual, and are often difficult to resolve.

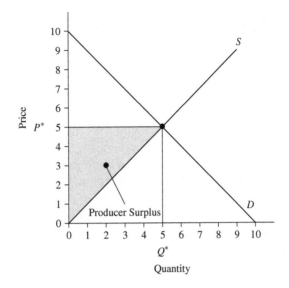

Figure 6-5 Producer surplus in a market with divisible goods.

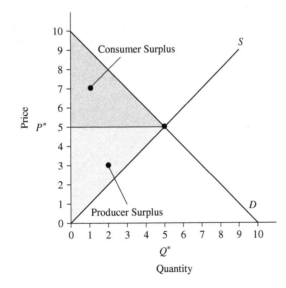

Figure 6-6 Consumer and producer surplus in a free market.

Changes in Consumer and Producer Surplus and Changes in Supply and Demand

Using the simple supply and demand model, it is possible to determine whether consumer and producer surplus increases or decreases after a change in supply and or demand. Economics is often concerned with such qualitative effects.

Consider the market equilibrium depicted in Figure 6-7a, where Point *B* is the original equilibrium, and the consumer and producer surplus are both depicted by the shaded areas. If demand increases, the new equilibrium is depicted in Figure 6-7b at Point *E*.

The shift in the demand curve reflects a greater willingness to pay by consumers. Even though the new equilibrium corresponds with a greater quantity sold at a higher price, the net effect on consumer surplus is ambiguous. As can be seen in Figure 6-7b, the new consumer surplus is the triangle defined by points *DEF*, whereas the original consumer surplus is the triangle defined by the points *ABC*. In Figure 6-7b the triangle *FED* has a greater area than triangle *ABC*, which would indicate that consumer surplus increased, but this is not guaranteed to happen every time demand increases.

On the other hand, the level of producer surplus at the original equilibrium is defined by triangle *OBC*, which is *unambiguously* smaller than the producer surplus at the new equilibrium, which in Figure 6-7b is defined as triangle *OED*. While the change in consumer surplus is ambiguous, the producer surplus increases because of the higher price and quantity that prevails at the new equilibrium.

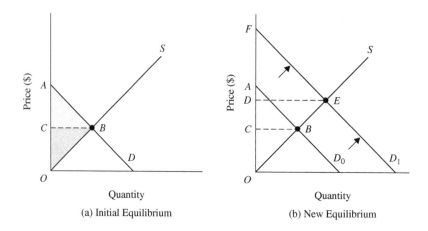

Figure 6-7   Change in demand and change in producer and consumer surplus.

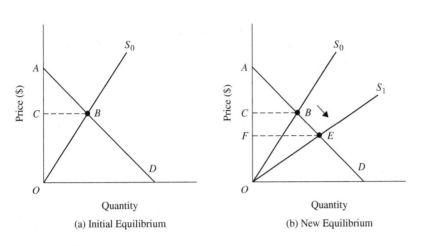

Figure 6-8   Change in supply and change in producer and consumer surplus.

Figures 6-8a and 6-8b depict the change in consumer and producer surplus after a change in supply. In this case, the increase in supply causes a reduction in the equilibrium price and an increase in the equilibrium quantity. On the consumer's side of the market, there is a greater amount of consumer surplus at each unit of output purchased (except for the equilibrium quantity which itself has zero consumer surplus). In Figure 6-8a, the original consumer surplus is defined by the triangle ABC and the original producer surplus is defined by the triangle OBC.

In Figure 6-8b, supply has increased and the new equilibrium is depicted by Point E. The new equilibrium corresponds with a consumer surplus defined by triangle AEF, which is unambiguously greater than the original consumer surplus defined by triangle ABC. This indicates that total consumer surplus in the market has increased. However, the change in producer surplus is ambiguous.

The new equilibrium in Figure 6-8b corresponds with a producer surplus defined by the triangle OEF, which may or may not be greater than the original producer surplus, defined by triangle OBC. The ambiguity lies in the fact that although the price has declined, there is more output sold at the new equilibrium. While it is possible that there is a greater level of producer surplus at the new equilibrium, this is not guaranteed.

The changes depicted in Figures 6-7 and 6-8 deal with an increase in demand and an increase in supply, respectively. The opposite conclusions can be reached if there is a decrease in demand or a decrease in supply. In the former case, the consumer surplus is not guaranteed to decline, and actually might increase, but the producer surplus is guaranteed to decrease. In the latter case, producer surplus might decline, but consumer surplus is guaranteed to decrease.

The Impact of a Sales Tax on Consumer and Producer Surplus

The previous two chapters have dealt with the impact of a sales tax in the supply and demand model. Chapter 4 outlined what will happen to the equilibrium price and quantity after a tax is imposed. Chapter 5 described the roles of the price elasticity of demand and supply on how much of the tax was borne by consumers and how much was borne by suppliers. This section will readdress the sales tax issue in the context of consumer and producer surplus.

Consider a market as depicted in Figure 6-9 where the original equilibrium condition is at Point B. In Figure 6-9, the original equilibrium corresponds with a consumer surplus defined by the triangle ABC and the producer surplus is defined by the triangle OBC. Notice that consistent with the free market, the natural equilibrium corresponds with maximum producer *and* consumer surplus.

Figure 6-10 depicts the same market after the per-unit sales tax of t has been imposed in the market. The original equilibrium is at Point B and the new equilibrium quantity is Q_t, where the new equilibrium price paid by consumers is P^d and the new equilibrium price kept by producers is P^s. The per-unit sales tax is $t = P^d - P^s$. In Figure 6-10, the consumer surplus is defined as the triangle ADF, which is unambiguously smaller than the original level of consumer surplus defined by triangle ABC.

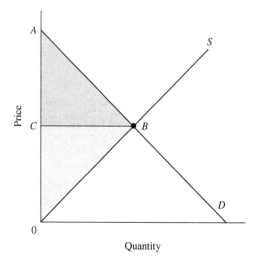

Figure 6-9   Producer and consumer surplus in a free market.

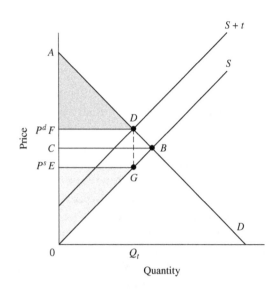

Figure 6-10   Producer and consumer surplus in a market with a per-unit sales tax.

Figure 6-10 also depicts the change in producer surplus that occurs after the sales tax. The original producer surplus is defined by the triangle OBC and the producer surplus after the tax has been imposed is defined by the triangle OGE, which is unambiguously smaller than the original producer surplus. The implication so far is that the total consumer surplus and the total producer surplus are both *less* after the sales tax has been imposed.

From Figure 6-10, it is also possible to calculate the total tax revenue generated in the market. This is determined as $t \times Q_t$, which is the area defined by the rectangle $EGDF$. As can be seen, a portion of the tax revenue remitted to the government is consumer surplus in a free market. Moreover, a portion of the tax revenue remitted to the government is producer surplus in a free market. In other words, if the government is going to raise revenue through a sales tax, the revenue doesn't come "free." The government's revenue comes from the pockets of producers and consumers (more accurately the surpluses of producers and consumers).

Notice that in Figure 6-10 there is a small triangle of what was producer and consumer surplus in the original equilibrium but that is not a portion of consumer surplus, producer surplus, or tax revenue after the tax has been imposed. This area is defined by the triangle DGB and is called dead weight loss. Dead weight loss is potential consumer or producer surplus that is not earned in a market. In the case of a sales tax, the tax distorts the market from its original surplus-maximizing equilibrium to the new equilibrium. While the new equilibrium does generate some consumer and producer surplus, as well as some tax revenue, the surpluses are not maximized.

Microeconomics Demystified

Because the tax distortion reduces the quantity sold in equilibrium, there are some gains in trade that are not recognized, in this case because the tax makes it too expensive for a consumer to purchase the product and producers wouldn't keep enough after the tax was paid to encourage them to supply the product. The tax revenue is therefore generated not only at a cost of actual producer and consumer surplus (which is what tax revenue comprises) but also potential surpluses that are not realized in the market. Dead weight loss is a measure of inefficiency in the market caused by government intervention (but also by other factors).

To more completely describe dead weight loss, consider Figure 6-11, which is an enlarged view of the dead weight loss triangle from Figure 6-10. In Figure 6-11, the dead weight loss triangle has been divided into two parts. The upper part, defined by the triangle *DBH*, is the consumption inefficiency brought about by the tax. The upper half of the dead weight loss triangle is the lost consumer surplus that would have been enjoyed by consumers had the tax not been in place.

The lower half of the dead weight loss triangle, defined by the triangle *HBG*, is the production inefficiency brought about by the tax. The lower half of the dead weight loss triangle is lost producer surplus that would have been enjoyed by suppliers had the tax not been in place.

Combined, the consumption and production inefficiencies define the dead weight loss of the sales tax. All taxes introduce a level of dead weight loss in the market, some more than others. At this point, we can combine the concepts of consumer and producer surplus, elasticity, and dead weight loss to provide a comprehensive analysis of a per-unit sales tax.

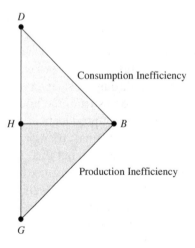

Figure 6-11   An enlarged view of the dead weight loss created by a per-unit sales tax.

Summary

This chapter extended the supply and demand model to recognize that the equilibrium quantity and price do not indicate the total value received in the market. Although consumers purchase each unit of the good for the equilibrium price, not every unit is valued at that price. The demand curve was reinterpreted as a willingness-to-pay curve in which consumers have been sorted by their willingness to pay. With this interpretation of the demand curve, it is easy to see that for most of the units sold in the market, the consumer would be willing to pay more than the market price. However, because suppliers have no way of telling exactly which person is which, they charge a single price for all the output they sell. The difference between the consumer's value for a unit of the good and the price they pay is called consumer surplus. In general, consumers like divisible goods because it allows for more consumer surplus.

Producer surplus is the difference between the price received and that required to produce the unit. The supply curve indicates how much suppliers must be paid to provide a unit of the good. Because it costs more to produce more, the supply curve is upward sloping. The market price is received for each unit sold even if that price is greater than the amount of money the supplier would have required to produce the good. In general, producers like divisible goods because they lead to greater producer surplus.

Therefore, while consumers are able to earn consumer surplus in a market, producers are also able to earn surplus. This result shows that the free market can provide *mutually beneficial* trade. In the free market, without any distortions or externalities, the interaction of supply and demand will lead to the maximum combined producer and consumer surplus. While it is possible to increase consumer surplus in a market, it is only possible to do so by reducing producer surplus. Similarly, it is possible to increase producer surplus in a market but only by reducing consumer surplus.

Quiz

1. What will happen if the demand for a product increases?

   a. Consumer surplus decreases.

   b. Consumer surplus increases.

   c. Producer surplus increases.

   d. Consumer surplus does not change.

2. What will happen if the supply for a product decreases?

   a. Consumer surplus will increase.

   b. Consumer surplus will decrease.

   c. Producer surplus will increase.

   d. Producer surplus does not change.

3. The more divisible a good is

   a. the greater the producer surplus.

   b. the greater the consumer surplus.

   c. the lower is both consumer and producer surplus.

   d. the greater is both consumer and producer surplus.

4. Willingness to pay

   a. is the most a consumer is willing to pay for the good.

   b. must be greater than or equal to the price of the good.

   c. is often much greater than the prevailing price of the good.

   d. often declines as more of a good is consumed.

5. Assume a consumer values a ticket to a concert at $50 and purchases a ticket for $25. What is the consumer's surplus?

   a. $50

   b. $25

   c. $75

   d. None of the above

6. If another consumer values the ticket at $80, what is the least amount for which the original buyer would be willing to sell the ticket?

   a. $51

   b. $25

   c. $50

   d. None of the above

7. If a baseball fan's value of attending a World Series game is $1000, which tour package is most likely to be chosen?

   a. Flight for $700, hotel for $200, ticket for $250

   b. Flight for $750, hotel for $100, ticket for $100

  c. Flight for $500, hotel for $250, ticket for $150

  d. Flight for $900, hotel for $250, ticket for $100

8. If the market price for a good is $45.95 and the first unit of the good costs suppliers $25.00, what is the producer surplus of the first unit of the good?

  a. $20.00

  b. $35.00

  c. $20.95

  d. $21.00

9. When a price floor is instituted in a market, what happens to consumer surplus relative to the free market equilibrium?

  a. It decreases.

  b. It increases.

  c. It is directly offset by gains in producer surplus.

  d. It does not change.

10. If the price of a pack of chewing gum increases from $0.30 to $0.50, which of the following is true?

  a. Consumer surplus must have declined.

  b. Producer surplus may have decreased.

  c. It is possible that consumer surplus increased even as price increased.

  d. Producer surplus might have decreased even as price increased.

  e. Both c and d.

Use Figure 6-12 for the next two questions:

11. The quantity quota increases consumer surplus.

  a. True

  b. False

  c. It is impossible to tell with the given information.

12. The quantity quota increases producer surplus.

  a. True

  b. False

  c. Perhaps, but it is not possible to tell with the given information.

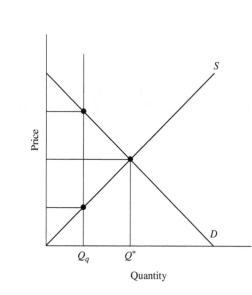

Figure 6-12   A market with a quantity quota.

Use Figure 6-13 for the next three questions:

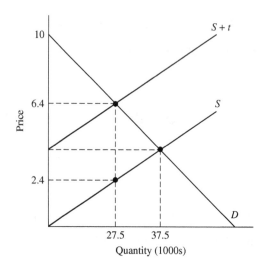

Figure 6-13   A market with a per-unit sales tax.

13. The per-unit sales tax generates how much tax revenue in equilibrium?

    a. $10,000

    b. $55,000

    c. $110,000

    d. $110

    e. None of the above

14. The per-unit sales tax induces how much dead weight loss?

    a. $50,000

    b. $25,000

    c. $10,000

    d. $20,000

    e. None of the above

15 The per-unit sales tax leads to how much consumer surplus?

    a. $100,000

    b. $49,500

    c. $250,000

    d. $500,000

Utility

In the previous three chapters, the basic supply and demand model was developed and extended to include the concept of elasticity and consumer and producer surplus. This chapter outlines the basics of household utility theory, which is the underlying source of each person's demand.

Consumption is the purchase of goods and services by a household. Households are typically assumed to *actually* consume the goods and services at the time of purchase, however this is not necessary. Two things influence consumption, preference and constraints. Preference essentially describes what the individual likes and doesn't like. Each person has their own set of preferences for the goods and services sold in the economy, and these preferences are fixed in the short to medium run. Preference is an easy concept, however preference is hard to quantify.

Economists avoid directly measuring preference and instead quantify preference through a measure called utility. Utility is a numerical measure of the level of satisfaction an individual obtains from their consumption and is measured in *utils*. If Good X is preferred to Good Y then $U(X) > U(Y)$, where $U(X)$ is the number of utils obtained from consuming Good X and $U(Y)$ is the number of utils obtained from consuming Good Y. Furthermore, if Good X is preferred to Good Y, and Good Y is preferred to Good Z, then $U(X) > U(Y)$, $U(Y) > U(Z)$, and $U(X) > U(Z)$.

The Utility Function and Indifference Curves

Utility can also be represented by a *utility function*, which is a mathematical equation that includes all the goods and services the consumer can consume. For simplicity, we will work with an economy that has only two goods, X and Y, and one consumer who has a utility function of $U(X,Y) = X \times Y$. With the utility function, it is possible to derive the utility enjoyed for different combinations of Good X and Good Y, as in Table 7-1

As shown in Table 7-2, an individual can obtain the same level of utility from different combinations of Good X and Good Y. What does this imply? Suppose an individual wants a utility level of 9 and has the same utility function that generated Table 7-1, $U(X,Y) = X \times Y$. Table 7-2 shows some of the combinations of Good X and Good Y that yield as utility level of 9.

The combinations of Good X and Good Y that yield the same level of utility can be plotted on a graph with Good X on the horizontal axis and Good Y on the vertical axis (Figure 7-1). The resultant curve is called an indifference curve because any combination of Good X and Good Y that falls on that particular curve yields the same utility.

Different combinations of Good X and Good Y will yield different levels of utility, as shown in Table 7-1. More of one or both goods will yield more utility. It is possible to draw an indifference curve for every possible level of utility, say 16, 20, or 200. A set of indifference curves is called an indifference curve map, as depicted in Figure 7-2, where moving further from the origin along the 45-degree ray corresponds to greater levels of utility, i.e., utility U_2 is greater than U_1, which in turn is greater than U_0.

Indifference curves are downward sloping, but why are they nonlinear? In general, indifference curves are not linear because of changing marginal rates of substitution. The marginal rate of substitution measures the additional amount of one good required to maintain a constant level of utility when a unit of another good

Good X	Good Y	$U(X,Y) = X \times Y$
0	0	0
3	4	12
4	4	16
5	4	20
4	5	20
4	3	12

Table 7-1   Utility Obtained from Different Combinations of Goods

Good X	Good Y	$U(X,Y) = X \times Y$
1	9	9
2	4.5	9
3	3	9
4.5	2	9
9	1	9

Table 7-2   Combinations of Good X and Good Y that Yield the Same Utility

is taken away. The marginal rate of substitution between Good Y and Good X is the slope of the indifference curve, i.e., the MRS is calculated holding utility constant. As the consumer has less of Good Y, more of Good X is required to maintain utility when a unit of Good Y is taken away. This is intuitively appealing: As a consumer has less of Good Y, it is more valuable in terms of Good X.

What if an additional unit of a good is consumed while the level of other goods is held fixed? The additional unit will cause utility to increase and the amount that

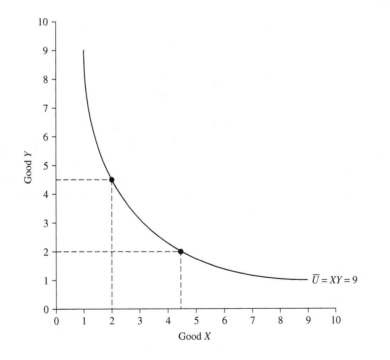

Figure 7-1   An indifference curve.

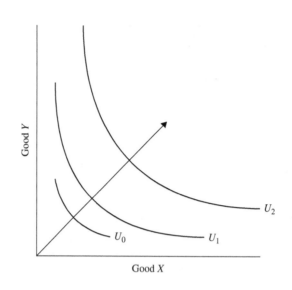

Figure 7-2 An indifference curve map.

utility increases is called marginal utility. Without introducing complicated mathe-matics, the MRS is equal to the ratio of the marginal utilities of the two goods being consumed:

$$\text{MRS}_{XY} = \frac{\text{MU}_X}{\text{MU}_Y}$$

Consumers want to maximize their utility from consuming goods and services. Unfortunately, consumers cannot simply consume all the goods they want to, be-cause consumption is not free. Goods and services are only available for a price and a household has limited income with which to purchase goods and services. Two things limit the ability of the individual to obtain the most utility possible: her in-come and the prices of the goods she wants to consume.

The Household's Income Constraint

A household's income is typically measured in dollars or some other currency, which is called *nominal income*. However, economists often find it useful to measure in-come in terms of one or more goods, which is called real income. To measure a household's income in terms of pizzas, divide the household's nominal (dollar) income by the nominal (dollar) price of a pizza. The result is a measure of real income measured in pizzas rather than dollars. For example, assume the household has $40,000 per year as disposable income and a pizza costs $10. The household's real income is $40,000/$10 per pizza = 4000 pizzas. In general, a consumer's real income can be stated in terms of any good and calculated as

$$M_j = \frac{I}{P_j}$$

where I is the household's disposable nominal income and P_j is the price of the good.

To determine exactly which combination of goods a household will consume to maximize its utility, it is first necessary to determine the combinations of goods and services the household can afford and which combinations it cannot afford. The budget constraint defines the limit between what is affordable and what is not affordable, given income and prices. The budget constraint is similar to the production possibilities frontier derived in Chapter 3. In our simple approach, we assume that the household does not have access to credit cards or bank loans.

For simplicity, assume only two goods, Good X and Good Y, one consumer with disposable income of $36, the consumer spends all he has, the price of Good Y is $3, and the price of Good X is $2. The household spends its disposable income on both goods and therefore will purchase a combination of Good X and Good Y that costs $36. Using our assumed values, we can rewrite the budget constraint as $36 = 2X + 3Y$.

If the household purchases 3 units of Good X, then the household can only purchase 10 units of Good Y. If the household purchases 15 units of Good X, then the household will only be able to purchase 2 units of Good Y.

The household could spend all of its income by purchasing 12 units of Good Y, but then it would have no money to spend on Good X. On the other hand, the household could spend all of its income by purchasing 18 units of Good X, but then it would have no money for Good Y. In all likelihood, the household will purchase a mix of both goods in order to maximize utility *given* the budget constraint.

More generally, the budget constraint can be written as $I = P_X C_X + P_Y C_Y$, where P_X and P_Y are the dollar prices and C_X and C_Y are the levels of consumption of the two goods. The budget constraint is actually the equation of a line, although it is not obvious at first. If C_Y is made the dependent variable, the budget constraint can be rewritten as $C_Y = (I/P_Y) - (P_X/P_Y)C_X$. The vertical intercept of this line is I/P_Y, which is the household's real income in terms of Good Y. The slope of this line, $-P_X/P_Y$, is

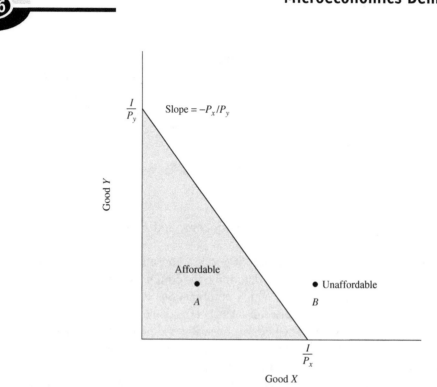

Figure 7-3　A budget constraint.

the relative price of Good X in terms of Good Y, i.e., how many units of Good Y it takes to purchase a unit of Good X. Figure 7-3 depicts a budget constraint.

Those combinations of goods that fall on or inside the budget constraint, such as Point A in Figure 7-3, are affordable. However, combinations that fall beyond the budget constraint, such as Point B in Figure 7-3, are not affordable.

How can the household afford a combination of X and Y that is beyond its budget constraint? Either the household's nominal income must increase or the price of Good X or Good Y must decline, or both there happen together. All three possibilities result in an increase in the household's real income, which makes more combinations of Good X and Good Y affordable.

If the price of Good X drops then the household can purchase more of Good X. On the other hand, if the price of Good X increases, then the household can purchase less of Good X. If the price of Good Y doesn't change then the most the household can buy of Good Y does not change. When the price of Good X increases (say, from P_x to P_x' in Figure 7-4), the budget constraint becomes steeper, and fewer

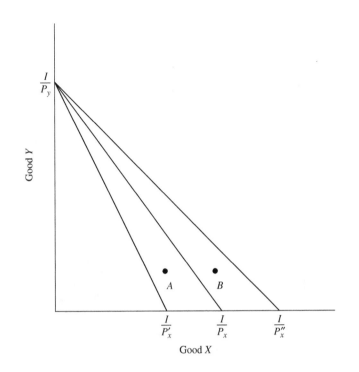

Figure 7-4   Changes in the budget constraint after changes in the price of Good X.

combinations of Good X and Good Y are affordable. When the price of Good X falls (say, from P_x to P_x'' in Figure 7-4), the budget constraint becomes flatter and more combinations of Good X and Good Y become affordable.

In a similar way, if the price of Good Y declines, the budget constraint becomes steeper because more of Good Y can be purchased, and more combinations of Good X and Good Y are affordable. On the other hand, if the price of Good Y increases, the budget constraint becomes flatter and fewer combinations of Good X and Good Y are affordable.

The budget constraint also changes if the household's disposable income increases. Holding prices fixed, if income increases (say, from I_0 to I_1 in Figure 7-5), real income increases and the budget constraint shifts to the right, and more combinations of Good X and Good Y are affordable. On the other hand, if nominal income declines (say from I_1 to I_0 in Figure 7-5), the budget constraint shifts to the left and fewer combinations of Good X and Good Y are affordable.

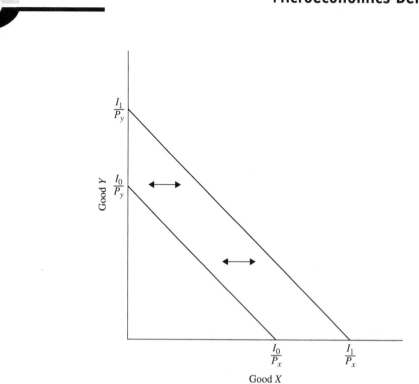

Figure 7-5 Changes in the budget constraint after changes in income.

The Household's Consumption Equilibrium

The consumer wants to maximize her utility, but she must recognize her budget constraint. To help determine the combination of Good X and Good Y that yields greatest utility subject to the consumer's income and the prices of Good X and Good Y, plot a set of indifference curves on the same graph as the budget constraint as in Figure 7-6

In Figure 7-6, the budget constraint defines the limit between what is affordable and what is not. The consumer cannot consume at Point D, even though it would yield a high level of utility—the combination at Point D is not affordable. On the other hand, the consumer could purchase a combination such as at Point A. However, at Point A, the consumer could afford more of Good X without buying any less of Good Y and vice versa. If the consumer spends all her income, she wants to purchase a combination of Good X and Good Y that maximizes her utility. She could consume at Point B or Point C, but Point E corresponds to the combination of Good X and Good Y that *simultaneously* spends all her income and maximizes utility.

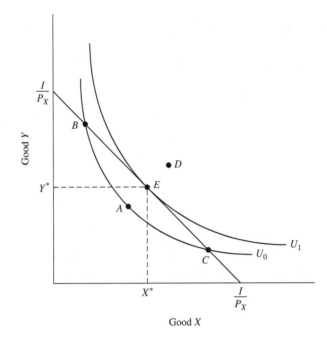

Figure 7-6   Household's consumption equilibrium.

The combination of Good X and Good Y that corresponds with Point E is unique; it represents a tangency between the budget constraint and the indifference curve. The tangency is unique because the slope of the budget constraint is the same as the slope of the indifference curve. As discussed earlier, the slope of the indifference curve was defined as the marginal rate of substitution, and the slope of the budget constraint is the price of Good X with respect to Good Y, that is, relative price. Therefore, at the household's utility maximizing combination of Good X and Good Y, the price ratio must be equal to the marginal rate of substitution, or

$$\frac{MU_X}{MU_Y} = \frac{P_X}{P_Y}$$

which can be rewritten as

$$\frac{MU_X}{P_X} = \frac{MU_Y}{P_Y}$$

The Law of Demand and Utility Theory

In Chapter 4, the law of demand was defined as follows: The greater the price, the lower the quantity demanded, and vice versa. Another way to interpret the law of demand is that the only way to induce consumers to purchase more of a product is to reduce the price. This intuitively appealing conclusion can be supported using the household utility theory developed thus far.

Consider Figure 7-7 in which the original equilibrium the price of Good X is P_X and the price of Good Y is P_Y. The household's original equilibrium is therefore at Point E. If the price of Good X drops, say to P_X', the household's budget constraint flattens out just a bit. The vertical intercept of the budget constraint does not change because the price of Good Y has not changed. However, the horizontal intercept is further out the on the horizontal axis because the consumer's real income in terms of Good X has increased after the price of Good X falls. The consumer's new equilibrium resides at Point E' and the household consumes more of Good X and less of Good Y.

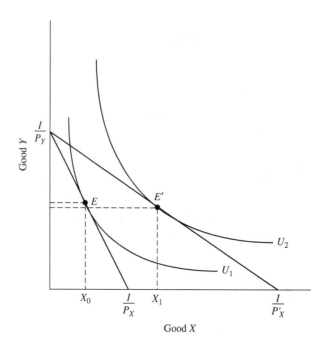

Figure 7-7   Price changes and consumption changes.

If the price of Good X falls yet again, say to P_X'', then the budget constraint becomes even flatter and the consumer's new equilibrium corresponds to even more of Good X being purchased and less of Good Y.

The different prices of Good X can be combined with the different levels of consumption of Good X to create the individual household's demand curve for Good X, as depicted in Figure 7-8. Notice that the demand curve in Figure 7-8 is downward sloping, just as the law of demand suggests. Each household has a different demand curve for each good because every household has different preferences for different goods. For instance, if Household 2 receives more marginal utility from Good X than Household 1, then Household 2's demand for Good X will be greater than the demand by Household 1. Hence, Household 2 would want the price of Good X to be lower (i.e., P_{X_2}) while Household 1 would be fine with the price P_{X_1}.

The market demand for a product is the horizontal summation of the demand curves for all the households in a market. At a given price, the quantity demanded of Good X in the market is the sum of the quantities demanded by each household at that price. For example, assume there are only two households in the market. If, at a price of $30, Household 1(Dennis) would purchase 25 units of Good X and Household 2 (Courtney) would purchase 15 units of Good X, the market demand for Good X at this price would be $25 + 15 = 40$. The derivation of the market demand for Good X is depicted in Figure 7-9.

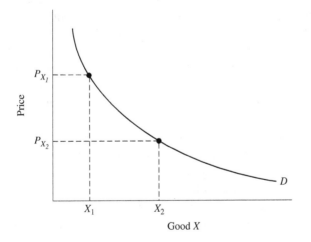

Figure 7-8   Derivation of the household demand curve.

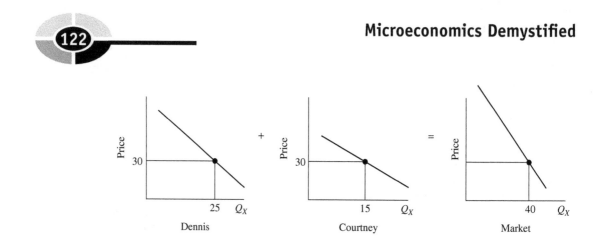

Figure 7-9 Derivation of a market demand curve.

Income and Substitution Effects

The previous section derived the demand curve by looking at what happens to the equilibrium level of consumption for the household as prices change, *holding nominal income constant.* However, the derivation of the demand curve in the previous section implicitly assumed that the reason the demand curve is downward sloping is because of diminishing marginal utility.

Diminishing marginal utility is a concept centered on the idea that, as more of a good is consumed, a marginal or additional unit of consumption contributes less to overall utility. For example, if you eat three slices of pizza you might have a utility level of 20 utils. Diminishing marginal utility suggests that the fourth slice of pizza will increase your utility but not by as much as the third slice of pizza, for instance your utility might increase to 24 utils. The fifth slice of pizza likewise increases your utility, say to 27 utils, but the increase of three utils is not as much as you enjoyed from the fourth slice of pizza.

The upshot of the theory of diminishing marginal utility is that because additional units of a good do not increase utility by as much as previous units, the price that a consumer is willing to pay for additional units declines. If prices are measured in real rather than nominal terms, the theory of diminishing marginal utility suggests that as you consume more of Good *A* you are not willing to pay as much in terms of Good *B* for additional units of Good *A*. This, in turn, leads to a downward sloping demand curve.

While the theory of diminishing marginal utility seems reasonable on the surface, the theory is in fact not universally correct. Although the theory of diminishing marginal utility will generate a downward sloping demand curve, the problem is, the only demand curve the theory of diminishing marginal utility can generate is downward sloping. Perhaps this is not a major problem; after all, the law of demand states that as price increases the quantity demanded will decrease. Yet, is it possible for a demand curve to be *upward sloping*, which would imply that a price decrease would correspond with a lower quantity demanded? If so, the theory of diminishing marginal utility is unable to explain why the demand curve would be upward sloping.

To explain why most, but possibly not all, demand curves are downward sloping requires an extension of the analysis of what happens when the price of a good changes. The shifts in consumption depicted in the previous section are what economists would term "net effects." The shifts in consumption are the end result of two different, and potentially offsetting, influences on consumption when the price of good changes: the income effect and the substitution effect. In general, the substitution effect suggests that as the price of a good drops, the consumer will purchase more of the good. The income effect indicates how the household's consumption level changes with a change in its income: Households consume more of a normal good when income increases and less of an inferior good when income increases. The combination of the substitution and income effects determines how much more (or less) of a good the household will purchase when the price of a good changes.

Substitution Effect

What happens to the household's utility maximizing consumption bundle when the price of a good changes? Figure 7-10 depicts the effect of a decrease in the price of Good X, which is on the horizontal axis.

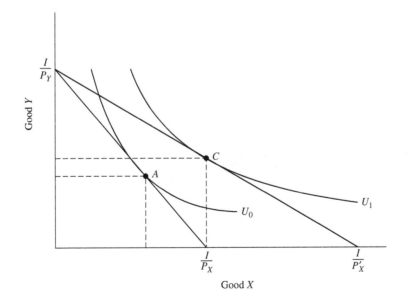

Figure 7-10 The total effect of a decrease in the price of Good X.

The decrease in the price of Good X swings the budget constraint out and increases the consumption possibilities set which makes it possible for the household to purchase a greater number of different combinations of Good X and Good Y. While the horizontal intercept of the budget constraint increases (because the price of Good X declined) the vertical intercept does not change (because the price of Good Y did not change). The total effect of the price change is reflected in the household moving their consumption equilibrium from Point A to Point C. Notice that in Figure 7-10, Point C indicates that the household will purchase more of *both* Good X and Good Y. This is an interesting result. The price of Good X declines and the household purchases more of both goods? How can this happen?

The answer lies in recognizing that there are two different impacts on household consumption when the price of Good X declines. The first is known as the substitution effect. The substitution effect reflects the change in the household's consumption after the price of Good X declines *holding utility constant.* The substitution effect is depicted in Figure 7-11.

In Figure 7-11, the original budget constraint is depicted as a solid line and the new budget constraint is depicted as the dotted line. The original level of utility U_0 is depicted as a solid curve and the new higher level of utility U_1 is depicted as a dotted curve. The substitution effect ignores the impact of a price change on income. Rather, the thought experiment requires reducing the household's disposable income such that they can just afford to purchase a combination of Good X and

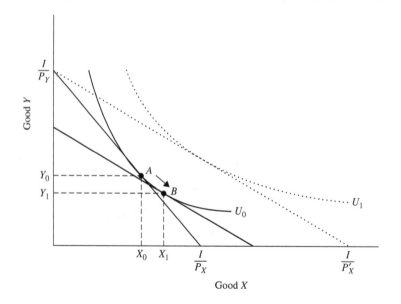

Figure 7-11 The substitution effect of a decrease in the price of Good X.

Good *Y* at the new relative prices but receive the same utility as they did before the price change. The substitution effect is depicted as the movement from Point *A* to Point *B* in Figure 7-11. In general, the substitution effect is positive. That is, if the price of Good *X* falls relative to the price of Good *Y* the household will *substitute* consumption into Good *X* and out of Good *Y*. The reverse also holds, if the price of Good *X* increases relative to the price of Good *Y*, the household *substitutes* consumption out of Good *X* and into Good *Y*.

For example, if the price of Tropicana orange juice increases relative to Minute Maid orange juice (and nothing else about Tropicana or Minute Maid orange juice changes), consumers will naturally purchase more Minute Maid orange juice and less Tropicana orange juice. The reverse holds as well. If the price of Tropicana orange juice declines, people are likely to purchase more Tropicana and less Minute Maid orange juice. This is the essence of the substitution effect.

The Income Effect

The substitution effect is relatively easy to understand. A little less obvious is what is called the income effect. The *income effect* suggests that as the price of a good decreases, those who consume the product experience an increase in their real income. This is because their nominal income will now purchase more of Good *X* and they experience an increase in their consumption possibilities set (the area *below* the budget constraint). Even though the substitution effect suggests that the household will buy more of the cheaper good, we also know from Chapter 4 that households change their consumption of goods based on the amount of (real) income they have. Households consume more of normal goods and less of inferior goods when their income increases, and vice versa.

The income effect is depicted in Figure 7-12 as the shift from Point *B* to Point *C*. The movement from Point *B* to Point *C* occurs *after* we have considered the substitution effect. In Figure 7-12, the original budget constraint is depicted as the dotted line, and the new budget constraint is depicted as a solid line. The new budget constraint and the "hypothetical" budget constraint used to determine the substitution effect are parallel to each other because they are based on the same relative price of Good *X* to Good *Y* (that is, after the nominal price of Good *X* has fallen). In Figure 7-12, the income effect reinforces the substitution effect and therefore we know that Good *X* is a normal good as the amount demanded increases with income.

To put Figure 7-11 in context, assume the household has $200 in disposable income, the price of Good *X* is originally $10, and the price of Good *Y* is $20. Assume the household spends $100 on Good *Y*, that is, it purchases 5 units of Good *Y*. The household would then have $100 left to spend on Good *X*. At the original price, the household could purchase only 10 units of Good *X*. If the price of Good *X* falls

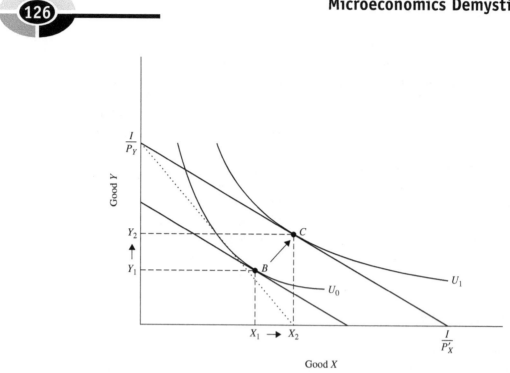

Figure 7-12   The income effect of a decrease in the price of Good X.

to $5, the household could purchase the same amount of Good Y and purchase 20 units of Good X rather than only 10 units.

However, it is also possible that the household could consume 10 units of Good X, spending only $50 on Good X, and spend the remaining $50 on Good Y (and purchase two and a half additional units) or on some other good.

Combining Substitution and Income Effects

The substitution effect of a price change is the change in a consumer's consumption of a good in response to an income-compensated price change. The income effect of a price change is the change in consumption of a good resulting from the implicit change in income because of a price change.

For a normal good, the substitution and income effects reinforce each other. In this case, if the price of Good X falls, the substitution effect contributes to an increase in the quantity of Good X demanded because the household substitutes consumption into Good X from other goods. If the price of Good X falls, the income effect indicates that the lowered price has increased the purchasing power of the

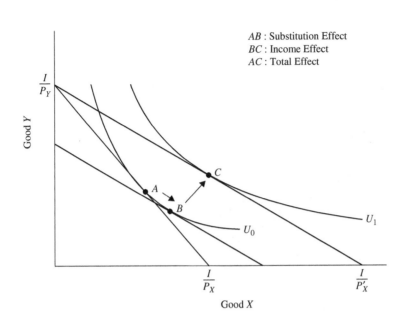

AB : Substitution Effect
BC : Income Effect
AC : Total Effect

Figure 7-13   The combined substitution and income effects of a price decrease for a normal good.

household, and therefore the household purchases more of Good X. This situation is depicted in Figure 7-13.

The reverse also holds. If Good X is a normal good, an increase in the price of Good X will motivate the household to substitute away from Good X into a relatively cheaper good, reducing the quantity demanded. The increase in the price of Good X will also reduce the purchasing power of the household's nominal income and will reduce the amount of Good X that the household can purchase, also reducing the quantity demanded.

However, for an inferior good, the income and substitution effects go in opposite directions. When the price of an inferior good falls, households substitute into the Good X and away from relatively more expensive products. Yet, the drop in price increases real income, which motivates the household to consume *less* of the inferior good. Such a case is depicted in Figure 7-14.

In Figure 7-14, when the price of Good X falls, the substitution effect indicates that the household will purchase more of the product, which is the movement from Point A to Point B. However, because the product is inferior, as the household's income increases the household purchases *less* of Good X. The substitution effect and the income effect offset each other, as indicated by the arrows along the horizontal axis.

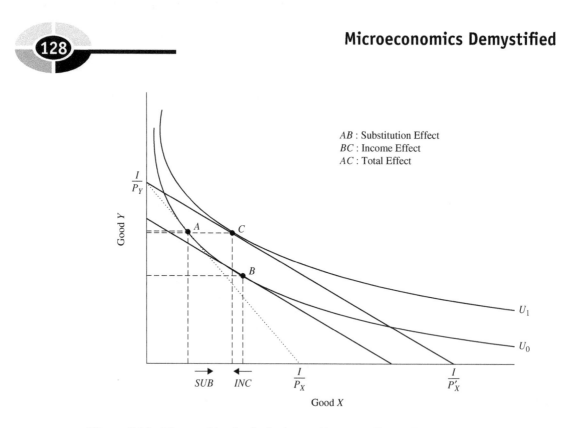

Figure 7-14 The combined substitution and income effects of a price decrease for an inferior good.

The dashed rectangles indicate the different consumption levels of Good X and Good Y at the various points of interest in Figure 7-14. Notice that the substitution effect suggests that the household will purchase more of Good X and less of Good Y after the price change. However, because Good X is inferior, the household purchases less X and more Y when he takes into account the impact of the price, change on his real income.

In general, the income effect is dominated by the substitution effect. Thus, many people use the law of diminishing marginal utility to explain downward sloping demand curves. However, it is theoretically possible that the income effect could dominate the substitution effect, in which case the household would purchase less of the product after the price declines, corresponding to an upward sloping demand curve. If this were the case, the law of diminishing marginal utility would not be able to explain the upward sloping demand curve; while the theory is intuitively appealing, it is not one hundred percent correct.

Summary

This chapter has outlined the basics of household utility theory. Previous chapters described the interaction of supply and demand, however they did not specify from where demand arises. The law of demand stipulates that the higher the price, the lower the quantity demanded, but utility theory provides the underlying reasoning for why the law of demand holds. Households wish to maximize their utility, or their level of satisfaction, given their income and the prices of the goods they wish to consume.

Households wish to maximize their level of satisfaction but are constrained by their income and the prices of the goods they want to purchase. A household will maximize its utility when it sets the marginal rate of substitution between two goods to their price ratio. Intuitively what this condition requires is that the individual balances the relatively dollar cost of purchasing one product or another with the internal preference tradeoff between one product and the other.

Quiz

1. The marginal rate of substitution is defined as

   a. the change in utility gained from a loss of a unit of a good.

   b. the amount of a good needed to maintain a given level of utility when a unit of another good is taken away.

   c. the amount of a good needed to obtain a higher level of utility when a unit of another good is taken away.

   d. the amount of a substitute good consumed with complement goods.

2. The benefit or satisfaction that a person receives from the consumption of goods and services is called

   a. marginal utility.

   b. utility.

   c. consumer demand.

   d. consumer equilibrium.

3. If the price of gasoline increases, what happens to the average household's real income?

   a. It increases.

   b. It does not change.

   c. It decreases.

   d. It is impossible to tell.

4. If a household wins the lottery, what will happen to the household's income constraint?

   a. It disappears.

   b. It shifts to the right because prices will drop.

   c. It declines because there is less of a constraint.

   d. It shifts to the right because nominal income has increased.

5. Assume a household maximizes utility by purchasing 6 units of Good X and 3 units of Good Y. If the price of Good X increases and the price of Good Y decreases, what will likely happen to the household's mix of Good X and Good Y at its new equilibrium?

   a. The amount of Good X will increase and the amount of Good Y will increase.

   b. The amount of Good X will increase and the amount of Good Y will decrease.

   c. The amount of Good X will decrease and the amount of Good Y will increase.

   d. The amount of Good X will decrease and the amount of Good Y will decrease.

6. Assume the relative price of Good X to Good Y is 4, person A has a marginal rate of substitution between Good X and Good Y of 4, and person B has a marginal rate of substitution between Good X and Good Y of 8. Which person will buy more or less of Good X to maximize their utility?

   a. Person A will buy less of Good X

   b. Person A will buy more of Good X

   c. Person B will buy less of Good X

   d. Person B will buy more of Good X

   e. Impossible to tell

7. Why might individuals on fixed incomes be anxious about inflation or a general increase in prices?

   a. Inflation reduces their real income and reduces what is affordable.

   b. Inflation increases their real income and increases what is affordable.

   c. Inflation has negative marginal utility.

   d. It is impossible to maximize utility in an inflationary environment.

8. Why might labor unions negotiate for regular cost of living adjustments?

   a. In deflationary environments, cost-of-living adjustments help maintain real income.

   b. In inflationary environments, cost-of-living adjustments help maintain real income.

   c. Because firms rarely give raises anymore and cost of living adjustments are one way for unions to reward their members.

   d. Cost of living adjustments typically make it easier to afford a new car.

9. If Kevin's utility function is 5 widgets + 6 gadgets + 0.5 (gadgets + widgets), how much utility would Kevin derive if he consumed 4 widgets and 10 gadgets?

   a. 87

   b. 97

   c. 109

   d. 0

   e. 400

10. If widgets cost $5 and gadgets cost $10, what is the relative price of a widget to a gadget?

   a. $1

   b. One half of a widget costs one tenth of a gadget.

   c. Two widgets cost one gadget.

   d. One widget costs two gadgets

   e. One widget costs one gadget.

8

Theory
of the Firm

A firm is an economic agent that converts factors of production (land, labor, and capital) into goods and services. In the process, firms make numerous decisions including what to produce, how much to produce, what inputs to purchase, and what technology to use to produce their product. There are thousands of other decisions firms make, including where to advertise, how much money to dedicate to research, when to innovate, and where to locate. Many of these decisions involve intricacies that are beyond the scope of this book. This chapter, therefore, outlines the general theory of how firms make decisions.

Why the Firm?

Why is the firm the preferred method of organizing production in today's modern economy? Why doesn't the government produce all goods and services? Economists have grappled with these questions for quite some time and offer four basic reasons why the firm is a preferred method of organizing production.

The primary reason to organize production with private firms is that private firms internalize risk. Households own private firms, and are called residual claimants in the sense that the owners of a firm will lay claim to whatever profits the firm generates. However, producing a profit is by no means guaranteed (otherwise no firm would go out of business), and therefore there is an inherent amount of risk in owning a firm. Not all people are willing to bear this kind of risk, and therefore organizing production in private firms allows those willing to bear risk (in the hopes of receiving a reward, called profit) to do so, and those not willing to bear risk to avoid doing so.

If the government produced every product in the economy, two things would happen. First, government bureaucrats would likely be extremely risk averse to innovation and new products for fear that they would lose their jobs if the product were a flop. Second, all the citizens in a country would involuntarily share any risk associated with a new product or innovation, which would be inefficient.

Economists also suggest that firms exist to reduce transaction costs. For example, suppose you wish to get fuel for your car. You normally drive to a fuel station, put fuel in your car, and pay the clerk. This is a pretty straightforward transaction. However, what if there were no fuel stations? You would have to trade with the owners of crude oil, the shippers of crude oil, the refiners of crude oil, and so on. The number of transactions you would have to complete would skyrocket, and the overall costs of obtaining fuel would be much greater than if you drove to the corner station.

Other reasons for firms to exist are to take advantage of the benefits of size and knowledge. The benefits of size are embodied in economies of scale, which occurs when the cost per unit of output decreases as output increases. Firms also internalize the benefits of knowledge, especially in research and development. When a firm's engineers or scientists make a new discovery or innovation, the firm is able to profit by producing products that incorporate this new knowledge. If all knowledge were immediately and freely available to everyone, the motivation for innovation would be dramatically reduced. Private firms actually generate more knowledge and innovations because of the profit motive.

While some might think the pursuit of profit is distasteful, economists consider the profit motive a powerful incentive to produce and provide goods and services that ultimately contribute to the utility of consumers (see Chapter 7). Economists do not consider profit to be a bad thing and typically model firms as profit maximizers.

However, much like consumers can't obtain an arbitrarily high utility because of income and price constraints, a firm cannot obtain arbitrarily high profits. Firms are constrained by the demand for their product, the prices of their inputs, and the technology they use. If the firm does make a profit, it is distributed to the firm owners, i.e., households. These households, in turn, use their share of the profit to buy goods and services from other firms. Other households sell their labor-time to the firm in return for a wage. Rather than bear risk and wait to share in any profits the firm might have in the future, employees typically want to be paid on a regular basis. While most employees do not share in the profits of the firm (at least directly), they also do not bear the same risk as firm owners.

Economists model a firm's decisions with the goal of maximizing the profit earned from the decisions. Every decision provides benefits to a firm, typically measured in terms of revenue, but also entails costs. The difference between the revenue generated from a decision and the cost incurred is the profit earned from the decision. This general concept is the same regardless of the decision being analyzed; the trick is accurately measuring the benefits and the costs of various decisions.

Consider the firm's choice of how much output to produce. It might seem natural to assume the firm would want to produce as much as physically possible, but this is not true. The firm's optimal level of production is that which maximizes profit, not the quantity produced. Total revenue is the total dollar receipts from selling goods, i.e., $TR = P \times Q$, where P is the price the firm can charge for its product and Q is the number of units the firm produces and sells. However, to produce and generate revenue the firm must incur costs. Total cost is the money paid to the factors of production used to produce the output the firm chooses to produce and sell, i.e., $TC = C(Q)$, where $C(Q)$ is the firm's cost function which tells the firm the minimum amount of money the firm will have to spend to produce a certain level of output. The difference between revenue and cost is total profit, denoted with the Greek letter π, i.e., $\pi = TR - TC = PQ - C(Q)$.

The Firm's Production Function and Isoquants

The goal of profit maximization is common to all firms. However, it is useful to describe in detail where a firm's cost comes from and to understand why firms will not simply produce the most possible. To produce output, the firm must hire factors of production, which are combined with a methodology or technology. The firm's

Capital (K)	Labor (L)	$Q = K \times L$
0	0	0
3	4	12
4	4	16
5	4	20
4	5	20
4	3	12

Table 8-1   Quantity Produced Using Different Combinations of Inputs

technology can be described by a production function. Assuming only two inputs, capital (K) and labor (L), an example of production function might be $Q = K \times L$, which is similar to the utility function used in Chapter. 7.

The production function is a mathematical equation that tells the firm the maximum it can produce with a given level of inputs (number of machines and workers) and its current technology. For example, Table 8-1 lists the production obtained using different combinations of capital and labor.

It is possible for a firm to produce the same amount of output with different combinations of inputs. A firm can choose different combinations of inputs to produce the same level of output. Suppose the firm decides to produce 9 units. Assuming the production function is the same $Q = K \times L$, the combinations of capital and labor that will produce 9 units as shown in Table 8-2.

The combinations of capital and labor that produce the same level of output can be plotted with labor (L) on the vertical axis and capital (K) on the horizontal axis. The resultant curve is called an isoquant (Figure 8-1) because any combination of capital and labor that falls on the curve can produce the same quantity.

Capital (K)	Labor (L)	$Q = K \times L$
1	9	9
2	4.5	9
3	3	9
4.5	2	9
9	1	9

Table 8-2   Combinations of Capital and Labor that Yield the Same Output

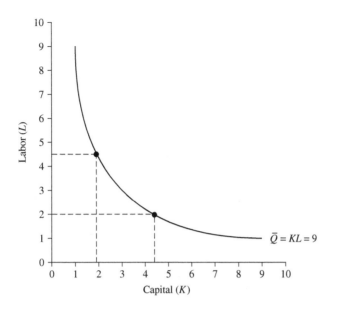

Figure 8-1   An isoquant.

Different combinations of capital and labor will produce different levels of output, as shown in Table 8-1. With more of one or both inputs, the firm can produce more. It is possible to draw an isoquant for each level of output, say, 50, 500, or 5000. A set of isoquants is depicted in Figure 8-2, where moving further from the origin along the 45-degree ray corresponds to greater levels of production

Isoquants are downward sloping, but why are they nonlinear? In general, isoquants are not linear because of the marginal rate of technical substitution. The marginal rate of technical substitution (MRTS) is the additional amount of capital required to maintain production at a certain level after a unit of labor is taken away. For example, if a worker is injured and can't return to work for some time, the MRTS tells the firm how many extra machines to hire to keep production at the same level. Of cource, the Firms may choose to hire a temporary replacement worker instead. The marginal rate of technical substitution between capital and labor is the slope of the isoquant curve, and is determined by the technology the firm uses.

The MRTS is calculated holding output constant. However, what if an additional unit of a capital is hired without decreasing the amount of labor employed? In this case, the additional capital will allow the firm to produce a bit more, which is the marginal product of capital, denoted MP_K. Likewise, if the firm hires another unit of labor without decreasing the amount of capital it uses, the firm will be able to produce a bit more. This increase in production is the marginal product of labor,

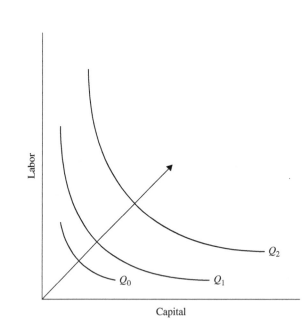

Figure 8-2 An isoquant map.

denoted MP_L. Without introducing complicated math, the MRTS is equal to the ratio of the marginal products of the two inputs used in production

$$MRTS_{K,L} = \frac{MP_L}{MP_K}$$

Firms want to produce as much as possible but, unfortunately, to produce more, the firm will have to hire inputs, which entails costs. Thus, firms cannot produce an arbitrarily large amount of output because production is not free. Two things limit the ability of the firm to produce as much as possible (consistent with maximizing profit): the technology the firm uses, embodied in the isoquant, and the prices of its inputs, embodied in its isocost curve.

Efficiency and the Firm

The firm's production function is a mathematical representation of a firm's production process. As a mathematical equation, the production function tells the firm the most it can produce when a certain amount of capital, labor, and other inputs are hired. However, facts of life are that machines break and workers get sick or are otherwise less than fully able or willing to work at any given time. This implies that it is possible, if not probable, that a firm will not produce the most that it could with a given level of inputs. This problem is called technical inefficiency.

Technical efficiency is defined as producing the most output possible with a given set of inputs. Technical inefficiency is the opposite: producing less than the maximum amount possible with a given set of inputs. Technical inefficiency can arise for a number of reasons, some are natural and beyond the control of a firm's management, while others are influenced by management decisions. For example, say, a firm hires 1000 employees in combination with 300 machines, purchases aluminum and steel as primary inputs, and purchases electricity from a local power plant. These inputs are combined to produce automobile radiators.

If all of the machines, workers, and other inputs are combined efficiently, suppose the firm can produce 2000 radiators in one eight-hour shift. However, it is highly likely that one or more inputs may not work at perfect efficiency. For example, during flu season there will likely be several employees who are sick and cannot come to work on a given day. Machines may break down, or some steel or aluminum may not be of sufficient quality to use in making car radiators. Additionally, power interruptions might occur during which all other inputs may be incapable of producing output.

These seemingly random effects are often beyond the control of the firm's management. After all, if a lightning storm knocks out the power, it is not something that the firm's management can easily foresee or forestall. These random events can cause a firm's output to drop below the maximum level of output that the production function predicts should occur. Firms try to insure against these random events as much as possible, perhaps by having surplus machines or spare parts with which to repair a broken machine, or a temporary employment agency that can provide short-term replacements for injured or ill employees. Unfortunately, these insurances are not guaranteed to make the firm efficient. In other words, the firm may still produce less than its production function indicates.

Technological efficiency is a problem for the firm because the firm's profits are the difference between revenue and costs. As a firm hires and pays inputs, this increases the firm's costs. If the inputs are expected to produce Q_0 units of output, the firm's revenue is expected to be PQ_0. However, if the inputs only produce eQ_0 where $e < 1$, then the firm's revenues are less than expected, PeQ_0. This, in turn, implies that the firm's profits are less when there is technological inefficiency because its revenues are not as great as they could have been.

Other sources of technical inefficiency may be purely engineering in nature. It might be possible for a firm to combine its existing inputs in a different way in order to produce more output. For that reason, firms often hire engineers to analyze the way their inputs are combined. For example, it might prove beneficial to move machines closer to each other to reduce the amount of time the yet-to-be-finished product moves from one portion of the production process to another. This was the primary source of the incredible efficiency gain from the assembly-line concept.

Another form of efficiency is allocative or economic efficiency. Allocative efficiency occurs when a firm produces a given amount of output with the *cheapest* mix of inputs.

The Firm's Cost Constraint

Much like a household has an income constraint, firms are constrained by the amount of money they are willing to spend in production. If the firm is willing to spend only $100 to produce its product, the firm will hire a combination of labor and capital that will spend the $100 and simultaneously produce the most output possible. The firm is not specifically concerned with *how much* labor or capital it hires, but how much the labor and capital it hires can produce.

The isocost curve is derived from the firm's *total variable costs*, which are those costs that change with output. As the firm hires inputs, it pays interest, r, for capital, and wages, w, for labor. Households own capital and labor, although they own different amounts of each input. Therefore, the firm pays households interest and wages. The firm's total variable cost is the sum of it's capital and labor costs, i.e., $TVC = wL + rK$. Given a specific total variable cost, various combinations of labor and capital will cost that amount. The total variable cost equation is the equation of a line, although it is not obvious at first. Consider making L the dependent variable, then the TVC equation can be rewritten as $L = TVC/w - (r/w)K$, where the slope $(-r/w)$ is the relative price of capital to labor. This isocost line can be plotted with labor on the vertical axis and capital on the horizontal axis as in Figure 8-3.

Much like the household's budget constraint changes with prices and income, the firm's isocost curve can change. If the firm decides to spend more on production, the isocost curve will shift right, making more combinations of capital and labor affordable and allowing the firm to produce more. On the other hand, if the firm decides to spend less on production, the isocost curve shifts left and fewer combinations of capital and labor are affordable and the firm will likely produce less.

If the price of capital falls, the isocost curve will shift out the horizontal axis, making the isocost curve flatter. If the price of labor falls, the isocost curve will shift out the vertical axis, making the isocost curve steeper. Whenever the price of an input falls, it makes more combinations of capital and labor affordable. Whenever the price of an input increases, it makes fewer combinations of capital and labor affordable.

How much the firm will produce and the combination of capital and labor it will hire is determined by combining the isoquant map with the isocost curve, as in Figure 8-4. The firm will produce as much as possible given the amount it is willing

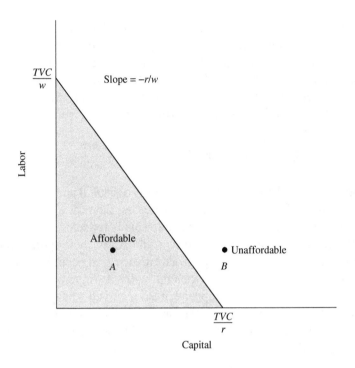

Figure 8-3   An isocost curve.

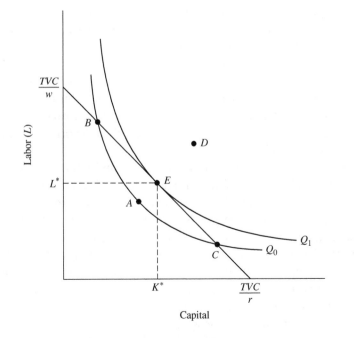

Figure 8-4   A firm's optimal combination of capital and labor.

to spend by hiring the combination of capital and labor that corresponds with Point *E*. At that point, the firm produces the most output given the amount it is willing to spend. Point *E* is a tangency between the isoquant and the isocost curves, indicating that the slopes of the two curves are the same at that point. At the firm's equilibrium, the relative price of labor to capital (the slope of the isocost curve) is set equal to the marginal rate of technical substitution (the slope of the isoquant curve), or

$$\frac{MP_L}{MP_K} = \frac{w}{r} \text{ which can be rewritten as } \frac{MP_K}{r} = \frac{MP_L}{w}$$

What happens to the firm's optimal combination of capital and labor if one or more input prices change? If the price of capital increases, then for a given level of Total Variable Cost, the firm can afford less capital. This is reflected in the isocost curve becoming steeper. In response, firms will typically adjust their optimal capital-labor mix to include more labor and less capital. The reverse will occur if the price of labor increases relative to capital. Firms, in general, will substitute out of inputs that are relatively more expensive and into inputs that are relatively cheaper.

Now that the firm's equilibrium level of inputs and output have been determined, it is possible to reconsider the efficiency issues addressed above, namely, technical and allocative inefficiency. Both sources of inefficiency can be depicted on the firm's isocost and isoquant.

Technical efficiency can be depicted on a firm's isoquant map. In Figure 8-5, if the firm spends $1000, the optimal level of capital and labor hired is K_0 and L_0. With perfect efficiency, the firm would produce 100 units. However, if output actually occurs at Point *A*, which corresponds, say, with 80 units, then output is less than expected given the amount of inputs hired. In this case, the firm would be operating at 80% technical efficiency. Either the firm could have produced more output with the given level of inputs or could have produced the 80 units by hiring fewer inputs, say, K_1 and L_1. The important issue from the point of view of the firm is that the combination of capital and labor at K_1 and L_1 would cost less than the original combination of capital and labor at K_0 and L_0.

Figure 8-5 also depicts combinations of capital and labor that are allocatively inefficient. The combinations of capital and labor at Points *B*, *C*, and *E*, will all produce 100 units. However, both Points *B* and *C* correspond to a total variable cost of $1100, whereas Point *E* corresponds with a variable cost of $1000. Therefore, Point *E* is allocatively efficient relative to Points *B* and *C*.

Moving from Point *C* to Point *E* entails replacing capital for labor, that is, firing some workers and replacing them with more machines. While this may not be good for the particular workers who lose their jobs, the firm is more efficient after moving from Point *C* to Point *E*. On the other hand, moving from Point *B* to Point *E* would entail replacing machines for workers. In this case, workers would stand to gain at the expense of the owners of capital. The desire for the firm to be efficient

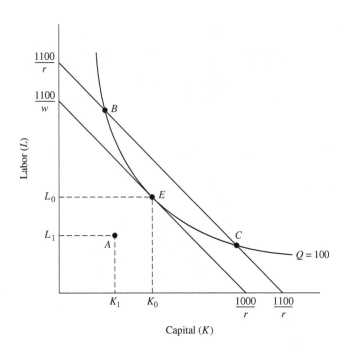

Figure 8-5   Technical and allocation efficiency.

is in the best interest of society as a whole, even if individual workers or owners of other inputs are made worse off.

Note that Point E is the only point where the firm is *simultaneously* allocatively and technically efficient. This simultaneous condition is a reinforcement for why the Point E is a firm equilibrium. As long as the firm can ensure efficiency, Point E is the best decision for the firm. Point E corresponds to producing the most possible, given a combination of inputs while at the same time minimizing cost for a given level of output. For the remainder of this book, it will be assumed that firms are both allocatively and technologically efficient.

A Firm's Cost Functions: Total Cost, Average Cost, and Marginal Cost

Economists assume that firms make decisions consistent with maximizing their profit. Profit was earlier defined as the difference between total revenue and total cost. The remainder of this chapter focuses on various measures of cost. In general, there are two types of costs that firms incur. Variable costs are those that change with output. Fixed costs are those costs that the firm incurs regardless of how much, or whether, it chooses to produce. An example of variable costs is hiring additional labor to work overtime. An example of fixed costs is the lease on a building that will be paid regardless of whether the business produces any output and the price on the lease does not change if the business does produce output. Total cost is the sum of variable and fixed costs.

Firms determine their total cost of production by adding the variable costs incurred after hiring the least cost combination of inputs to produce the level of output and any fixed costs. These combinations can be plotted on a total cost curve, which is drawn with cost (in dollars or some other currency) on the vertical axis and output on the horizontal axis. If there is no fixed cost, the total cost curve extends from the origin and total cost is equal to total variable cost. If there is a fixed cost, the total cost curve has a vertical intercept at the fixed cost. From the total cost curve it is possible to determine the least amount of money the firm will spend to produce a given amount of output. An example of a total cost curve is depicted in Figure 8-6.

The total cost curve in Figure 8-6 seems to have a weird shape. In certain ranges of production, costs do not increase very fast, but in other ranges, costs increase rather quickly. The total cost curve in Figure 8-6 has a couple of inflection points that, as shown below, are indicative of the type of technology the firm uses. The total cost curve is useful in its own right, however a couple of measures can be derived from the total cost curve that are also very useful. The average cost or per-unit cost is total cost divided by the amount of output the firm has produced.

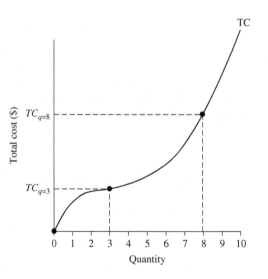

Figure 8-6 A total cost curve.

From the total cost curve in Figure 8-6, a ray from the origin to any particular point on the total cost curve has a slope that equals average total cost. Average total cost is comprised of two elements, average variable cost and average fixed cost, or ATC = AVC + AFC. Average variable costs can increase or decrease with the level of output, however average fixed cost approaches zero (but never quite gets there) as more output is produced. Average variable cost, average fixed cost, and average total cost can be calculated for each level of output and plotted as in Figure 8-7.

The average variable cost and average total cost curves in Figure 8-7 are U-shaped because of a technological phenomenon known as returns to scale. Not every technology exhibits this phenomenon but many do. Returns to scale reflects how much output increases after all inputs have been increased by the same proportion. If the amount of all inputs used to produce were to double, the variable costs paid by the firm would likewise double. If twice the inputs produce more than twice the original output, the firm's technology exhibits increasing returns to scale (IRS). In the case of increasing returns to scale, the average cost of production declines, indicating a downward sloping average variable and average total cost curve. An alternative is that doubling all inputs yields just double the original output level. In this case, the firm's technology exhibits constant returns to scale, and average variable and average total costs do not change with output. The final possibility is that doubling all inputs yields less than double the original output. In this case, the firm's technology would exhibit decreasing returns to scale, and the firm's average variable and average total cost would increase with output.

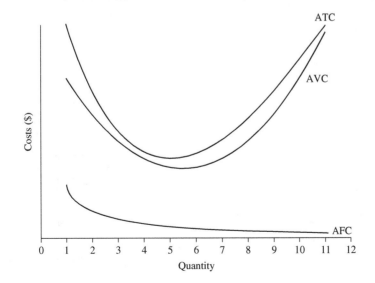

Figure 8-7   Average variable cost, average fixed cost, and average total cost curves.

The average variable and average total cost curves depicted in Figure 8-7 exhibit all three forms of returns to scale at different points of production. At relatively low levels of production, the firm's per-unit costs decline with additional output, indicating increasing returns to scale. When a firm produces at the lowest possible average total cost, the firm reaches minimum efficient scale, beyond which the firm's technology exhibits decreasing returns to scale.

Another useful measure that helps firms make profit-maximizing decisions is marginal cost, which is the change in total cost after producing an additional unit of output. The marginal cost can be calculated from the total cost curve. At each level of output, the slope of the total cost curve is the marginal cost of that unit of the good. Because the total cost curve does not have a constant slope, the marginal cost is calculated as the slope of a tangent line at each level of output. Figure 8-8a depicts the marginal cost at two different levels of output. As can be readily seen, marginal cost changes with output. The various marginal costs can be plotted on a marginal cost curve, as depicted in Figure 8-8b.

Figure 8-9 combines average total cost and marginal cost curves on the same graph. Notice that the marginal cost curve intersects the average total cost curve at the minimum of average total cost, or minimum efficient scale.

Firms can only maximize profits if they know how their decisions impact their revenues and their costs. The decision to produce an extra unit of output increases cost by some amount because the firm must hire more inputs. The change in revenue that occurs when the firm is able to sell another unit of output is called marginal revenue. If the firm sells the extra unit for more than what it cost to produce, marginal

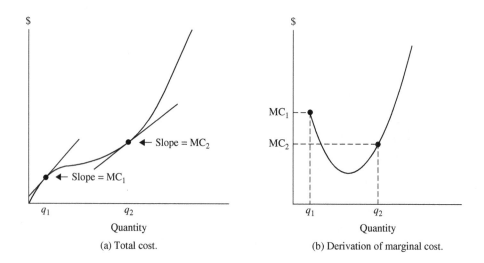

(a) Total cost. (b) Derivation of marginal cost.

Figure 8-8 (a and b) Derivation of marginal cost.

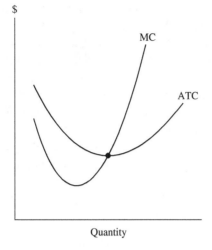

Figure 8-9   Average total cost and marginal cost.

revenue is greater than marginal cost, and the firm's profit will increase. If the firm sells the extra unit for less than what it cost to produce, marginal revenue is less than marginal cost, and the firm's profit will necessarily decrease. Finally, if the firm sells the extra unit of production for exactly what it cost to produce, marginal revenue equals marginal cost, and the firm's profit will not change.

In general, firms should produce output until their marginal cost is just equal to their marginal revenue. At this point, the firm's profit is maximized, although it is not guaranteed to be positive (otherwise no firm would ever go out of business). In the next three chapters, various scenarios are investigated in turn. While each scenario has its own general conclusions, the solution to the firm's problem in each case is the same: Set marginal revenue equal to marginal cost.

Summary

This chapter has discussed the basic theory of the firm. After discussing why economists believe organizing production in private firms is superior to alternative frameworks, the decision of what combination of inputs to hire was investigated. Firms are assumed to maximize profit. Given a target level of output, firms seek to produce that output with the cheapest combination of inputs. Firms end up hiring inputs such that the monetary trade-off between hiring one or the other input is just balanced with the production trade-off between hiring one input or the other. Because different firms use different technologies, labor is not always as productive in one industry as it might be in another, similarly for capital. Therefore, depending on the firm's technology and the relative prices of inputs, firms might decide to employ more workers and fewer machines, or more machines and fewer workers. While it is common to lament a firm replacing workers with robots, such a decision is often consistent with changing relative prices of inputs and the goal of maximizing profit.

The remainder of the chapter discussed various measures of cost, including total cost, comprised of fixed and variable cost, average total cost, average variable cost, average fixed cost, and marginal cost. Average costs curves tend to be U-shaped if the technology of the firm exhibits various returns to scale. These concepts of cost, especially marginal and average total cost, are important elements to the firm's profit-maximizing output decision.

Quiz

1. At the point of equilibrium for the firm, which of the following is true?
   a. The amount of capital and labor used is the same.
   b. The price of capital and labor are the same.
   c. The slope of the cost constraint is the same as the slope of the isoquant.
   d. The slope of the cost constraint is different than the slope of the isoquant.

2. The difference between fixed costs and variable costs is that
   a. fixed costs vary with quantity produced.
   b. variable costs depend upon the quantity produced.
   c. there is no difference.
   d. variable costs are included in profit maximization while fixed costs are not.
   e. none of the above.

3. A firm's cost constraint can shift outward due to which of the following:
   a. An increase in the price of any factor of production
   b. A decrease in the price of any factor of production
   c. An increase in the marginal productivity of labor
   d. A decrease in the total cost the firm is willing to spend
   e. None of the above

4. The Average Total Cost curve can shift due to all of the following except:

   a. Improvements in technology

   b. Shifts in the product's supply curve

   c. Shifts in the supply curve for a factor of production

   d. Shifts in the preference structure of the households

   e. Both (b) and (d)

5. At profit maximization,

   a. marginal revenue is equal to average cost.

   b. marginal cost is equal to average revenue.

   c. marginal cost is equal to marginal revenue.

   d. marginal profit is equal to average profit.

   e. marginal cost is equal to average cost.

6. Which of the following was not offered as a reason for the firm to exist?

   a. Firms minimize transaction costs.

   b. Firms are easier to regulate.

   c. Firms internalize risk.

   d. Firms internalize benefits of size.

   e. Firms internalize benefits of knowledge.

7. Increasing returns to scale is identified by

   a. average cost decreasing as quantity decreases.

   b. average cost increasing as quantity increases.

   c. average cost decreasing as quantity increases.

   d. average cost equal to zero.

   e. the prices of the factors of production.

8. An increase in the price of labor causes a decrease in the supply of the product because

   a. each firm is going out of business.

   b. barriers to entry exist in the market.

   c. each firm produces less at profit maximization.

   d. each firm produces more at profit maximization.

9. Minimum efficient scale occurs at

    a. the maximum of the average cost curve.

    b. the minimum of the marginal cost curve.

    c. the smallest quantity possible to produce.

    d. the minimum of the average cost curve.

10. Assume the relative price of capital to labor is 0.50. If Firm A has an MRTS of 8 and Firm B has an MRTS of 0.25, which of the following statements is true?

    a. Firm A should hire less capital and more labor.

    b. Firm A should hire more capital and less labor.

    c. Firm B should hire more capital and less labor.

    d. Firm B should hire the same amount of capital as Firm A.

11. If a firm can produce more output without hiring any more inputs, then the firm is

    a. allocatively efficient.

    b. technologically inefficient.

    c. allocatively inefficient.

    d. technologically efficient.

    e. none of the above.

12. If a firm can produce a given output with a mix of inputs that cost $1000 or a mix of inputs that cost $850, the firm is allocatively efficient if it chooses

    a. $850.

    b. $500.

    c. $1000.

    d. none of the above.

Use Figure 8-10 for the following three questions:

13. Which point is both technologically and allocatively efficient?

    a. A

    b. B

    c. C

    d. D

    e. E

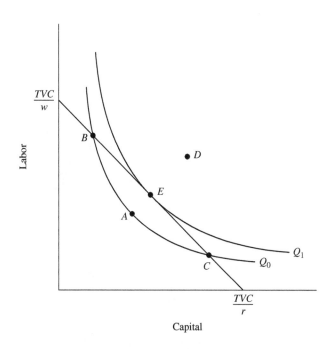

Figure 8-10 Firm's equilibrium.

14. Which points are allocatively inefficient?

   a. *B* and *E*

   b. *A* and *E*

   c. *B* and *C*

   d. *D* and *E*

   e. *C* and *D*

15. What must happen to make Point *D* feasible?

   a. A decrease in the price of labor

   b. A decrease in the price of capital

   c. An increase in the amount of money the firm is willing to spend

   d. An improvement in the firm's technology

   e. All of the above

Perfect Competition

Firms maximize profits when their marginal revenue equals marginal cost. The previous chapter outlined how firms determine their marginal cost of production. This chapter (and the next two) focuses on how firms measure their marginal revenue and how firms interact with each other and their customers in various market structures. There are numerous different market structures, including perfect competition, perfect monopoly, monopolistic competition, and oligopoly. The most intense form of market competition is modeled as perfect competition.

Like other economic models, the theory of perfect competition entails assumptions that lead to implications. The assumptions of perfect competition include:

1. There are many sellers.

2. There are many buyers.

3. Firms sell a homogeneous good.

4. Firms and consumers can freely enter and exit the industry.

5. Consumers and firms have perfect information.

6. There are no transaction costs.

7. There are no externalities in production or consumption.

The first implication of the seven assumptions enumerated above comes from assumptions 1, 2, and 3. Because firms sell a homogeneous good, that is, one that all consumers consider perfect substitutes, and there are many (perhaps thousands) buyers and sellers in this market, it is impossible for any single seller or buyer to unilaterally change the price of the product. In other words, both buyers and sellers are price takers.

Consider buying apples at a local farmer's market. Because you are only going to buy a few apples relative to the overall size of the apple market you are not able to negotiate the price lower. Try this sometime and you will quickly see that you have no individual influence over the price of apples. However, the farmer you buy the apples from has no control over the price of apples either. The price of apples is determined by the overall interaction of supply and demand, as described in Chapter 4, and once the market-clearing price is determined, the farmers and the customers take that price as given. Of course, if there is only one farmer selling apples, he will likely command a higher price. However, this would violate assumption 1 of the model of perfect competition.

Even if the seller cannot unilaterally increase the price of the good he is selling, is it at all desirable for him to lower the price of his product? In general, a firm in a perfectly competitive industry can sell as much as it desires without shifting the market supply curve enough to change the market equilibrium price. Because the firm can produce and sell as much as it wants at a given market price, lowering the price of the product will not provide additional revenue for the firm.

Because each firm must act as a price taker, the individual firm's demand curve is perfectly flat at the market-clearing price, as depicted in Figure 9-1. Because the firm is small relative to the overall market, the firm can produce q_0 or q_1 in Figure 9-1 and not influence the market price of its product. If the market-clearing price were to increase or decrease, the firm's demand curve will increase or decrease accordingly.

The perfectly competitive firm's goal is to maximize its profit. However, because the market is characterized by freedom of entry and exit, a firm might want to leave one market and enter another. The competitive firm must make the following decisions:

1. Whether to enter, stay, or leave the industry

2. Whether to produce or to *temporarily* shut down

3. How much to produce

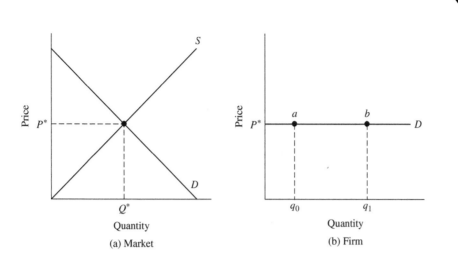

Figure 9-1 A perfectly competitive firm's demand curve.

Assume the firm decides to stay in the industry and that it is going to produce. The firm wants to choose a level of production that is consistent with maximizing profit. What quantity does the firm choose? We know that the firm's total revenue is TR = PQ, and we can define the firm's average revenue or revenue per-unit sold as

$$\text{AR} = \frac{\text{TR}}{Q} = \frac{PQ}{Q} = P$$

and the firm's marginal revenue is MR = ΔTR/ΔQ, which is the change in total revenue caused by a change in quantity produced and sold.

To calculate marginal revenue is rather straightforward, simply calculate the to-tal revenue at two different levels of output and calculate the difference. For example, let price be $10 and the original quantity produced and sold be 20 units. In this case, the firm's total revenue is $10 × 20 = $200. If the firm produces an extra unit of the good and sells it, its total revenue increases to $10 × 21 = $210. The $10 difference between the two levels of revenue is the marginal revenue of the 21st unit. Because the firm is a price taker and is very small relative to the overall market, the marginal revenue will always be the market-clearing price determined by the interaction of supply and demand. In other words, in a perfectly competitive market, the firm's marginal revenue equals price, i.e., MR = P.

The total revenue curve depicts the total revenue generated at each quantity pro-duced. The total revenue curve of the competitive firm is linear with the slope of P^*, which is the market-clearing price, as depicted in Figure 9-2.

CHAPTER 9

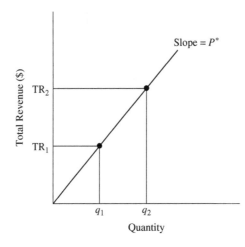

Figure 9-2 A perfectly competitive firm's total revenue curve.

To determine the firm's profit at each possible level of production, the total revenue curve (TR) and the total cost curve (TC) can be drawn on the same graph as in Figure 9-3.

The firm's profit is the difference between total revenue and total cost, which can be determined from Figure 9-3. At each unit of output, the total profit can be determined and plotted on a total profit curve as in Figure 9-4.

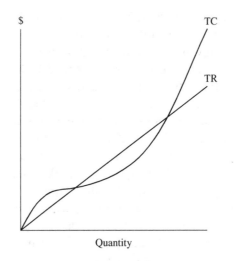

Figure 9-3 Total revenue and total cost.

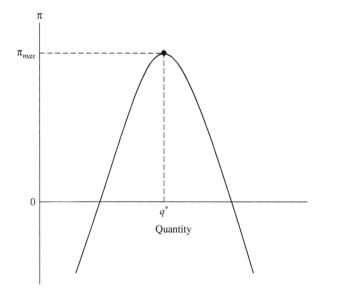

Figure 9-4   A competitive firm's profit curve.

The firm's maximum profit is obtained at the peak of the profit curve. In Figure 9-4, the firm's profit is maximized when it produces q^* units of output. If the firm chooses to produce more than q^*, its costs will increase more than its revenue will increase, and hence its overall profit will decline. If the firm chooses to produce less than q^*, its revenue will fall faster than its cost, and therefore its profits will drop.

The firm's profit curve incorporates a lot of information in one graph. However, the firm can also choose its profit maximizing quantity by setting the marginal revenue of output equal to the marginal cost of output. Because the firm's demand curve, average revenue curve, and marginal revenue curve are all horizontal lines at the market-clearing price, it is possible to determine the firm's profit maximizing quantity by drawing marginal revenue and marginal cost on the same graph as in Figure 9-5.

To determine where the firm will produce in order to maximize profit, the firm sets marginal revenue equal to marginal cost. However, in Figure 9-5 there are two points where marginal revenue equals marginal cost. For each unit produced from 0 to q_1 units, the firm earns a negative marginal profit. However, between Points a and b, the firm earns positive per-unit profits. The firm maximizes its profit by producing where marginal cost equals marginal revenue and marginal cost cuts marginal revenue from below, as at Point b in Figure 9-5.

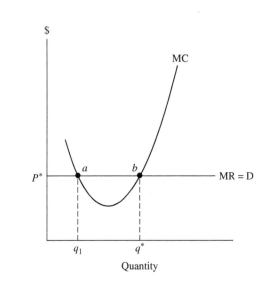

Figure 9-5 A competitive firm's choice mechanism.

What is the profit of the firm at quantity q^*? To determine this, it is possible to calculate total revenue and total cost as in Figure 9-3, or we could depict the average total cost on the same graph as marginal revenue and marginal cost, as in Figure 9-6. Because profit is defined as $\pi = \text{TR} - \text{TC} = PQ - \text{TC}(Q)$, it is possible to rewrite profit as $\pi = (P - \text{ATC})Q$, where $\text{ATC} = \text{TC}(Q)/Q$. If we draw the Average Total Cost

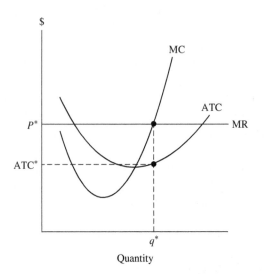

Figure 9-6 Determining profitability for a competitive firm.

curve on the same graph as marginal revenue and marginal cost, as in Figure 9-6, it is possible to determine very quickly whether the firm is making a positive, negative, or zero profit by comparing the price and average total cost at q^*.

If the firm's price is greater than average total cost, the firm is making a positive profit. If the firm's price is equal to average total cost, then the firm is making zero profit. Finally, if the firm's price is less than its average total cost, then the firm is making negative profits.

However, just because a firm is making a negative profit, does the firm want to shutdown or leave the industry? The firm will shut down temporarily only if price falls below the firm's average variable cost and the firm believes that price will increase in the future. If price is greater than the firm's average variable cost but less than the firm's average total cost, the firm's profit is negative. However, the firm does not want to shut down because to do so, the firm will have to pay it's fixed cost, and if the firm does not produce, it will have no revenue. Therefore, the firm finds it best to produce, pay off the variable cost of production, pay off a portion of its fixed costs, and hope that price will increase in the future. On the other hand, if the price falls below average variable cost and the firm does not anticipate that the price will increase in the future, the firm will choose to leave the industry.

A firm with a positive profit in the short run might find itself pushed into a negative profit in one of two ways: Either the price in the market declines or the costs of the firm increase. How can costs increase? Either the prices of the inputs used by the firm increases or the government might increase the regulations with which the firm must comply, resulting in an increase in cost.

The other way a firm might be pushed towards zero or negative profit is if the price in the market declines. Yet, the first implication of perfect competition is that the firm does not have any control over the price it charges—it has to take the market-clearing price as given. So, how might price change in a competitive market? The answer lies in the assumption of freedom of entry and exit.

Freedom of entry and exit means that firms can come and go in the industry with little trouble. Farming is such an industry as farmers can use their land to grow corn or, say, to raise cattle. If the corn market is not as profitable as the cattle market, competitive farmers will leave the corn industry and enter the cattle industry. If the corn market is more profitable than the cattle market, the reverse will hold: Farmers leave the cattle industry and enter the corn industry. The movement of firms from or to an industry influences the industry's supply curve (see Chapter 4). As entry occurs, there are more firms in the market and the supply curve increases or shifts right. If exit occurs, there are fewer firms in the market and the supply curve decreases or shifts left.

If incumbent firms in a perfectly competitive market make positive profits, the assumption of perfect information implies that everyone knows that the market is profitable. The freedom of entry, coupled with the assumption that all firms produce the same product, implies that firms will want to enter the market. As entry occurs, the industry's supply curve shifts right and the market-clearing price in the market declines (see Figure 9-7a). As the market price declines, the market quantity increases, even while the quantity that the firm produces declines (see Figure 9-7b).

Over time, as more entry occurs, it is entirely possible that the market price will decline far enough so that some firms are forced to shutdown temporarily, i.e., price is less than average variable cost. When firms shutdown temporarily, or leave the industry for other markets where profits are higher, the industry's supply will decline, shifting the supply curve to the left and causing price to increase (the reverse of what happens in Figures 9-7a and 9-7b). As price increases, firms see their marginal revenue increase and therefore they produce more. This cyclical entry and exit will continue as long as profits are positive or negative.

The long-run equilibrium of a perfectly competitive market occurs when neither entry nor exit occurs. This will happen when firms in the market are not making positive profits, which would encourage entry, nor are they making negative profits, which would encourage exit. The long-run equilibrium occurs when profits are zero.

If perfectly competitive firms are assured zero profit in the long run, why do perfectly competitive firms exist? One explanation is that the firm owners, who are the residual claimants, are paid as employees of the firm, and therefore even if the firm technically makes a zero profit, the firm owners are paid enough to keep them in the market. Economists refer to these profits as normal profits. Normal profits are not average or standard profits but refer to a zero profit condition in which firm owners stay in their industry.

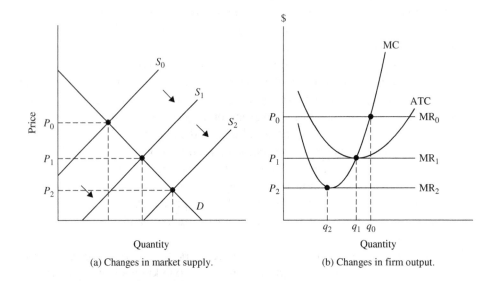

(a) Changes in market supply.   (b) Changes in firm output.

Figure 9-7   (a and b) Long-run changes in perfect competition.

What happens if there is an increase in the demand for a product produced in a perfectly competitive industry? When demand increases, the market-clearing price will increase in the short run, and existing firms produce more. However, existing firms will experience higher profits, which will encourage entry. Over time, entry will push the supply curve to the right, thereby increasing the quantity sold in the market but reducing the market-clearing price and the profitability of the firms in the industry. On the other hand, if there is a decline in demand, prices fall and some firms are pushed out of business, supply shifts to the left, eventually price increases, and the market quantity declines.

Seasonal effects can cause changes in demand. For example, the demand for pumpkins in the United States is very high during October through December, but is very low in April. Therefore, pumpkin farmers tend to produce a lot of pumpkins when price is high and not when the price of pumpkins is low. Other influences on demand might be from changes in information available to consumers. For example, if it were discovered that drinking two cups of orange juice every morning would cure cancer, it is likely that the demand for orange juice would permanently increase and, over time, we would see a permanent increase in the supply of orange juice.

Profits in the Movie Industry

The movie industry doesn't seem to be perfectly competitive at first glance. Indeed, very few industries meet all the assumptions of the perfectly competitive market. However, there is a relatively large number of movie studios; there are clearly a lot of consumers in the movie industry; there is relatively good information about the quality of the movies, what movies contain, and the actors who star in the various movies. While there is not necessarily free entry into the industry, movies come and go on a regular basis, and therefore in many ways, the movie industry might be considered somewhat competitive.

Because some of the most famous movie stars are often paid several millions of dollars for a single movie, it might seem that every movie is guaranteed to make positive profits for the studio. However, this is far from the case. There have been some notable flops (both artistically and economically) in the movie industry over the past several years, as well as some sleeper movies that cost very little to make but generated huge profits for their studio. An example of the former is *Water World* and an example of the latter is the *Blair Witch Project*.

Movies are produced and the majority of the expenses of the movie are incurred before the movie is even released to the general market. Before and immediately after release, the major expense of the movie is likely to be advertising efforts. Therefore, the majority of the costs of a movie can be considered fixed costs in the sense that they do not change after the movie has been completed. Unfortunately for the movie studio, the movie's revenue is not determined until after the studio has incurred the costs of production. While many movie stars negotiate for a share of the film's profits, many times stars are satisfied being paid a lump sum at the time of production.

Because the film's costs are borne before its revenues are generated, it is not guaranteed that any particular film will generate a positive profit, even if it features a well-known actor or actress. To demonstrate, the graph in Figure 9-8 depicts the expenditures and the profits for twenty selected movies from 2004.

The various movies are plotted with their costs in million dollars on the horizontal axis and their revenues in million dollars on the vertical axis. As a film generates positive profits if its revenues are greater than its costs, those movies that fall above the diagonal line earned positive profits. Those movies that fall below the diagonal axis earned negative profits. Those movies that fall on the diagonal generated zero profits.

Included in the movies depicted were the top ten in terms of domestic gross revenues. Of these ten films, nine earned a positive profit, the lone exception was *Polar Express* which lost $2 million in its U.S. run. Amongst the top ten films, the average revenue was $267.41 million and the average cost was $106.71 million for an average profit of $161.71 million. Amongst these top ten films are several blockbusters such as *Shrek 2*, *Spiderman 2*, *The Passion of the Christ*, and *National Treasure*.

The other 10 films were ranked between 89 and 100 in total revenues, and included films such as *Garden State*, *Jersey Girl*, *The Life Aquatic*, and *Agent*

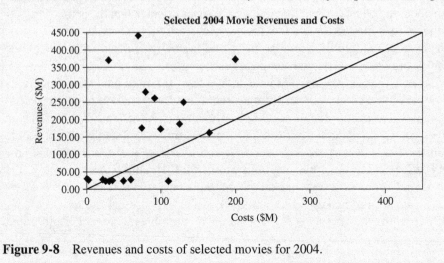

Figure 9-8 Revenues and costs of selected movies for 2004.

Cody Banks 2: Destination London. The average revenue of these films was $25.89 million, while the average cost was $38.70 million, leading to an average *loss* of $12.81 million. Notice that having a big star does not guarantee positive profits. *National Treasure* starred Nicholas Cage, *Jersey Girl* starred Ben Affleck, and *The Life Aquatic* starred Bill Murray.

This example shows that even in markets where positive profits would seem guaranteed, this is not necessarily the case. The movies included in this example, their budgets, and revenues were obtained from the website <http://www.boxofficemojo.com> and are listed in Table 9-1.

U.S. Revenue Rank	Movie Title	Total U.S. Revenue ($ millions)	Total Cost ($ millions)	Total Profit ($ millions)
1	Shrek 2	441.23	70	371.23
2	Spiderman 2	373.59	200	173.59
3	The Passion of the Christ	370.27	30	340.27
4	Meet the Fockers	279.25	80	199.25
5	The Incredibles	261.44	92	169.44
6	Harry Potter and the Prisoner of Azkaban	249.54	130	119.54
7	The Day After Tomorrow	186.74	125	61.74
8	The Bourne Supremacy	176.24	75	101.24
9	National Treasure	172.98	100	72.98
10	The Polar Express	162.78	165	−2.22
89[1]	Open Water	30.61	0.5	30.11
91	After the Sunset	28.33	60	−31.67
92	The Prince and Me	28.18	22	6.18
93	Garden State	26.78	2.5	24.28
94	Jersey Girl	25.27	35	−9.73
95	Twisted	25.20	50	−24.80
96	The Life Aquatic	24.02	50	−25.98
97	Around the World in 80 Days	24.01	110	−85.99
98	Agent Cody Banks 2: Destination London	23.63	26	−2.37
100	Ella Enchanted	22.92	31	−8.08
	Average	**146.65**	**72.70**	**73.95**

[1] The films ranked 90 and 99 in U.S. revenue did not report production costs and therefore were not included in this table.

Table 9-1   Top U.S. Movies in 2004 Ranked on the Basis of the Revenue Generation

Summary

Perfect competition is the most intense form of competition. Consumers and firms are each very small relative to the overall market and therefore act as price takers. The market price is determined by the interaction of supply and demand. The analysis of perfect competition focuses primarily on the decisions of firms, namely whether to stay in the industry or leave, whether to produce or temporarily shut down, and if they decide to produce, how much to produce. Each decision on the part of the firm aims to maximize the profit the firm can earn. Unfortunately, in perfect competition firms that make positive profits today are unable to deter entry into their market—other firms want to share in the positive profits. Entry in the market increases the supply in the market, which, in turn, puts downward pressure on price. As price falls, firms find their profitability reduced and, indeed, firms might actually earn negative profits in the short run.

When firms earn negative profits, some firms temporarily shut down or leave the industry altogether. This reduces supply, putting upward pressure on price, and increases profitability. The entry and exit into a competitive industry will continue as long as profits are positive or negative, respectively. In the long run, however, neither entry nor exit occurs. This occurs when all firms earn a normal profit, or zero economic profit. Whether an industry is ever in long-run equilibrium is an open question because any failure in the assumption of *ceteris paribus* can start the entire entry or exit process over again.

Perfect competition is valuable as a benchmark against which to compare other market structures. The benefits of perfect competition are that price equals marginal cost, both producer and consumer surpluses are maximized, and in the long run, firms operate at minimum efficient scale, indicating that all increasing returns to scale have been realized. From consumers' point of view, perfect competition is an ideal arrangement. However, from the point of view of firms and firm owners, perfect competition is far from ideal. The individual firm has no control over price and has little advantage against their competition.

Quiz

1. A firm will temporarily shut-down when

    a. it cannot cover average fixed cost.

    b. it cannot cover average variable costs.

    c. it cannot cover average total cost.

    d. it cannot cover average marginal cost.

    e. it cannot cover average regulatory cost.

2. If a competitive firm finds that it can produce additional output for less than the market price, the firm should

    a. produce less output.

    b. not change the amount it is producing.

    c. produce more output.

    d. look at what the competition is doing.

3. If government passes an increase in the minimum wage,

    a. firms that hire minimum wage labor will see their marginal revenue increase.

    b. firms that hire minimum wage labor will see marginal cost decrease.

    c. firms that hire minimum wage labor will see average and marginal costs increase.

    d. firms that hire minimum wage labor will see only average cost increase.

    e. firms are guaranteed to see profits increase.

4. If a competitive firm faces $P = 10$, ATC $= 5$, and $q = 20$, what is its profit level?

    a. 10

    b. 1000

    c. 2000

    d. 150

    e. 100

5. If a firm earns positive profits in a perfectly competitive environment, it can expect

    a. price to decrease in the future.

    b. price to remain the same in the future.

    c. price increase in the future.

    d. profits increase in the future.

    e. the profit maximizing quantity to increase in the future.

6. Consider that, at a highway exit, the price of gasoline is the same at all four gas stations. This can be explained by

    a. an obvious attempt to price gouge the consumer.

    b. price taking behavior.

    c. the fact that the Federal government controlled prices in 1973.

    d. the fact that the Federal government imposed a price ceiling on gasoline after 1991.

7. Christian's Hamburgers hires minimum wage labor and sells hamburgers in a competitive market. Christian's Hamburgers is at a long-run equilibrium when Congress increases the minimum wage. Which of the following *would not* apply to Christian's Hamburgers?

    a. The price will not change in the short-run.

    b. The profitability of Christian's Hamburgers will go down.

    c. Christian's Hamburgers will unilaterally increase its price.

    d. The quantity of hamburgers sold by Christian's Hamburgers will decrease.

    e. All of the above apply.

8. Assume a competitive firm finds itself at long-run equilibrium wherein it produces 40 units. If the federal government levies a corporation fee on the competitive firms, what will happen to the profit maximizing quantity?

    a. It will increase.

    b. It will not change.

    c. It will decrease.

    d. Not enough information to answer the question.

    e. None of the above.

9. What will happen to the profitability of the firms in the above question?

    a. It will increase.

    b. It will not change.

    c. It will decrease.

    d. Not enough information to answer the question.

    e. None of the above.

10. If price decreases in a perfectly competitive industry,

    a. the federal government will often intervene.

    b. consumers benefit while firms are harmed.

    c. firms benefit while consumers are harmed.

    d. firms and consumers benefit while the government is harmed.

Use Figure 9-9 for the following three questions:

11. The firm in Figure 9-9 is making

    a. short-run positive profits.

    b. short-run negative profits.

    c. long-run positive profits.

    d. long-run negative profits.

    e. long-run zero profits.

12. The firm in Figure 9-9 can expect

    a. its profit maximizing quantity to increase.

    b. its profit maximizing quantity to decrease.

    c. its profit maximizing quantity to stay the same.

    d. its profit maximizing quantity to change, but it's not clear in what direction.

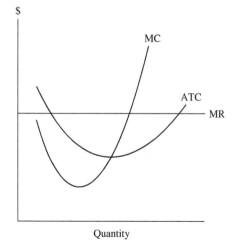

Figure 9-9

13. The consumers in Figure 9-9 can expect

    a. prices to increase in the future.

    b. prices to not change in the future.

    c. prices to decrease in the future.

    d. prices to change in the future, but it is not clear in what direction.

Use Figure 9-10 for the following two questions:

14. Which points are technologically and allocatively efficient?

    a. Points *A* and *C*

    b. Points *B* and *D*

    c. Points *A* and *B*

    d. Points *O* and *D*

15. Between which two points is the firm likely to maximize profit?

    a. Points *O* and *D*

    b. Points *B* and *D*

    c. Points *O* and *A*

    d. Points *A* and *C*

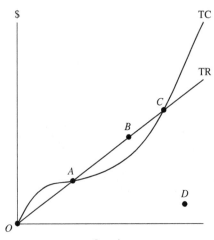

Figure 9-10

10

Theory of Monopoly

Static Monopoly

Perfect competition is a market structure with many sellers of a homogeneous product and is the most intense form of market competition. Perfectly competitive firms are guaranteed zero profit in the long run, but firms rarely find this prospect very appealing. One reason firm owners attempt to differentiate their firms or product from their competition is that with differentiation it is possible to earn more profit. The next two chapters consider variants of what is generally called imperfect competition. This chapter focuses on monopoly. The next chapter considers monopolistic competition and oligopoly.

The alternative extreme to perfect competition is perfect monopoly, which is characterized by a single seller. Monopolies can be local, regional, or national, but the analysis is the same.

The standard static monopoly model assumes:

1. There is only one seller in the market.
2. There are many buyers in the market.
3. The firm's product is unique and has no close substitutes.
4. The firm chooses only one price.
5. There are barriers of entry to the industry.
6. There is asymmetric information.

One of the most important aspects of monopoly is the existence of barriers to entry in the industry. A barrier precludes entry to a market, especially when firms in the industry are making a positive profit. There are two major types of barriers: legal and natural. A legal barrier to entry is a law passed at the local, regional (state), or national level that makes it illegal to enter and compete in the market. For example, it is against the law for a private company to directly compete with the U.S. Postal Service in the delivery of first-class mail. Other examples include patents and copyrights. Both of these legal protections to innovation and intellectual advancements act as legal barriers to entry.

Some markets have *natural barriers to entry*, which can be caused by geography or technology. A firm can have a monopoly because it owns the only source of an input, for example, the only gold mine in the state of Colorado. The firm who owns the only gold mine would be able to extract gold or lease the mine to others, but as long as the firm has well-defined property rights to the gold mine, no one can legally compete against it. A different type of natural barrier to entry is technology. If the technology used to produce the firm's good exhibits increasing-returns to scale at very large quantities, one firm might become a natural monopoly. In such cases, the monopolist can continue to lower per-unit cost by producing more. An entrant that would produce less than the monopolist would thus have higher per-unit costs and could not survive.

There are three primary questions of interest when studying a monopoly.

1. What quantity of output will the monopolist produce?
2. What price will the monopolist charge for the output?
3. Are consumers made worse off with a monopoly?

Because the monopolist is the only firm in the market, the monopolist does have a bit more control over the price of its product. In contrast to the common belief that firms choose prices, firms (be them monopolists or competitive firms) choose the level of output that maximizes their profit. After the firm has chosen the amount to produce, it charges the highest price consumers are willing to pay.

Unlike the perfectly competitive firm, which faces a perfectly horizontal (perfectly elastic) demand curve, the monopolist will influence the price it can charge as it produces more or less output. In essence, the demand for the monopolist's product is the market demand for the product, because the monopolist is the only firm that produces and sells this product. If the market demand is downward sloping, then the monopolist's demand is downward sloping. This is depicted in Figure 10-1. Say the monopolist originally produces three units of output. The demand curve indicates that the monopolist would be able to charge $7 per unit. However, if the monopolist decided to produce and sell seven units of output, the demand curve indicates that that monopolist would only be able to charge $3 for each unit of output. This indicates that a monopolist faces a bit of a dilemma. If it produces more, it can sell more and hopefully generate greater revenue and hence profit. However, if it produces too much it might push the price of its product too low, thereby reducing profit.

In essence, every time the monopolist produces an additional unit of output and tries to sell it on the market, it competes with itself rather than competing with other firms in the market. Unlike the perfectly competitive firm, which cannot unilaterally influence the price of the good, the monopolist does influence the price of its good. However, it is important to remember that while a monopolist might influence the price of its product, it is not able to arbitrarily choose an artificially high price. If a monopoly wants to maximize profits, it cannot choose just any price it wants; it must choose a price consistent with $MR = MC$.

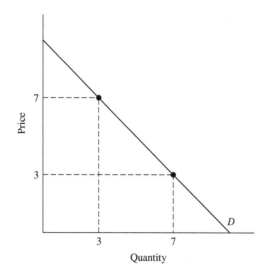

Figure 10-1   The demand for a monopolist.

We proved earlier that every firm will maximize profits when marginal revenue equals marginal cost, that is, $MR = MC$. In the case of the perfectly competitive firm, marginal revenue was simply the market price, and the firm's choice was to select a level of output whose marginal cost was equal to the market price. The monopolist will also maximize profits when $MR = MC$, however now the monopolist must be a bit more careful about marginal revenue. As the monopolist produces more, it can sell the extra unit for a price. However, that price will necessarily be lower than the price that the monopolist could charge with less output. Because the monopolist charges only one price, it must lower the price of all the other units it wants to sell. This implies that the marginal revenue of the monopolist is not constant.

Figure 10-2 shows the tradeoff the monopolist faces when it decides to produce more output. The marginal revenue of any unit is the sum of lost revenue from having to drop price on all the other units (Box A in Figure 10-2) and the additional revenue gained from selling the extra unit (Box B in Figure 10-2). Because of this, the monopolist's marginal revenue is less than its price. From Figure 10-2, whenever Box B is greater than Box A, the firm's marginal revenue is positive. On the other hand, if Box A is greater than Box B, the firm's marginal revenue is negative. This last point is important. If the monopolist produces too much, its revenues will actually drop (because it has to lower price to sell more), and when marginal revenues are negative, it is impossible for the monopolist to maximize profit. Where the MR curve cuts the quantity axis (i.e., $MR = 0$), is the output that will yield maximum total revenue. The monopolist's marginal revenue curve is depicted in Figure 10-3.

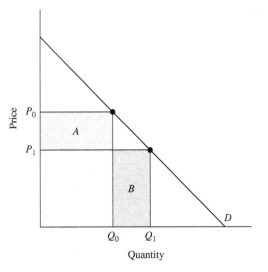

Figure 10-2 Changes in total revenue for an extra unit of output.

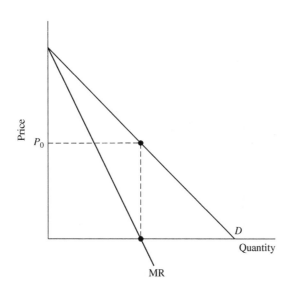

Figure 10-3   Marginal revenue for a monopolist.

The monopoly's choice mechanism is depicted in Figure 10-4. The graph shows the firm's demand, the firm's marginal revenue, the firm's marginal cost, and the firm's average cost. The monopoly chooses to produce Q_M where marginal revenue equals marginal cost, Point A. The monopoly then chooses the highest single price it can charge for its level of production, P_M, which coincides with Point B on the demand curve. The monopolist knows that it is maximizing profit, but how much profit does it earn? Compare price to the firm's average total cost at Q_M, and if price is greater than average cost, the monopolist earns a positive profit.

Figure 10-4 provides a graphical analysis of the monopoly's choice of output and price. However, it is informative to consider a mathematical representation of the monopoly's profit maximizing decision. Without adding too much confusing math, it is possible to rewrite the monopolist's MR = MC condition as

$$\frac{P - MC}{P} = \frac{1}{\varepsilon}$$

where P is the monopoly's price, MC is the monopoly's marginal cost and ε is the absolute value of the firm's price elasticity of demand. The equation above is commonly called the Lerner Condition and simply states that the optimal markup over cost, $(P - MC)/P$, is equal to the inverse of the absolute value of the price elasticity of demand. An important implication from the Lerner Condition is that as long as MC is positive and $P > MC$, then to maximize profit the monopolist must operate

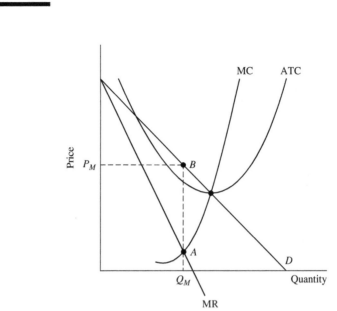

Figure 10-4 The monopoly's choice mechanism.

on the elastic portion of its demand curve ($\varepsilon > 1$). Further, the more elastic the firm's demand, the closer price will be to marginal cost. The less elastic the firm's demand, the greater the difference between price and marginal cost.

Competition and Ticket Prices in Professional Baseball

Monopoly theory suggests that prices are greater when there is only one firm than if there is perfect competition. However, perfect competition suggests that there are hundreds if not thousands of firms in an industry. How many firms does it take for there to be a substantial reduction in prices? We can address this question in the context of professional baseball. Most Major League Baseball teams are local monopolies. Although there might be minor league teams playing in or near a city that has a major league baseball team, there are only four cities that have more than one team: San Francisco/Oakland, New York, Chicago, and Los Angeles/Anaheim.

If the theory of monopoly is correct, those teams that are local monopolies should have higher ticket prices than those teams that share a city with a competing team, *ceteris paribus*. Using data published by the trade publication *The Team Marketing Report,* it is possible to compare the prices of tickets to professional baseball teams that are local monopolies to those of teams that share their host city with another big-league team.

The comparison of ticket prices uses a technique known as econometrics, which is the statistical analysis of economic data. Because the various host cities have different characteristics, including population size, per capita income, and the number of other professional sports franchises (football, basketball, and hockey), it is necessary to control these different characteristics before we can accurately measure the impact on price of having an additional competitor.

Using data from 1991–2001, it is possible to estimate the relationship between the various city characteristics and average nominal ticket prices charged by baseball teams. While a full description of econometric techniques is well beyond the scope of this book, the estimation results are discussed here as an example of the power of econometric analysis.

During the sample period, the average nominal ticket price charged by professional baseball teams was $12.57, with the maximum average ticket price being $34.86 (charged by the Boston Red Sox in 2001) and the minimum average ticket price being $7.00 (charged by the Seattle Mariners in 1991). The econometric exercise entails relating the nominal ticket prices of the various baseball teams during the 1990s to the host city population, the host city per capita income, the number of non-baseball professional sports franchises, and the number of baseball franchises in the host city.

The estimation results suggest that for every additional million people in the host city, the average ticket price increases by approximately $0.18. In other words, if there are two host cities, one with 7 million people and the other with 3 million people, then, *ceteris paribus*, the team in the larger host city can charge approximately $0.52 more per ticket. While this might seem a small price increase, the average baseball team had 2.20 million fans attending games during this period. Thus, the additional $0.52 per ticket would represent $0.52 × 2.2 million = $1.14 million in additional revenues to the team in the bigger city.

The estimation results indicate that for every additional thousand dollars in per capita income in the host city, a team can increase ticket prices by $0.60. This suggests that baseball is a normal good, that is, demand increases as income increases. If one team plays in a host city with a per capita income of $24,000 and another plays in a host city with a per capita income of $28000, the team in the city with the higher income could charge $2.40 more per ticket, $0.60 \times (28 - 24) = \$2.40$, where the term in parentheses reflects the difference in per capita income measured in thousands of dollars. If the team in the wealthier city enjoyed average attendance of 2.20 million fans, the ticket price increase would represent approximately $\$2.40 \times 2.20$ million $= \$5.28$ million in additional revenue.

Teams that share their host city with more professional sports franchises are able to charge more for their tickets than teams that play in cities with fewer franchises. For each additional professional sports franchise, baseball teams can charge approximately $0.38 more per ticket. This is likely explained by the fact that cities with more sports franchises have populations that are more interested in and willing to pay more to see sports in general. If a team plays in a host city with two other professional franchises and another team plays in a host city with four other professional franchises, the team in the city with more franchises could charge $0.74 more per ticket. If the team enjoys average attendance, this increase in ticket price would represent $\$0.74 \times 2.20$ million $= \$1.68$ million in additional revenue.

The major purpose of the exercise, however is to see what happens to a team's ticket prices when they share their host city with another baseball team. Unlike a franchise in a different sport, another baseball team in a host city represents a direct competitor. If the theory of monopoly (and competition) is correct, then ticket prices should come down when there are more firms selling in a market. Indeed, the estimation results suggest that an additional baseball team in a host city *reduces* ticket prices by approximately $3.17 per ticket. At the average attendance level, the team would stand to loose approximately $\$3.18 \times 2.2$ million $= \$6.99$ million in revenue.

The theories of monopoly and perfect competition are supported by this simple exercise. The ability to price at monopoly levels is undermined when there are more firms in the market. Because baseball teams stand to lose a considerable amount of money if they share their host city with another baseball team, it is understandable that baseball team owners are very reluctant to let new or existing teams relocate to their host city. Moreover, teams that seek to relocate away from their existing host city are not highly motivated to locate to a city that already has a baseball team, even if that city is very large.

Next, we can see reports of the sample averages and the estimation results for those who are familiar with econometric techniques.

Variable	Mean	Standard Deviation	Minimum	Maximum
Ticket price	12.57	4.33	7.00	34.86
Number of other baseball teams in host city	0.303	0.46	0.00	1.00
Number of other sports franchises in host city	2.262	1.54	0.00	6.00
Host city population	6.227	5.47	1.60	21.31
Host city per capita income	28.385	5.12	20.27	47.18

Independent Variable	Coefficient
Number of baseball teams	−3.178
	$(4.04)^2$
Number of other sports franchises	0.378
	$(2.65)^2$
Host city population (millions)	0.175
	$(2.62)^2$
Host city per capita income (thousands)	0.604
	$(11.10)^2$
Constant	−5.548
	$(4.17)^2$
Observations	290
R-squared	0.54

Note: Robust t statistics in parentheses
[1] significant at 5%; [2] significant at 1%

Having determined how much the monopoly will make and what price the monopoly will charge, the last question is whether the consumer is worse off because of the monopoly. This question is important for public policy reasons. If a monopolist makes consumers worse off than they would be under an alternative market structure, public policy might try to correct this problem by encouraging the market to become more competitive. Perfect competition is typically used as a benchmark in comparing market structures. In perfect competition, MR = MC = P, and consumer surplus—the extra value to consumers beyond what they paid for the goods,

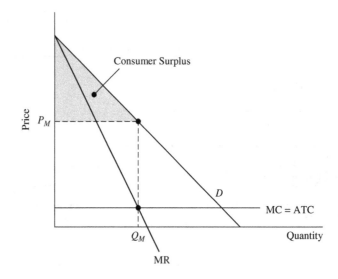

Figure 10-5   Consumer surplus in a monopoly.

and producer surplus—the value received beyond what suppliers required to sell the goods, are both maximized. In the case of a monopoly, price is greater than marginal cost ($P > MC$), and therefore it is unlikely consumer and producer surpluses are maximized.

In Figure 10-5, the monopoly sells Q_M at price P_M, and the consumer surplus is the shaded area below the demand curve and above price. This indicates that in a monopoly situation, there is some consumer surplus. However, is consumer surplus greater than or less than what would have been enjoyed in perfect competition? To determine this, we need to compare the actual monopolistic market to a hypothetical competitive market.

Efficiency Aspects of Static Monopoly

Assume a hypothetical competitive industry that has the same technology as the monopolist. The marginal cost curve for the competitive industry and the monopolist would then be the same. As the market supply curve in perfect competition is the industry marginal cost curve, the marginal cost (MC) curve for the monopolist would be the same as the supply curve of the hypothetical competitive market.

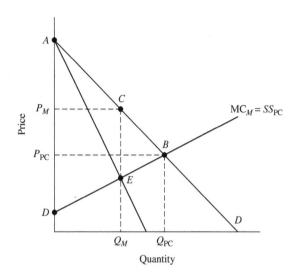

Figure 10-6 Perfect competition and monopoly compared.

In Figure 10-6, the hypothetical competitive market would produce quantity Q_{PC} and price at P_{PC}, whereas the monopolist would produce at Q_M and price at P_M. In this case, the monopolist curtails output and raises price because the monopolist seeks to maximize profit not consumer surplus, and there are no other firms in the market to force the market price to decline towards marginal cost.

Figure 10-6 also depicts the consumer and producer surplus that would prevail if the market were competitive instead of monopolistic. If the market were competitive, the consumer surplus would be the triangle defined by Point A, Point P_{PC}, and Point B, whereas with the monopoly, the consumer surplus is the triangle defined by Point A, Point P_M, and Point C.

It is clear that the consumer surplus in competition would be greater, and therefore consumers are worse off with the monopolist (note that this is not always the case). However, it is one thing to say that consumers are made worse off and still another to say that society is worse off with the monopolist.

To determine the impact of the monopoly on society, it is necessary to compare total surplus with the monopolist and total surplus with competition; consumer surplus is only one portion of total surplus.

The other portion of total surplus is producer surplus. In competition, the producer surplus would be area DBP_{PC} in Figure 10-6. The monopolist earns what economists call "monopolistic rents," which are similar to producer surplus. In Figure 10-6, the monopolistic rents are area P_MDEC. A portion of the monopoly rents would have been consumer surplus and another portion of monopoly rents would have been producer surplus in competition. Combined, these surpluses are transferred to the monopolist in the form of revenues.

Potential consumer and producer surpluses do not accrue to consumers or producers when the monopoly chooses its single-price profit maximizing level of output. Figure 10-7 shows these two areas. The upper shaded triangle would have been consumer surplus in competition but is not transferred to the monopolist in the form of revenues. The lower triangle would have been producer surplus in competition but was not transferred to the monopolist in the form of revenue. Combined, the lost producer and consumer surplus is total dead weight loss (see Chapter 6).

If the dead weight loss in a market is greater than zero, the market is inefficient. Even though some producer and consumer surplus was transferred to the monopoly in the form of monopoly rents, the positive dead weight loss depicted in Figure 10-7 indicates that society would rather have perfect competition if it were possible to somehow create a competitive market from a monopolistic market.

It is not always the case that a monopolist leads to dead weight loss. One example would be a monopolist that creates a bad or something that is undesirable, say, nuclear waste. Another example would be if the monopolist has economies of scale at very large quantities. In this case, it is possible that the monopolist would actually price lower than competition because the small competitive firm is unable to grow large enough to take advantage of increasing returns to scale. Such a market is depicted in Figure 10-8, and it can be seen that the monopoly would produce more and price lower than competition.

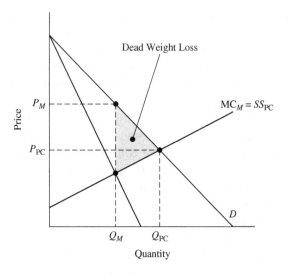

Figure 10-7   Dead weight loss in a monopoly.

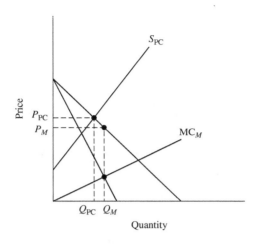

Figure 10-8   Monopoly performs better than competition.

Price Discrimination

One of the important assumptions of the static monopoly model is that the monopolist charges a single price for its product. This is often consistent with what is observed in the real world, but many times firms charge different customers different prices for what seem to be the same goods. When a firm charges two different consumers different prices for the same good, the firm is practicing price discrimination. An important aspect of price discrimination is that the marginal cost of the two goods must be the same. If the marginal costs differ, and prices differ as well, the firm engages in price differentiation.

First Degree Price Discrimination

There are three types of price discrimination that firms can employ: first, second, and third degree price discrimination. First degree price discrimination (also called perfect price discrimination) occurs when the monopolist charges each customer his or her reservation price, i.e., the highest price each different customer is willing to pay. If successful, perfect price discrimination transfers the entire consumer surplus that would be obtained in a competitive market to the monopolist, as depicted in Figure 10-9.

The perfectly discriminating monopolist sells the same level of output as a perfectly competitive market. Moreover, because the monopolist charges each consumer

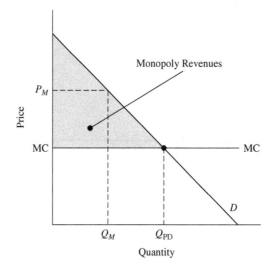

Figure 10-9   Perfect price discrimination.

her maximum willingness to pay, there is no dead weight loss. All consumer surplus for each unit sold is transferred to the monopolist in the form of monopoly rents.

Third Degree Price Discrimination

Not many monopolists practice perfect price discrimination because it can be expensive for the monopolist to determine the maximum amount each consumer is willing to pay. Often firms take an easier approach by charging different prices to different types of consumers using third degree price discrimination. This form of price discrimination entails charging different prices to different groups of consumers, sorted on some easily confirmed characteristic such as age or time of purchase.

Discriminating firms take advantage of the different willingness to pay by different groups of consumers. In other words, different groups have different price elasticities of demand. If the firm can identify a characteristic that correlates strongly with high price elasticity of demand and another characteristic that correlates strongly with low price elasticity of demand, then the firm can take advantage of these characteristics to increase their profits relative to charging a single price.

Figure 10-10 depicts the demands for older and younger consumers in the market for movies. Because younger folks have fewer options than older folks, it is likely that younger movie consumers have a lower price elasticity of demand, i.e., their demand is steeper than the demand of older people. Assuming the marginal

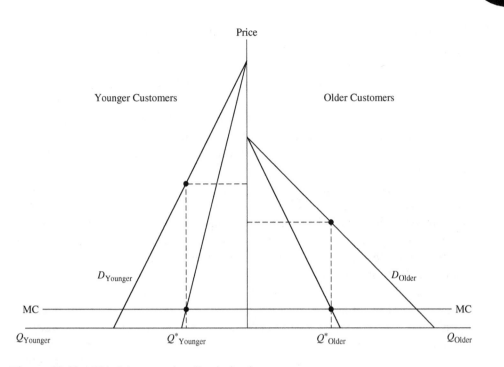

Figure 10-10   Third degree price discrimination.

cost of a movie attendee is the same, regardless of whether the customer is older or younger, the firm can take advantage of the two different demands by charging a higher price to young consumers and a lower price to older consumers.

Third degree price discrimination is a common practice for many companies. Examples include airlines, which charge different prices to those who purchase weeks in advance and those who purchase few hours before the flight. Movie theaters often charge a lower price for a matinee or afternoon show than for the evening show. Many restaurants provide a senior-citizen discount (or a children-eat-free discount). All of these examples clearly align with the theory that the firm should choose an easy-to-confirm characteristic of customers on which to sort those who are charged a high price and those who are charged a low price. Further, in each of these examples it is fairly easy to deduce that those who are charged the lower price likely have the more elastic demand.

However, it is possible that a firm might falsely sort an individual into a low-price group when they would have been willing to pay a higher price (perhaps even as much as the high-price group). For example, there might be one or more individuals willing to pay the same price for a matinee as for an evening show. Yet, the

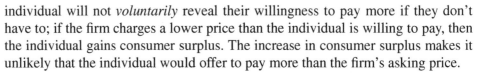

individual will not *voluntarily* reveal their willingness to pay more if they don't have to; if the firm charges a lower price than the individual is willing to pay, then the individual gains consumer surplus. The increase in consumer surplus makes it unlikely that the individual would offer to pay more than the firm's asking price.

Nevertheless, if the firm asked a higher price, some people who would have been sorted into the low-price group, either by age or time of purchase, might be willing to pay the higher price. If so, the firm stands to earn more revenue if they can charge a higher price to enough people who would have been incorrectly sorted into the low-price group.

Therefore, many times firms would rather let the consumer voluntarily reveal which group they belong to—the high elasticity group that is charged a lower price or the low elasticity group that is charged a higher price. While this seems like a reasonable desire on the part of the firm, after all the firm simply wants to maximize its profit, the firm cannot simply ask which price an individual wishes to pay—the consumer will always choose the lower price.

However, all is not lost for the firm. There are ways the firm can shift to consumers the burden of revealing the group they belong to. These methods allow the firm to earn extra revenue that they would not have earned if some customers were incorrectly sorted into the low-price group. These measures differ primarily by *when* customers reveal which group they are in. One allows customers to sort themselves *before* the sale takes place. Another allows customers to sort themselves *at the time* the sale takes place. A final method allows customers to sort themselves *after* the sale takes place.

The first method requires customers to sort themselves before the sale takes place. Firms can use coupons to accomplish this. Coupons are familiar to most of us; they are printed in local newspapers, are available on the Internet, and are sometimes delivered in so-called junk mail. Coupons provide customers with a discount, either in percentage terms, for example 10%, or by a fixed dollar amount, for example $0.50. Any customer who presents a coupon at the time of the sale receives the discount, those who do not, pay a higher price. It seems that coupons actually sort customers at the time of purchase, but customers must clip, collate, and keep coupons *before* they purchase. Those who are willing to incur these costs are likely to have a more elastic demand and therefore should be charged a lower price. Coupons are a good way for firms to shift the burden of sorting to the customers.

It is estimated that less than ten percent of all coupons printed in major newspapers in the United States are redeemed. Therefore, it seems that relatively few people actively seek out coupons and sort themselves into the lower price group. There are several plausible explanations for the low rate of redemption, including sufficiently high costs of collecting coupons, any psychic cost of redeeming a coupon, the lower readership levels of newspapers, and the increasing income of the general population.

While the coupon is very effective, though a little recognized form of third degree price discrimination, firms also employ a means of customer sorting when the sale takes place. In what can be considered somewhat sneaky on the part of the firm, the firm might offer a discount if a person simply asks. This is often the case with senior citizen discounts. Firms offer a discount for older customers who indicate that they have relatively elastic demand by asking for the discount.

Finally, firms also have a means of sorting customers after the sale: the rebate. The rebate is a form of third degree price discrimination similar to the coupon. Rebates entail the firm remitting some portion of the purchase price to customers who redeem the rebate. Much like coupons, rebate redemption rates are surprisingly low, in the area of ten percent. Therefore, rebates are also a good way for firms to sort customers into high-price and low-price groups. Both coupons and rebates shift the burden of sorting to the customers themselves and increase the revenues of the firm.

Second Degree Price Discrimination

Second degree price discrimination includes many types of advanced and clever pricing techniques that firms can use. The most common form of second degree price discrimination is the quantity discount. In this case, the more quantity purchased in a given transaction the lower the per-unit price. It often costs more in total to purchase a greater quantity, but the firm offers a quantity discount to induce consumers to purchase more quantity in a given transaction. There are many practical reasons why both firms and consumers like the ability to purchase different quantities, and there are also practical reasons why firms offer and consumers require quantity discounts to purchase larger blocks of product.

Examples of quantity discounts would include subscriptions to magazines and newspapers, the "family-size" jar of mayonnaise, and season tickets to the opera or a sports team. All of these examples provide the consumer with a per-unit discount over purchasing either a single unit at a time or a different size unit (in the case of the mayonnaise). For instance, a magazine subscription will often have a per-issue price that is substantially less than the single-issue or newsstand price. The same generally holds for season tickets to sports teams, and in the case of the jar of mayonnaise, the price per ounce is often less if you purchase more ounces in a single jar.

While we observe quantity discounts in many instances, simple observation does not provide any insight as to why such discounts are offered. Firms are not legally obligated to offer discounts, so there must be some other reason discounts are offered. Firms use the discounts to induce consumers to purchase higher quantities than they otherwise would. Firms do this because it benefits their bottom line.

This intuition relies upon an important concept in economics. In general, a good is something for which an economic agent is willing to pay to consume or something for which an economic agent must be compensated if they cannot consume. On the other hand, a bad is something for which an economic agent is willing to pay to avoid consuming or for which they must be compensated to consume. For example, if you do not like garbage filling up in your backyard, you are willing to pay a garbage company to take it away from your house and put it in a landfill. Likewise, because garbage is a bad, you would demand compensation if the garbage company came and built a landfill in your backyard. For many reasons, consumers purchase auto and home insurance in order to share the risk of an accident. Many people consider bearing the full risk of an accident a bad, and therefore they are willing to pay to avoid bearing the full risk of an accident. However, insurance companies must be compensated to bear part of the risk of a consumer being in an accident, which it is done in the form of insurance premiums.

We can apply this same logic to the phenomenon of quantity discounts. If consumers are offered a discount to purchase a greater quantity at a single time, it must be the case that consumers find the greater quantity a net bad and/or the firms find selling the greater quantity a net good. In other words, firms are willing to pay, through lower prices, if consumers will purchase more, and consumers are only willing to purchase more if they are compensated, through lower prices.

Does this intuition make sense? From the point of view of the firm, selling a greater quantity in advance provides several benefits, including assured and predictable revenue, lower storage and inventory costs, and the time value of money. Finally, firms face substantial risk of not selling their product or at least of not selling as much as they anticipate at any given time, and being able to sell more today rather than a little today and a little tomorrow reduces risk to the firm. Risk is something the firm is willing to pay to avoid.

Consider a professional baseball team that plays in an open-roof stadium. When the season begins in April, demand for the team's tickets might be brisk and the team enjoys a number of sell-outs. However, if over time the team's poor quality is revealed to the fans, the might not attend games later in the season, causing the team's demand and revenues to fall. The team owner might be able to avoid this problem if he can sell season ticket packages to a substantial number of fans. Those who purchase season tickets pay in advance for the entire season, regardless of whether the team is terrible or wins the championship. Therefore, the team owner can avoid some of the risk involved with selling his product, something for which he is willing to pay.

Many times firms produce product in advance of taking the product to market. This advanced production makes it easier for the firm to respond to demand changes or might be the nature of the firm's production process, but in this case the firm incurs the cost of storage and transportation. If the firm can induce customers to purchase more quantity today rather than half today and half next week, the firm can avoid the cost of storage and transportation, something for which the firm is willing to pay.

Finally, the firm has a time value of money. If the firm would rather have, say, 95 cents today rather than a dollar next week, the quantity discount might be a way for the firm to induce the consumer to spend today rather than a little today and a little next week. The firm pays to get access to money today rather than waiting for money in the future by offering consumers a lower price if they purchase more today.

Therefore, it seems that a firm has a strong incentive to offer quantity discounts if it gains more by selling today rather than selling some today and some next week. However, is it enough that firms are willing to pay for the benefits of selling greater quantity or do consumers consider the costs and benefits of buying greater quantities?

Consumers incur benefits and costs from purchasing a higher quantity in advance. The benefits include assured delivery and reduced transaction costs, whereas consumers incur costs in the form of storage, time value of money, and uncertainty about future quality. The benefits are fairly straightforward. By purchasing a greater quantity today, the consumer is guaranteed to have access to the product in the future. Especially in the case of a newspaper or magazine subscription, by purchasing a subscription the consumer insures that the publisher will deliver future issues. Moreover, the consumer saves additional transaction costs. Instead of incurring the expense of, say, twelve transactions for a year's worth of a magazine, the subscription entails only one transaction.

Unfortunately, the higher quantity does come with some costs. The household must find a place to store the product, which in the case of baseball tickets would not be a major problem, but if the household were to buy twenty cases of cola, the storage costs might be significant. Further, the household sacrifices any interest it could have earned on the greater amount of money it spends on the greater quantity. Finally, the consumer is locked into delivery of future issues; she cannot opt out of future purchases. For example, if a consumer purchases season tickets to a local sports franchise and the quality of the team is very poor, she cannot opt out of the games towards the end of the season. If she purchases tickets game-by-game, she can opt out of games at the end of the season if the team is bad, but if the team is very good, she is not guaranteed to have access to tickets.

In general, firms use quantity discounts to enhance their revenues and increase their profits. However, the firms would not offer quantity discounts if they didn't have to. Firms offer quantity discounts for two reasons. First, selling larger quantities provides a number of benefits for the firm, for which the firm is willing to pay. Second, customers are not always naturally inclined to purchase large quantities, and therefore they must be compensated to do so.

Cartel Theory

The last topic to cover in the area of monopolization is cartel theory. Cartels are groups of firms that work together in an attempt to monopolize an industry. Examples of cartels include OPEC, shipping industries, sports leagues, and labor unions. The goal of a cartel is to maximize joint profits rather than individual profits. Consider a market as depicted in Figure 10-11.

The previous discussion on the monopoly problem focused on the potential dead weight loss created by the monopoly. However the monopoly graph can be also be used to understand why firms may want to create a cartel, and also why it is difficult to maintain a cartel.

If the industry were initially competitive, all firms would be guaranteed zero profits in the long run and the industry would produce at Q_{PC} and P_{PC} in Figure 10-11. However, if the market was monopolized it would produce at Q_M and P_M in Figure 10-11, and long-run profits could be positive. Hence, if the perfectly competitive firms could cooperate and reduce output from Q_{PC} to Q_M, they could raise price from P_{PC} to P_M and enhance their profits. If the cartel were able to earn monopoly profits, each firm could have an egalitarian share of those profits and they would exceed the long-run profits from perfect competition.

The problem with trying to form a cartel is maintaining solidarity amongst the cartel members. Notice that the cartel will create a level of dead weight loss in the market. Dead weight loss was defined in Chapter 6 as potential consumer and producer surplus that could be earned in the market but for some reason is not. In case of a cartel the consumer and producer surplus that comprise the dead weight loss are potential gains in trade that are not realized in the market. Some consumers are willing to pay less than the cartel price P_M but greater than the marginal cost of production.

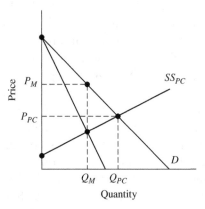

Figure 10-11   A cartel arrangement.

Therefore, for at least one cartel member the marginal benefit of producing and selling an additional unit of output is greater than the marginal cost of production, even if the price of the extra output is a little bit less than P_M.

To formalize this a bit more, consider the total output produced by the cartel as Q_M and assume there are N firms in the cartel. A simple way to allocate the cartel quantity across the cartel members is to give each firm an equal share or cartel quota to produce, in this case, Q_M/N. If each member abides by the agreement, the total output will be Q_M and the price the cartel will charge for its output is P_M, and each firm stands to earn some positive profit, which is more than they will earn in perfect competition.

The problem is the dead weight loss the cartel output creates. The dead weight loss represents potential profit for one or more cartel members. Now, suppose Firm A is a member of a cartel and believes the other $N - 1$ members will abide by the agreement. Firm A could then produce just a little bit more output and sell it for a price greater than the marginal cost of production. If a large enough number of cartel members behave the same as Firm A, the cartel arrangement will break down. Total output exceeds Q_M and approaches Q_{PC}, which requires a reduction in price from P_M to P_{PC}.

This incentive to cheat on the agreement is called the free rider problem. Each cartel member that cheats ignores the impact of their extra production on the market price and therefore anticipates being able to earn extra profit while not bearing the full cost of their cheating. Unfortunately for the cartel, all of the cartel members are motivated to cheat. Cartels often find it difficult to maintain solidarity unless it can monitor and punish cheaters. Monitoring requires the cartel members to police themselves or to hire a "manager" to make sure that all of the members abide by the agreement.

Although it might be possible to monitor the behavior of a cartel's members in order to keep output curtailed to Q_M, there are several elements of a market that make it more conducive to a cartel. In markets where demand is relatively inelastic, there are relatively fewer firms, and there is a central location at which the product is sold, it is easier to create a cartel. The cartel will raise price to the monopoly price and curtail output from the competitive level. Initially, things look pretty good for the cartel members because they are able to earn profits that they were not able to earn acting as price takers.

While cartels are often a source of concern in the popular press, for example, OPEC *seems* to have a large influence in the world oil market, economists tend to discount the long-run viability of cartels because of the free rider problem. Although OPEC seems to be a powerful cartel, most of its power is historical because over the past twenty years more oil production occurred outside of the Middle East, including the North Sea and the Gulf of Mexico.

Contestable Market Theory

The static monopoly model predicts that monopolies tend to price higher and produce less than competition. The reason for this is that the monopoly, because it is the only firm in the market, is able to "internalize" the downward pressure on price that is inherent in competitive markets. In markets with more than one firm, each firm has an incentive to continue producing as long as there is profit to be made on the marginal unit. Unfortunately, extra production by one firm puts downward pressure on the price of *all* firms. One of the best attributes of a competitive market is this downward pressure on price—it increases consumer surplus and ensures efficiency in the market.

Monopolists, on the other hand, do not face any outside pressure on their price. Even if the static monopolist faced a potential entrant into its market, the barriers-to-entry assumption of the static monopoly model ensures that entry will not occur, and if the monopolist is making a positive profit in the short run, it can expect to make positive profits in the medium to long run.

Unfortunately, the pure static monopoly is not very commonly observed in the real world. Beyond a few governmental monopolies such as the Postal Service, local cable television franchises, some power plants, and municipal trash pickup, the privately held monopoly is extremely rare. In reality, most private monopolies, if they were to exist, would quickly be undercut by entrants into the market. The natural barriers to entry described earlier in this chapter are much less common than legal barriers.

This does not imply that it is impossible to maintain a monopoly for a short while. ALCOA was one company found guilty of anti-trust laws because they were "too good." During the middle part of the twentieth century ALCOA precluded entry into the aluminum ingot industry precisely because the company continually improved its production process, reducing costs and making it impossible for any other firm to effectively compete. In return for these increased efficiencies and cost savings, ALCOA was found in violation of anti-trust laws, which seek to curtail the ability of firms to exercise market power.

If ALCOA was a monopoly, why would ALCOA feel obligated to improve its technique, cut costs, and importantly, pass some of those cost savings on to the customer? Why wouldn't ALCOA just sit back and enjoy its monopoly status?

The theory describing why ALCOA and other near-monopolies *must* continue to reduce their costs or improve their product is embodied in a theory called Contestable Markets. This theory is essentially that of a *dynamic* monopoly. The model recognizes that monopolies are very rarely static and sufficiently protected from the entry of competitors to make the static monopoly model appropriate. Rather, contestable market theory suggests that monopolies respond to the threat of entry to their markets.

If a monopolist perceives the possibility that an entrant might come into their market, the monopolist might reduce its price so that the residual demand, that is the demand left over for the entrant, causes the entrant to earn zero profit. If this were the case, the entrant would be indifferent to entering the market, competing against the monopolist and earning zero profits or going to some other market.

Contestable market theory suggests that the static monopoly model is insufficient to explain why firms can remain monopolists for long periods of time without strict government protection. Moreover, the contestable market theory is able to explain why ALCOA continued to improve its production process and cut costs. The threat of entry into the aluminum market was all that was needed to encourage ALCOA to lower prices, to the benefit of customers.

Summary

This chapter has developed the theory of monopoly. Perfect competition is the most intense form of competition and the static monopoly is the least intensive, namely because there is only one seller in the market. Monopolists are not guaranteed a positive or unreasonable profit, however, because they are still constrained by their technology and factor prices, which help determine costs, and the demand for their product, which helps determine marginal revenue. Monopolists determine their output level in the same manner as other firms, i.e., by setting marginal revenue equal to marginal cost. However, unlike the perfectly competitive firm who could take price and marginal revenue as given, the monopolist recognizes that to sell more, it will have to lower its price. Hence, marginal revenue changes with the amount of product the monopolist wishes to sell. In fact, marginal revenue can actually become negative, in which case the monopolist cannot possibly be maximizing profit.

The monopolist's optimal output and price are not guaranteed to lead to a positive profit. However, unlike the case of perfect competition, if a monopolist does make positive profits in the short run, barriers to entry preclude entry which ensures that the monopolist can continue to earn positive profits until another market develops a relatively close substitute (such as cellular phones or satellite television) or until the monopolist no longer enjoys the protection of the law or technology.

Quiz

1. Monopolies that price their good lower than a perfectly competitive industry would often have

   a. decreasing Returns to Scale.

   b. diminishing marginal returns.

   c. monopolies that do not exercise market power.

   d. increasing Returns to Scale.

2. The Postal Service is an example of

   a. a competitive firm.

   b. a natural monopoly.

   c. a legal monopoly.

   d. a public good.

3. The long-run equilibrium in a monopolistic market is characterized by

   a. a positive profit, guaranteed.

   b. a negative profit, guaranteed.

   c. a zero profit, guaranteed.

   d. a positive, negative, or zero profit.

   e. guaranteed positive dead weight loss.

4. A monopolist is different from a competitive firm in that

   a. the competitive firm always has marginal revenue greater than price.

   b. the monopolistic firm always has marginal revenue greater than price.

   c. the monopolistic firm always has a lower quantity than a competitive firm.

   d. the monopolistic firm always has marginal revenue less than price.

   e. the competitive firm always has marginal revenue less than price.

5. In order for a cartel arrangement to be beneficial to its members,

   a. the cartel members must be willing to restrict output in order to raise the cartel price.

   b. the cartel members must be willing to expand their plants in order to produce the necessary increased output.

   c. the cartel members must produce at an output level where marginal cost is greater than marginal revenue.

   d. the cartel members must be willing to retrain their labor forces.

6. The major threat to a cartel is

   a. product homogeneity.

   b. an increase in input prices.

   c. cost reductions by one or more members.

   d. the free rider incentive.

7. In third degree price discrimination, the group with the higher price elasticity of demand will

   a. pay the same price as the uniform price.

   b. pay a lower price.

   c. pay a higher price.

   d. will be priced out of the market.

8. If a monopoly price discriminates, consumer surplus _____ and its economic profit _____.

   a. decreases; does not change

   b. increases; increases

   c. decreases; decreases

   d. decreases; increases

   e. increases; does not change

9. Price in a monopoly is determined by

   a. supply only.

   b. the monopolist.

   c. demand, technology and factor prices.

   d. the government.

   e. technology only.

10. The definition of dead weight loss is

   a. potential surplus in a market that is not obtained by any agent.

   b. potential surplus in a market obtained by the government.

   c. potential surplus to consumers transferred to the government or a monopolist.

   d. actual surplus transferred to the government or a monopolist.

11. If a firm wants to engage in third degree price discrimination, which of the following is not a likely candidate for sorting customers?

   a. The age of its customers

   b. The time of purchase

   c. The income of its customers

   d. The sex of its customers

Use Figure 10-12 for the next four questions:

12. If the firm only charges one price, what price will maximize profits?

   a. $7

   b. $2

   c. $5.5

   d. $10

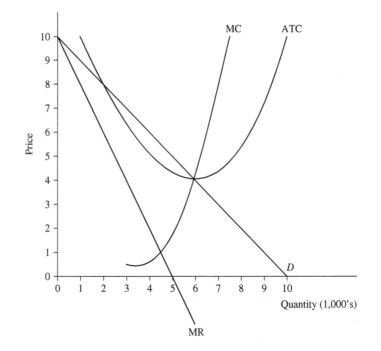

Figure 10-12

13. If the firm only charges one price, what quantity will it sell?

    a. 5,000

    b. 10,000

    c. 6,000

    d. 4,000

    e. 4,500

14. If the firm wishes to sell as many tickets as possible without losing money, how many will it sell?

    a. 5,000

    b. 10,000

    c. 6,000

    d. 4,000

    e. 45,000

15. At what quantity is the firm's demand unitary elastic?

    a. 5,000

    b. 10,000

    c. 6,000

    d. 4,000

    e. 4,500

Monopolistic Competition and Oligopoly

The previous two chapters explored the extremes of market structures: perfect competition and perfect monopoly. Most markets fall somewhere in between these two extremes and are called imperfect competition. Unfortunately, unlike perfect competition and perfect monopoly there is no single model to describe imperfect competition because small differences in markets lead to very different outcomes. This chapter outlines two broad areas of imperfect competition: monopolistic competition, which is characterized by product differentiation, and oligopoly models, which model strategic interaction amongst firms.

Monopolistic Competition

Monopolistic competition is characterized by a large number of firms making slightly different products, in contrast with perfect competition in which all firms make the same good and perfect monopoly in which the firm makes a unique good. Examples might include potato chips, cereal, televisions, and automobiles. As monopolistically competitive firms differentiate their products, some consumers find that they like certain brands more than others, which in turn provides a firm a bit of consumer loyalty. If a firm chooses to increase the price of its product, the firm does not lose all of its consumers. This is called market power and implies that the demand for a monopolistically competitive firm is downward sloping (much like a monopolist's but at a smaller scale).

Product differentiation can be actual or perceived. Obviously, a luxury automobile is very different from an economy car. However, differences may only be perceived. A firm might produce two products that have different names and different reputations even if the two products come off the same assembly line. Automobile manufacturers often produce two or more cars that look very similar even though they have different names. Regardless of why consumers think the products are differentiated, from the firm's point of view the impact is the same.

The assumptions of monopolistic competition are a blend of the assumptions of competition and monopoly. Three important assumptions are: products are differentiated; there are several firms; and there are no barriers to entry or exit. The first implication of these assumptions is that firms have downward sloping demand curves. In this sense, monopolistic competition differs from perfect competition and seems more akin to perfect monopoly. However, the freedom of entry assumption implies that if firms make a positive profit, entry will occur and new products will be introduced to the market. The demand for all firms' products will decline and entry will stop when firms make zero economic profit. In this sense, monopolistic competition is similar to perfect competition.

Figure 11-1 depicts the short-run choice of a monopolistically competitive firm. In Figure 11-1, the firm maximizes profit by producing where marginal revenue equals marginal cost. The firm produces q_{SR}^* and chooses price P^* and, as in Figure 11-1, earns a positive profit. Notice that there is a small amount of dead weight loss generated by this firm (the shaded area in Figure 11-1), although the inefficiency is not as large as would prevail in a monopoly.

As mentioned, because the firm in Figure 11-1 makes a positive profit, other firms want to enter the industry and share in the positive profits. New firms enter the industry and produce products slightly different than the products produced by

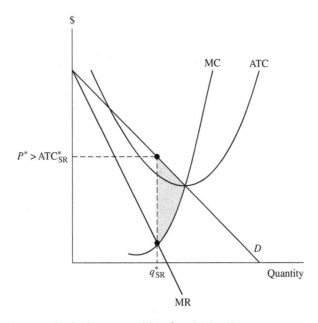

Figure 11-1   A monopolistically competitive firm in the short run.

incumbent firms. These new products match the preferences of some consumers better than other products, and incumbent firms see their demand decline or shift left. Entry will continue as long as firms make positive profits. A long-run equilibrium in which all firms earn normal profits is depicted in Figure 11-2. Each firm produces q^*_{LR} and price equals average total cost for each firm.

An interesting feature of monopolistically competitive industries is that at long-run equilibrium, firms are producing less than minimum efficient scale. In other words, each firm has excess capacity at equilibrium. This is a potential source of inefficiency: If only firms would produce more, per-unit costs would fall and so would price. However, individual firms want to maximize their profits, not minimize per-unit costs.

Nevertheless, at times, excess capacity might be appreciated. For instance, if you are in an accident and need to go to the hospital, you would like the hospital to have a bed waiting for you and doctors and nurses with time to treat you for your injuries. If the hospital operated at full capacity at all times, you would have to wait for a bed to become available in order to get medical care. In times of emergency, product recalls, or other short-run increases in demand the excess capacity inherent in monopolistically competitive industries can be beneficial.

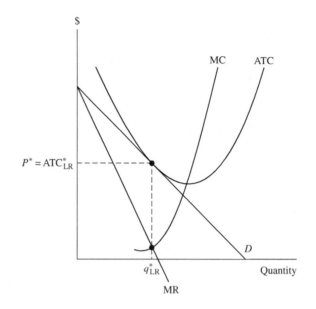

Figure 11-2 A monopolistically competitive firm in the long run.

Oligopoly

Oligopoly is a market structure in which a few firms compete with each other, typically in a strategic fashion. In the previous market structures, firms make decisions without considering how their decisions influence the decisions of other firms. Oligopolistic models explicitly recognize that the decision of one firm likely impacts the decisions of other firms.

For example, assume Airline A reduces the price of a flight from Atlanta to New York City. In the short run, Airline A expects to see its sales and short-run profits increase. However, other airlines will experience a decrease in their market share and will likely reduce their prices as well. After this occurs, Airline A will see its market share and profits decline, thereby perhaps offsetting the short-run gains that Airline A hoped to receive from lowering its price. The managers of Airline A likely take the potential responses of other airlines into account before making the final decision to lower price. This is the essence of strategic interaction. Oligopolists face challenging questions when making decisions: How will one firm's decision impact the decisions of other firms? Two different approaches to oligopoly markets will be considered: traditional and game theoretic.

The Kinked Demand Model

The kinked demand model has four basic assumptions for each firm in the market:

1. If I lower my price, everyone else will.
2. If I raise my price, no one else will.
3. If someone else lowers price, so will I.
4. If someone else raises price, I will not.

The interesting implication of the four assumptions of this model is that the firm's demand curve has a kink at the prevailing market equilibrium price, as depicted in Figure 11-3

Where does the kink come from? Suppose the market price is P^* and the firm decides to raise its price, say to Point a in Figure 11-3. The quantity it can sell will decline significantly because none of its competitors will increase price. Consumers will purchase from other firms because they will have lower prices. Therefore, above price P^*, the firm's demand is relatively elastic. If, on the other hand, the firm decides to lower its price below P^*, say to Point b in Figure 11-3, all of its competitors follow suit. Since all firms lower their price, the individual firm does not enjoy a large increase in the amount it can sell. The demand curve below price P^* is relatively inelastic.

The kinked demand curve has implications for the firm's marginal revenue curve. In monopoly, demand is continuous (i.e., has no kink), and MR is continuous as well. In the kinked demand model of imperfect competition, MR is discontinuous at price P^* as depicted in Figure 11-4.

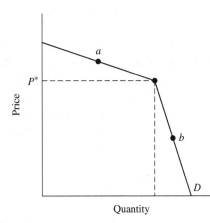

Figure 11-3 A kinked demand curve.

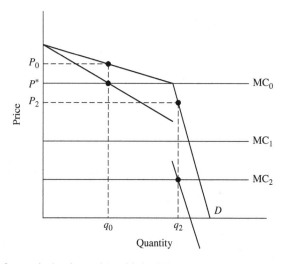

Figure 11-4   Profit maximization with a kinked demand curve.

The gap in marginal revenue is not important unless the firm's marginal cost happens to fall in the gap. If this were the case, the firm would not change price from P^*.

Oligopoly with a Dominant Firm

A different approach to the oligopoly problem is to consider a near monopoly or dominant firm that shares its market with a competitive fringe. There is no fixed amount of market share that the dominant firm must have, but a market with a single firm holding 65 percent of the market and all other firms having considerably less than 5 percent market share would be an example. The firms in the fringe operate as price takers, regardless of how price is determined. The question addressed in this model is what the dominant firm will want to do. The dominant firm has three options and chooses that which it thinks will yield the greatest profit.

First, the dominant firm could drive the fringe out of business and become a monopolist. This would allow the dominant firm to earn the greatest amount of profit possible in its market but would also invite investigation and possible litigation by the federal government. It is illegal to actively attempt to monopolize a market according to the Sherman Antitrust Act of 1890. Therefore, if the dominant firm chooses this option, it must take into account the probability that it will be sued, have to defend itself and pay millions of dollars in legal fees, and perhaps be fined even more money for violating federal law. The prospect of being sued reduces the appeal of this option.

Another option would be the dominant firm joining in with the competitive fringe and acting as a price taker. In this case, the dominant firm would earn a zero profit in the long run. An appealing third possibility would yield more profit than either perfect competition or driving the fringe out of business.

Assume that the market demand for taxi cabs in New York City is downward sloping. Assume that Red Cab is the dominant firm with 70 percent market share and there are 10 other firms that share the remaining 30 percent. Figure 11-5 depicts the market demand, the supply that would prevail with only the 10 smaller firms (SS_F), and the supply that would prevail if all firms, including the dominant firm, acted as price takers (SS_{F+D}).

If the smaller firms were the only firms in the market, in Figure 11-5 the market-clearing price and quantity would be P_F and Q_F, whereas if the dominant firm acted as a price taker, the market-clearing price and quantity would be P_{F+D} and Q_{F+D}, respectively.

The dominant firm might recognize that for every price below P_F, the quantity supplied by the fringe is less than the quantity demanded in the market. The difference between the quantity demanded and the quantity supplied is the excess demand in the market. The only firm that can supply to the residual demand at prices less than P_F is the dominant firm. In fact, at all prices below P_F, the dominant firm is a quasi-monopolist and can choose the quantity to produce that maximizes its profit from the residual demand. The dominant firm then chooses its price from the residual demand; the fringe takes that price as given and produces according to their

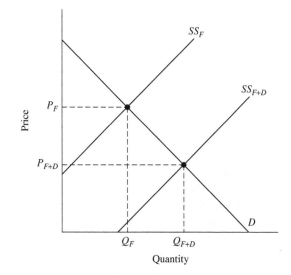

Figure 11-5   Market demand and supply for taxi cabs.

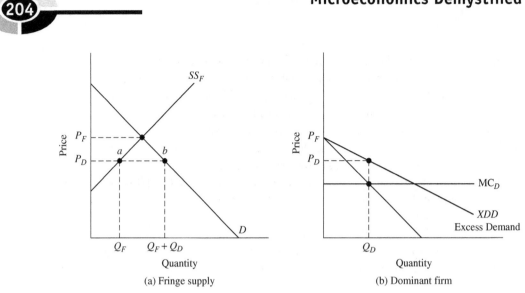

Figure 11-6 (a and b) The dominant firm as a price leader.

supply schedule. The dominant firm will choose this option, if it yields the greatest profit, of the three possibilities.

This process is shown in Figure 11-6 (a and b). In this case, the price is less than the monopoly price, and the total quantity supplied is greater than both the monopoly quantity and the quantity that would be supplied by the fringe alone. However, price is greater and total quantity is lower than it would be if the dominant firm acted as a price taker. Thus, the dominant firm market performs better than perfect monopoly but not as good as perfect competition.

Strategic Interaction

There are numerous oligopoly models, many of which use the concepts from game theory to model firm decisions. In game theory, players of a game take into consideration how their actions might influence the actions of other players and how the actions of other players influence their decisions. In a game of chess, it is easy to see how your moves will alter the strategies chosen by your opponent, how what your opponent does will influence your choices, and how there are likely feedbacks between the two sets of strategies.

In previous market structures, firms simply set marginal revenue equal to marginal cost and did not concern themselves with how their marginal revenue might be influenced by their actions or the actions of others. However, in markets with relatively few firms, it is hard to imagine that firm managers are not aware of what their competitors are doing, and this awareness might influence decisions.

While there are literally hundreds of different game theoretic models, two primary models that convey much of what game theory has to offer are developed here.

Cournot Duopoly Game

The Cournot model assumes two firms, a homogeneous good, constant marginal cost, and no entry and is named after Augustin Cournot who developed his model in the early 1800s. Cournot assumed that each firm maximizes its profit using the residual demand available after the other firm has selected its profit-maximizing level of output. In other words, each firm responds to the changing level of output of its competitor by changing its profit-maximizing level of output. The idea that one firm would "respond" to another firm's decisions was very unique when Cournot derived this model, but given the advancements in game theory since the 1940s, Cournot's concept is now universal.

Cournot suggested that the two firms would find an equilibrium in which neither firm would want to change their level of output given the output of their competitor. This type of equilibrium is now called a Nash Equilibrium (after the Nobel winning economist John Nash who pioneered many advancements in game theory in the 1950s). The Cournot model assumes that each firm sets its own marginal revenue equal to marginal cost, but that the marginal revenue of each firm is influenced by the decisions of its competitor.

The optimal choices of Firm A in response to decisions by Firm B can be plotted in a two-dimensional space with the quantity of Firm A on the horizontal axis and the quantity of Firm B on the vertical axis as in Figure 11-7.

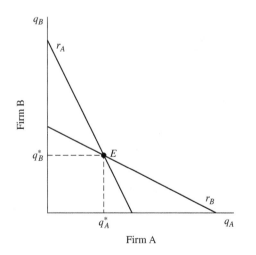

Figure 11-7   Reaction functions in a Cournot duopoly.

Firm A has a reaction function (r_A) and Firm B has a reaction function (r_B). When plotted on the same graph, the Cournot-Nash equilibrium resides at Point E, which corresponds with q_A^* and q_B^*. Firm A's reaction function tells Firm A exactly what to do given what Firm B has chosen to do. Likewise, Firm B's reaction function tells Firm B exactly what to do given what Firm A has chosen to do. The equilibrium is unique because at Point E, neither Firm A nor Firm B wishes to alter their level of output given what the other firm wants to do.

There is more to the Cournot reaction functions than immediately meets the eye. Figure 11-8 redraws the Cournot reaction functions including two dashed lines that connect the endpoints of the reaction functions.

The reaction functions tell each firm their best strategy given what the other firm decides to do. Thus, if Firm B decides to produce *nothing*, Firm A will be a monopolist in the market. The profit maximizing level of output for Firm A would then be the monopoly output q_M. This is reflected in the horizontal intercept of the reaction function for Firm A, denoted r_A in Figure 11-8. The same holds for Firm B if Firm A decides to produce nothing. Therefore, the *vertical* intercept for Firm B's reaction function, denoted r_B in Figure 11-8, is also the monopoly quantity, q_M.

On the other hand, the only time Firm A finds it in its best interest to produce nothing is if Firm B has already produced the amount consistent with perfect competition, q_C. In this case, if Firm A produced any positive amount, the profits of both firms would be negative. The same holds true for Firm B; the only time Firm B finds

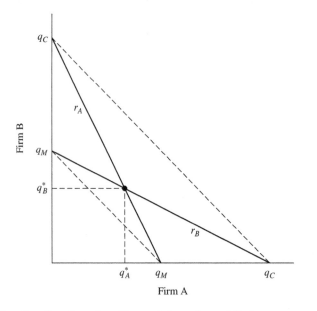

Figure 11-8   Reaction functions in a Cournot duopoly revisited.

it profit maximizing to produce nothing is if Firm A produces the perfectly competitive level of output, q_C. Therefore, the vertical intercept of Firm A's reaction function and the horizontal intercept of Firm B's reaction function are denoted as q_C.

Each combination of q_A and q_B that falls on the dashed line connecting the monopoly quantity q_M on the vertical axis and the monopoly quantity q_M on the horizontal axis corresponds to a combined output by Firm A and Firm B of q_M (i.e., $q_M = q_A = q_B$). In other words, all the combinations on this dashed line correspond to output combinations consistent with the two firms colluding in a cartel arrangement. However, it is also clear that none of the combinations on this dashed line lie on the reaction functions of either of the two firms. Because none of the combinations can possibly be a Nash equilibrium, the cartel is destined to fail.

On the other hand, the dashed line that connects the two perfectly competitive output levels corresponds to shared competition. If both firms decided to act as price takers and ignore the potential benefits of strategic interaction, their combined output would fall on the dashed line connecting the perfectly competitive quantity q_C on the vertical axis and that on the horizontal axis. However, if the two firms behave as perfectly competitive firms (even though there are only two of them), they will guarantee themselves zero profit. The Cournot equilibrium generally leads to some positive profit being earned by both firms, and therefore the Cournot outcome is preferred to shared competition.

Bertrand's Duopoly Game

Joseph Bertrand suggested a model similar to Cournot's, with a few twists. Bertrand assumed: firms choose prices instead of quantities; each firm can produce for the entire market; and consumers are indifferent about the firm from which they purchase and buy from the firm offering the lowest price.

The Bertrand model leads to a perplexing result: Firms are motivated to undercut their competition in order to corner the market. What has been called the Bertrand Paradox is that the price war eventually leads to each firm pricing at marginal cost. In other words, Bertrand's model suggests that two firms engaged in price competition will obtain the perfectly competitive outcome, as depicted in Figure 11-9.

Many economists have tried to "solve" the so-called Bertrand Paradox. The most common criticism of Bertrand's model is the assumption that one firm can provide product to the entire market at any given price. Other criticisms focus on the other assumptions of the model. In general, economists have dismissed the original Bertrand model as being too unrealistic. However, one of its benefits is showing how slight changes in the assumptions of game theoretic models can lead to dramatically different outcomes.

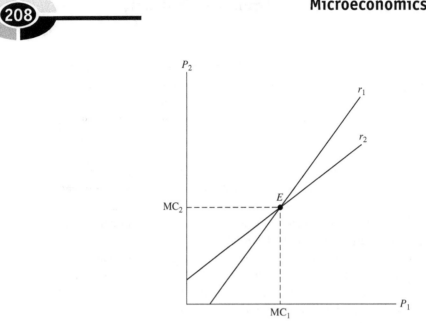

Figure 11-9   Reaction functions in a Bertrand duopoly.

Summary

This chapter has outlined the general approach to monopolistic competition and oligopoly. Most markets are characterized as monopolistically competitive, in which firms produce slightly differentiated products but earn zero economic profits in the long run, or oligopolistic, in which a relatively small number of firms produce similar goods and interact strategically. Unfortunately, there is no single theory of monopolistic competition because different markets reflect different conditions and each set of conditions can lead to a different result.

However, the models discussed here do allow for some generalization. First, in monopolistic competition, firms can earn short-run profits, but entry will eventually drive profits to zero in the long run. At the long-run equilibrium, however, firms do not produce at minimum efficient scale and there is excess capacity in the market. Second, monopolistically competitive markets lead to some positive dead weight loss, but it is considerably less than what would prevail in a monopolistic market.

Various oligopolistic markets were developed, and those included here are only a small number of existing models. In general, oligopolistic markets involve some strategic interaction in which one firm's decision is influenced by and influences the decisions of other firms. In such models, it is entirely possible that strategic interaction changes the decisions of a firm. Strategies can be modeled intuitively, as in the kinked demand model or explicitly as in the Cournot and Bertrand models. Explicitly modeling strategies entails game theory, developed in the 1940s and 1950s, which is a highly mathematical yet intuitively appealing way to model decision-making.

Quiz

1. The dominant firm's demand curve is

    a. identical to the competitive market's demand curve.

    b. the excess demand from the market of smaller firms.

    c. not related to the competitive market's demand curve.

    d. none of the above.

2. The market characteristic that insures that economic profit is reduced to zero in long-run equilibrium in a monopolistically competitive market is

    a. homogeneous products.

    b. differentiated products.

    c. entry and exit.

    d. a large number of sellers.

3. Because firms do not produce at minimum efficient scale, many argue that monopolistic competition charges _____ a price and produces _____ output.

    a. too high, too much

    b. too low, too little

    c. too high, too little

    d. too low, too much

4. A monopolistically competitive firm is producing at an output level where average total cost is $3.00, price is $3.50, marginal revenue is $1.50, and marginal cost is $1.50. This firm is operating

    a. with an economic loss in the short run.

    b. at the break-even level of output in the long run.

    c. with an economic profit in the short run.

    d. with an economic profit in the long run.

5. The firm in Question 4 can expect to see its demand curve

    a. shift to the right in the future.

    b. shift to the left in the future.

    c. not change in the future.

    d. become one with the next largest competitor.

6. The dominant firm hypothesis predicts

    a. the dominant firm will charge a price greater than in perfect competition but less than in monopoly.

    b. the dominant firm in each industry is necessarily the firm with the highest quality.

    c. the dominant firm will drive all of its competition under.

    d. the dominant firm is better off acting as a price taker.

7. Assume that each firm in a monopolistically competitive industry incurs short-run losses. In the long run,

    a. firms will leave the industry; those that remain will experience an increase in demand for their products.

    b. demand for the industry's product will increase.

    c. all firms in the industry will move their resources to a different industry.

    d. cost curves will shift lower because producers will demand price concessions from their suppliers.

8. Monopolies and monopolistic competitors are both characterized by

    a. constant marginal cost.

    b. price taking behavior.

    c. unique and hard to substitute goods.

    d. downward sloping demand curves.

9. A firm with a kinked demand curve will find it

    a. easy to increase price and increase revenues.

    b. easy to decrease price and increase revenues.

    c. hard to increase price and decrease revenues.

    d. hard to decrease price and increase revenues.

10. In oligopolies,

    a. output is greater than in perfect competition.

    b. strategic interaction is paramount.

    c. prices are greater than in monopolies.

    d. there are too many firms to realistically implement strategy.

Use Figure 11-10 for the next five questions:

11. The strategies depicted in Figure 11-10 are

    a. strategic complements.

    b. strategic substitutes.

    c. strategically independent.

    d. doomed to failure.

12. In the game depicted in Figure 11-10, the equilibrium strategies are

    a. Player A makes nine units; Player B makes eighteen units.

    b. Player A makes eighteen units; Player B makes zero units.

    c. Player A makes nine units; Player B makes nine units.

    d. Player A makes six units; Player B makes six units.

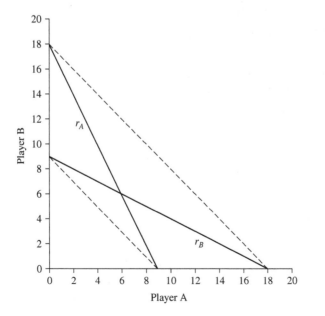

Figure 11-10

13. In the game depicted in Figure 11-10, if the two players choose to collude, how much will they produce together?

    a. Eighteen units

    b. Twelve units

    c. Nine units

    d. Six units

14. In the game depicted in Figure 11-10, if the two players tried to collude, which of the following would be the best explanation for the collusion failing?

    a. The cartel level of output is not the same as the competitive level of output.

    b. The cartel level of output is not a Nash equilibrium for either player.

    c. The cartel level of output is not a Bertrand equilibrium for either player.

    d. The competitive level of output is the Nash equilibrium level of output.

15. Given your understanding of the game depicted in Figure 11-10, which of the following statements is true?

    a. At the Nash equilibrium, price is greater than that which would prevail in a monopoly.

    b. At the Nash equilibrium, quantity is greater than that which would prevail in competition.

    c. At the Nash equilibrium, price is the same as would prevail in Bertrand competition.

    d. At the Nash equilibrium, price is greater than would prevail in competition but less than would prevail in monopoly.

CHAPTER 12

Factor Markets

The previous three chapters discussed various market structures in which firms make decisions. This chapter develops the markets for the three factors of production: land, capital, and labor. Factor markets are not much different from other markets. A major hurdle for most students is remembering who *supplies* and who *demands* factors. Households are assumed to own the factors of production and firms hire factors to produce goods and services. Therefore, households supply factors and firms demand factors. The returns to factors flow from firms to households: labor receives a wage; capital owners receive interest; and landowners receive rent.

The price of a factor of production is determined in a market, which obeys the laws of supply and demand like any other market. An example of a generic factor market is depicted in Figure 12-1. In this market, the factor's supply reflects the law of supply in that more of the factor is made available with higher prices. On the other hand, the quantity of a factor demanded declines as its price increases, reflecting the law of demand. The equilibrium in this factor market resides at Point E, with the factor's price being w^* and the total amount of the factor hired being Q^*. The total amount paid to the factor is the factor's income and is calculated as $I = w^* \times Q^*$.

What if firms demand more or less of a factor over time? If demand increases, such as a shift of D_0 to D_1 in Figure 12-2, more of the factor will be hired at a higher price,

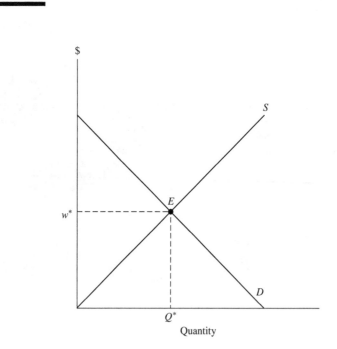

Figure 12-1 A sample factor market.

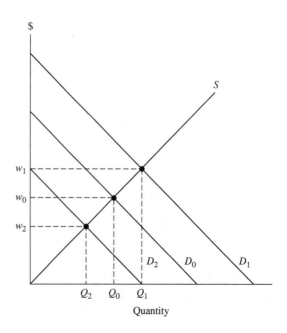

Figure 12-2 Changes in demand for a factor of production.

and the total income earned by the factor will increase. On the other hand, if the demand for the factor decreases, such as the shift of D_0 to D_2 in Figure 12-2, then the total amount of the factor hired decreases, as does the price paid to the factor, and the factor's income will decline.

The impact of a change in demand on a factor's income can be inferred from the factor's elasticity of supply. If the supply of a factor is elastic, then a change in demand will lead to a large change in quantity but a small change in price. Although the total income paid to the factor will increase, individual households may not experience a dramatic increase in the price they receive for the amount of their factor they are willing to sell to firms. On the other hand, if the supply of a factor is inelastic, then a change in demand will cause a relatively small change in the equilibrium quantity of the factor hired but there will be a large change in the factor's price.

Labor

Labor Demand

Labor is a primary factor of production for many firms. The individual household owns its labor and is assumed to be able to freely sell its labor to firms or to withhold its labor from the market. If the household decides to sell its labor to a firm, the firm pays a wage rate to the household (compensation could also be in the form of a set salary, but this could always be converted to an hourly wage). If the household decides not to sell its labor to firms, the household is assumed to have no income from working. Firms demand labor but only inasmuch as labor helps them earn profit.

In Chapter 8, marginal product was defined as the additional production from hiring another unit of a particular factor, holding the levels of other inputs fixed. In the case of labor, each additional hour of labor hired will help the firm produce some additional output, which is the marginal product of labor. Firms are only willing to pay a worker inasmuch as the worker's output is worth to the firm. A worker's value to the firm is therefore not measured by marginal product but by marginal revenue product—the change in total revenue after hiring another unit of labor. This distinction is important, and failure to remember it can cause confusion while analysing labor markets. The marginal product of a worker is the additional amount produced, whereas the marginal revenue product is the additional total revenue the firm earns by selling the worker's marginal product.

If labor receives a wage of w for each hour, the marginal cost to the firm of hiring an additional unit of labor is equal to that wage. In general, economists assume w

incorporates all wages, taxes, and fringe benefits. Therefore, firms pay more for each unit of labor they hire than households *take home* in pay. This is an important point because firms hire labor to the point where the marginal cost of labor is equal to the marginal benefit of labor. A firm demands labor consistent with the marginal revenue product curve. At a given wage rate w, the firm will hire labor to the point where the marginal revenue product is equal to the wage rate, as depicted in Figure 12-3.

What can alter the demand for labor by a firm or an industry? If the demand for the final good increases, it would cause the product's price to increase in the short run. As marginal revenue product is defined as price times marginal product, the marginal revenue product will increase if the good's price increases.

Another reason the demand for labor might increase is if firms change their technology such that the marginal product of labor increases. Even if the price of the product does not change, the marginal revenue product, that is, the demand for labor, will increase.

Unfortunately, the reverse also holds. The demand for labor in a particular industry can decline if the demand for the industry's product declines, which would cause a decline in the good's price and a decline in the marginal revenue product of labor. Moreover, an industry might move to a different technology in which the marginal product of labor declines and so too does the marginal revenue product of labor.

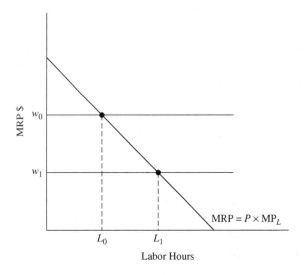

Figure 12-3   The demand for labor.

Labor Supply

Labor is owned and supplied by households. Unfortunately, households have a limited amount of time to dedicate to their desired activities. Economists divide the household's time into two parts: labor time, during which households are assumed not to consume and leisure time, during which households are assumed not to work. In reality, households often consume while they are working, for example, the refrigerator is running and consuming electricity while a household is at work. However, the delineation of time between work and leisure makes it easier to determine the amount of time the household is willing to work at a given wage rate.

The first unique aspect of labor supply is that each household has a reservation wage below which the household will supply no labor. At the reservation wage, households are willing to offer labor for firms to use. As wages increase, it is natural to assume that the household will be willing to sell more of its labor time to firms. However, as the household sells more labor time to a firm, the household necessarily has less time to dedicate to leisure activities. As wages increase there are two offsetting effects upon the household's decisions. The first is the substitution effect, which motivates households to increase the amount of time they dedicated to work and reduce the amount of time dedicated to leisure. The intuition behind the substitution effect is that an increase in wages makes work time more valuable relative to leisure time and therefore the household substitutes labor for leisure.

However, as wages increase, the household is able to earn more money for a given amount of labor time. The household's increased income makes more leisure opportunities affordable. This makes the household want to work less and consume more leisure. This is known as the income effect because higher wages cause a disincentive to work.

Whenever wage rates increase, these two offsetting effects are at work. If the substitution effect dominates the income effect, the household will supply more labor. If the income effect dominates the substitution effect, the household will supply less labor even though wages are increasing. The interaction of the two effects can cause the household's labor supply curve to be backward bending, as depicted in Figure 12-4.

At a low wage rate, the substitution effect dominates the income effect. In other words, as wages increase, the household is willing to work more hours, substituting away from leisure and into labor. However, as wages increase, the household is able to afford more leisure opportunities and is able to earn a target income with fewer hours worked. Eventually, the substitution and income effects just offset each other; say at wage w_0 in Figure 12-4. At this point, a small increase in the wage rate will not affect the quantity of labor supplied. As wages rise beyond w_0, the income effect dominates the substitution effect and the household begins to substitute out of labor

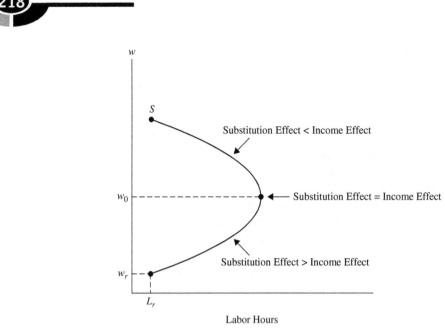

Figure 12-4   The household's supply of labor.

and into leisure by supplying less labor, causing the backward bending nature of the household labor supply curve.

Every household has a different reservation wage and a different wage at which the income effect just offsets the substitution effect. For this reason, the market supply of labor typically has a larger portion that is upward sloping than most household labor supply curves. While it is entirely possible for an individual to operate on the backward bending portion of their labor supply curve, it is highly unlikely that an entire market would operate on the backward bending portion of the market's labor supply curve.

Labor Market Equilibrium

Labor market equilibrium occurs when the supply of labor is equal to the demand for labor. Figure 12-5 depicts a labor market in equilibrium. At equilibrium, all workers are paid the same wage rate w^* and L^* workers are hired. The firms in the market pay $w^* \times L^*$ in total wages. If the demand for labor increases in this market, then the wage rate and the number of workers employed in the market will increase. If the demand for labor falls, then the wage rate and the number of workers employed will both decrease.

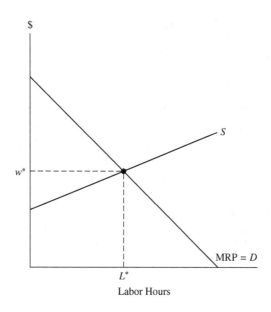

Figure 12-5   Labor market equilibrium.

If the equilibrium wage rate in this industry is relatively high, people may be motivated to enter the labor market, pushing the supply curve to the right and lowering the equilibrium wage rate. In many cases, the individual worker does not have the ability to unilaterally affect their wage rate, and therefore entry by other workers can reduce the wages that incumbent workers earn. This, in turn, might motivate incumbent workers to try to bar entry into their labor market. How do people already working in a particular sector keep the supply of labor from increasing? Labor markets might require specialized training (as with doctors, lawyers, and mechanics); it might become harder to get into schools that provide specialized training (even if it is not harder to graduate from the schools), or labor may try to unionize and limit the number of people allowed to work in the sector.

However, it is possible that the equilibrium depicted in Figure 12-5 corresponds with a low wage rate and a relatively high number of workers hired. The equilibrium wage in a labor market reflects the marginal revenue product of the last worker hired and does not necessarily indicate the value of all workers. After all, some workers provide high marginal product and are very valuable to the firm, and other workers provide lower marginal product and are therefore not as valuable to the firm. In the end, however, if all workers are paid the same, then all workers receive the value of the marginal worker and not necessarily a true reflection of their own value to the firm.

Additional Topics in Labor Markets

The labor market depicted in Figure 12-5 implicitly assumes that all workers and all firms act as price takers, that is, they take the wage rate as fixed. However, it is possible that firms, workers, or both, could have some level of market power, which might help them influence the prevailing wage rate. Monopsony power occurs when there is only one purchaser of a product. In the case of household labor, if one or a very few firms purchase a particular kind or labor, they will have market power in purchasing labor. This, in turn, is likely to reduce the level of employment and wages in a market. On the other hand, although an individual worker is rarely able to dramatically influence the wages, workers can organize in the form of a quasi-cartel in an attempt to increase wages and employment. These quasi-cartels are called labor unions. A final possibility is that workers unionize and have some level of market power at the same time that firms enjoy some measure of monopsony power.

Monopsony

In Chapter 10, we discussed the influence of a monopolist on equilibrium price and quantity in a market. In that chapter, we showed that a typical monopolist will produce less and price higher than what would prevail in a perfectly competitive market. In the process, the monopolist is able to earn more profit relative to perfectly competitive firms while imposing some level of dead weight loss on the market.

A monopsonist is the opposite of a monopolist. A pure monopsonist is the only purchaser of a good or service, typically an input to production such as land, labor, or capital. For example, a one-mill town with a single major employer might hire the vast majority of the workers in that town. Other examples include professional sports leagues where there are a limited number of firms who are in the market for, say, baseball pitchers. Like monopolists, a monopsonist will tend to reduce the equilibrium quantity relative to what would prevail in perfect competition. Unlike a monopolist, a monopsonist tends to push the equilibrium price to less than what would prevail in perfect competition.

Before we derive the monopsonistic market in detail, consider whether the monopsony equilibrium makes sense. In the case of a single seller, the monopolist wants to price as high as it can while producing as little as possible and still maximize profit. This is exactly what monopolists do. In the case of a single buyer, the monopsonist wants to pay as low of a price as possible while still purchasing enough of the input so that they can maximize profit. In both cases, it makes sense that the equilibrium quantity would be less than would prevail in perfect competition. A single buyer would want to push price down, if it can, and a single seller would want to push price up, if it can. In both cases, because price and quantity differ from what would prevail in perfect competition, both monopolists and monopsonists can impose a dead weight loss in the market.

To derive the equilibrium in the monopsonist market, we start with an upward sloping market labor supply curve as depicted in Figure 12-6

From Figure 12-6, it is possible to determine the prevailing wage rate that will induce a certain amount of labor to be supplied on the market. For example, at a wage rate of $6.50 per hour, the labor supply curve indicates that 100 hours of labor would be supplied in the market. If the prevailing wage rate were $6.50, the firm would pay $650 for the 100 hours of labor.

As the monopsonist is the only purchaser of labor in the market, if the monopsonist wants to induce another 10 hours of labor to be supplied in the market, it will have to increase the wage, say to $7.15 per hour. For the last 10 hours of labor hired, the firm would pay $7.15 per hour or $71.50 in total. However, if the workers that are included in the market supply curve depicted in Figure 12-6 are homogeneous, (i.e., they are basically the same), the firm can't pay one person $7.15 and not pay the other workers the same as well.

This implies that the monopsonist will have to pay $7.15 for every hour of labor hired, not just the last ten. Because the monopsonist has to pay $7.15 not $6.50 for all the hours worked, the first one hundred hours would now cost the firm $715 instead of $650. The last 10 hours hired at $7.15 per hour would cost the firm $71.50 and the additional expenditure on the first 100 hours is $65. This will make the total

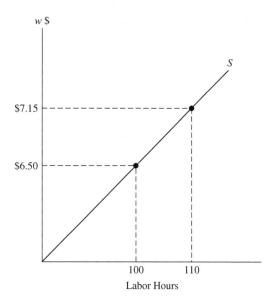

Figure 12-6   A labor supply curve.

wage bill for 110 hours $786.50 = $650 + $65 + $71.50. In other words, the last 10 hours would actually cost $71.50 + $65 = $136.50 or $13.65 per hour not $7.15 per hour. The marginal factor cost is the change in total cost that occurs when the monopsonist hires more of an input. The marginal factor cost includes the new, higher price that must be paid to the additional input that is hired *and* the additional cost incurred from paying inframarginal, or previously hired, inputs a higher price. In this case, the marginal factor cost is $13.65 per additional hour hired.

The market supply curve depicted in Figure 12-6 is not the curve the monopsonist uses to determine the equilibrium amount of labor to hire and the equilibrium wage to pay. Rather, the monopsonist uses the Marginal Factor Cost (MFC) curve depicted in Figure 12-7, which takes into account the fact that to hire more of the factor (in this case, labor), the firm has to raise the price for all the input it hires. In Figure 12-7, the MFC lies strictly above the supply curve.

The monopsonist demands labor based upon the marginal revenue product of labor. The marginal revenue product of labor is, in turn, determined by the production technology the firm uses and the market price of the product the firm makes. The monopsonist's decision of how much of an input to hire is determined by setting the

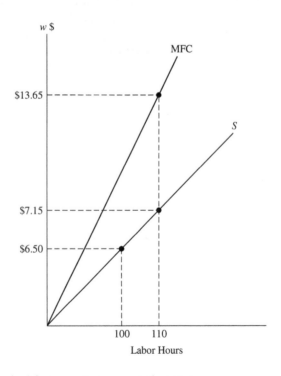

Figure 12-7 Marginal factor cost versus supply curve.

marginal benefit of an additional unit of an input equal to the marginal cost of an additional unit of an input. Unlike the case of perfect competition where the firm can take the market wage rate as given and hire according to $w = \mathrm{MRP}_L$, the monopsonist sets $\mathrm{MFC} = \mathrm{MRP}_L$ as depicted in Figure 12-8.

As can be seen in Figure 12-8, the monopsonist hires labor up to the point where the $\mathrm{MFC} = \mathrm{MRP}_L$, which occurs at L^*_M. The monopsonist pays a wage rate of w^*_M. This equilibrium is in contrast to what would have prevailed if the monopsonist market were replaced with a perfectly competitive market. In this case, the equilibrium would correspond to L^*_{PC} units of labor being hired at a wage rate of w^*_{PC}. In a competitive labor market equilibrium, there would be more labor hired at a higher wage.

The difference between the amount of labor hired in competition and that hired in monopsony represents lost opportunities for gains in trade. As discussed in Chapter 6 and Chapter 10, lost opportunities for gains in trade represent inefficiency in a market. The dollar value of the lost gains in trade is dead weight loss. In Figure 12-9, the dead weight loss created by the monopsony market is depicted by the triangle defined by the Points ABC.

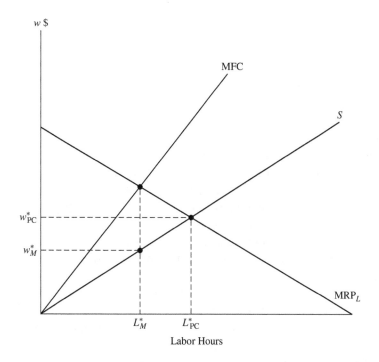

Figure 12-8   Monopsonist equilibrium.

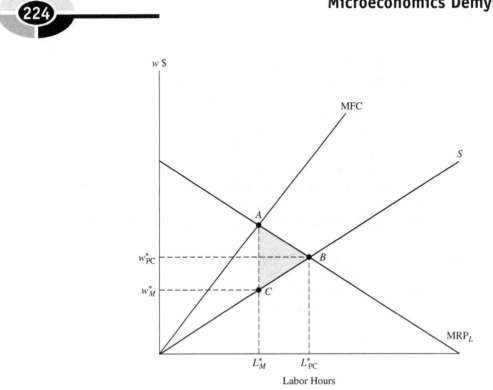

Figure 12-9 Dead weight loss created by monopsony.

Labor Unions

While it might be the case that a labor market has only one buyer, as in the one-mill-town, monopsony markets are relatively rare. Labor is most often free to work when, where, and for whom they wish. However, often a worker has little control over the wages he will be paid. This is because in many labor markets workers are somewhat interchangeable, that is, they are relatively homogeneous. While workers have their own strengths and weaknesses, in the market for taxi drivers most people will be fairly good substitutes for each other. For this reason, workers in markets with more homogeneous labor cannot influence their wage rate and must take wages as given.

Often the individual worker finds it nearly impossible to influence his wage rate or other aspects of his job, including working hours, vacation and benefits, and so forth. This does not mean that workers are completely without recourse. The labor union is one way for workers to collectively bargain with the firm in order to secure higher wages, more or better hours, or better fringe benefits. Regardless of the political aspects of labor unions, in a basic framework the labor union allows workers to negotiate as a group in hopes of securing a higher wage.

Instead of negotiating one-on-one with the firm owners, which would put the individual worker at a significant disadvantage, the union negotiates for *all* workers simultaneously. While the individual workers cede their ability to negotiate with the firm's owners, such negotiating power is often limited. In return for ceding their negotiation rights, the workers hope to convince the firm owners to pay them more or to otherwise meet their demands. In most cases, the firm must negotiate with the union in good faith because the union, if it can maintain solidarity, holds the threat of a strike against the firm.

A strike is essentially a voluntary reduction of the supply of labor to zero, which, if effective, will significantly reduce the amount of output the firm can produce and therefore reduce the firm's profitability. The viability of a strike is significantly reduced if the firm can hire replacement workers to cross any picket line that would be formed by a strike.

While unions are often beneficial for their members, unions can either artificially restrict the supply of labor, increase the demand for labor, or both. If the union is unable to encourage the firms to hire more workers at a higher wage rate, the union may find it acceptable (if not preferable) to artificially restrict the supply of labor. In this manner, the union would be able to increase the equilibrium wage paid to those union members who remain employed but at the expense of some people becoming unemployed, as the firms will hire fewer workers at the higher wage. Such a situation is depicted in Figure 12-10, where the supply of labor has

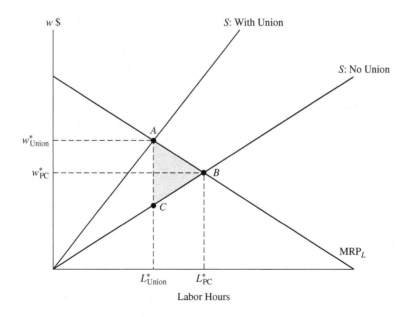

Figure 12-10   A union that restricts supply.

been curtailed and the equilibrium wage increases while the equilibrium amount of labor hired decreases.

How does a union effectively reduce the supply of labor offered in a market? A few elements are required. First, the union must represent a substantial portion of the workers in the market. If the union only represents a minority of the workers in the market, then the threat to strike and significantly reduce the firms' profits is not as credible. Moreover, if there is a substantial number of workers who are not in the union, those workers are not bound by union-firm agreements, nor do they necessarily share the same goals as the union members. Therefore, it is possible that non-union members could undercut the union members by offering to work more hours, work for a lower wage, or both.

If the union is able to represent most or all of the workers in the market, it can then try to limit the entry into and exit from the market. This can occur by requiring those who want to be in the union, to work as an apprentice for a number of years, to pass certification requirements, or by requiring that individuals have certain qualities or characteristics before being allowed to join the union. In this manner, a union can restrict the supply of labor to be less than it would be in perfect competition.

Regardless of how a union restricts the supply of labor in the market, the end result is a higher wage but fewer people working in the market. As depicted in Figure 12-10, the number of workers hired with the union in place is reduced from L^*_{PC} to L^*_{Union}, whereas wages increase from w^*_{PC} to w^*_{Union}. While some workers are paid a higher wage, some workers are unable to work at all. Whether the cost in lost employment is worth the benefit of higher wages for those who remain employed is unclear.

Because an effective union that restricts supply alters the equilibrium from Point B to Point A in Figure 12-10, the union induces a dead weight loss in the market, defined by triangle ABC. Note that the dead weight loss created by a union is similar to the dead weight loss created by a monopsonist. In both cases, the equilibrium level of workers hired is reduced. In the case of a monopsony, wages are depressed below natural market wages. In the case of a supply-restricting union, wages are pushed above natural market wages.

It is not guaranteed that a union will induce a dead weight loss. Some unions attempt to increase the demand for their workers, which can only occur with an increase in the marginal revenue product of the labor the union represents. Thus, unions may lobby to increase the marginal product of its workers, perhaps through investing in new technology. A labor union might lobby to make certain inputs relatively more expensive than labor, thereby increasing the demand for labor on the part of firms (see Chapter 8). Unions might also lobby or advertise their products in order to increase the demand for the goods the union members produce. If the demand for a union product increases, the price of the product is likely to increase, and this, in turn, will increase the marginal revenue product of labor. If a labor union simply tries to increase the demand for labor, but does not influence the supply of labor, the impact of the union is as depicted in Figure 12-11.

In Figure 12-11, it is apparent that the union is beneficial to workers because it has increased the wage and the amount of labor hired in equilibrium. In general, such unions are not thought to create significant dead weight losses.

However, if a supply restricting union also attempts to enhance demand, then the union might be able to increase the wages of the workers while ensuring that more workers are hired (even at the higher wages). From the point of view of most unions, it would seem that the combination of increasing demand and decreasing supply would be the perfect combination. By restricting supply, the union guarantees a higher wage but with fewer workers hired in equilibrium. By enhancing demand, it guarantees yet another increase in wages and an increase in the number of workers hired. What is not clear is whether the union can increase demand sufficiently to ensure that more workers are hired with the union than without the union.

As depicted in Figure 12-12, the perfectly competitive equilibrium is at Point A. The restriction in labor supply and the enhancement of labor demand shift the equilibrium to Point B. At Point B in Figure 12-12, wages increase, as does the number of workers hired, relative to the perfectly competitive outcome. However, this is not guaranteed to happen all the time.

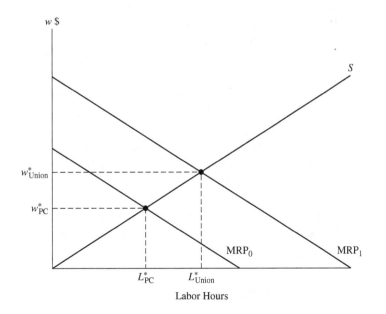

Figure 12-11   A union that enhances demand.

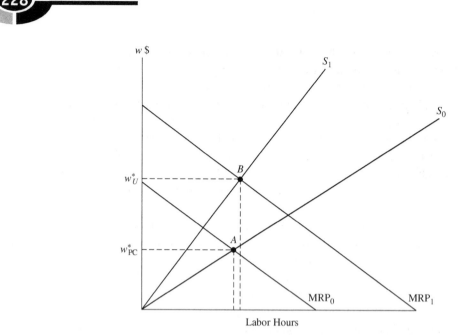

Figure 12-12 A union that restricts supply and enhances demand.

In some labor markets, it is possible for individual workers to negotiate their wage with firm owners. These markets require at least some level of worker heterogeneity that can be objectively measured by the firm and proven by the worker. For instance, a professional basketball player can provide evidence of his productivity and his impact on the team's revenues. Actors, lawyers, doctors, and professors, are other examples of markets where it is relatively easy to discern the quality of one worker relative to another. Notice that in most of these markets, unions are very loose associations, if they exist at all. In professional sports, players unions rarely negotiate salaries but rather a general agreement in which negotiations will take place. In these types of markets, workers have some measure of market power and are less prone to cede the market power to a union negotiator.

The lesson here is to recognize that a union can be a monopsony fighter, essentially increasing the amount of labor hired, increasing the wage rate, and reducing dead weight loss. On the other hand, it is possible for a union to become a monopolistic seller of labor and thereby increase wages, reduce the amount of labor hired, and generate dead weight loss.

One-on-One Wage Negotiations

Look back at Figure 12-5, which depicts a labor market equilibrium where all workers and firms take the wage rate as given. Assume that workers cannot unilaterally alter the wage rate. For those labor units to the left of L^*, the marginal revenue product of labor is greater than the marginal cost, which is the wage rate. In other words, the firm owner is able to earn a profit on the efforts of the worker because, on the margin, the worker is more valuable than his wage.

A worker might try to negotiate for a wage that is closer to his marginal revenue product. The problem is that in most markets it is difficult to discern one worker's marginal revenue product from another. This is where worker heterogeneities are valuable. If those workers who are very productive and very valuable to the firm can prove their value, they may be able to negotiate for a higher wage.

If the worker engages in a negotiation with the firm, how high can the employee bid up his wage? The wage can only be bid up to his marginal revenue product; any higher and the firm would be paying more than the worker is worth. On the other side of the negotiation process, the firm wants to negotiate the worker's wage as low as it can. However, the natural limit to how low the firm can bid the wage is the worker's reservation wage.

What can be termed the "contract zone" is determined by the difference between the worker's reservation wage and the worker's marginal revenue product. Assuming that the worker knows his reservation wage but can only estimate his marginal revenue product and the firm knows the worker's marginal revenue product but not his reservation wage, the contract zone is the natural area in which the negotiated wage will fall. An example of contract zone is depicted in Figure 12-13.

Where the negotiated wage falls, depends upon the relative negotiating skills and power of the worker versus the firm. If the worker has more leverage, the negotiated wage will be closer to the worker's marginal revenue product. On the other hand, if the firm has more leverage, the negotiated wage will lie closer to the worker's reservation wage.

If the worker anticipates that they do not have enough leverage to negotiate a wage significantly higher than their reservation wage, the worker might hire an agent to negotiate for him alone (such as a sports agent or acting agent), or the worker might be interested in hiring an agent to negotiate for a large number of employees, such as a union.

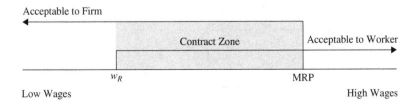

Figure 12-13   A sample contract zone.

Capital Markets

Capital markets are similar to labor markets. Households are assumed to own capital and they sell their capital to firms that demand the capital as an input to production. Firms are only willing to pay, for a given amount of capital, to the extent that the marginal cost of capital is equal to the marginal benefit of capital. Capital is paid an interest rate. Capital is typically defined as machines and other physical goods used to produce other goods and services. However, it is equally valid to consider capital as financial capital, that is, money that households save from their disposable income and are willing to "lend" to firms in return for an interest payment.

The interest rate is therefore the return to households for saving. As any money saved by households could have been used to purchase consumption goods, households must be compensated in order to let firms use their saved money. Interest rates can therefore be interpreted as the price that firms must pay households not to spend their money on current consumption.

Demand for Capital

Firms demand capital according to the marginal revenue product of capital. As capital will exhibit diminishing returns, holding fixed the amount of labor and land employed, the marginal revenue product of capital will decline as more capital is hired, *ceteris paribus*. This implies that the demand for capital is downward sloping as shown in Figure 12-14.

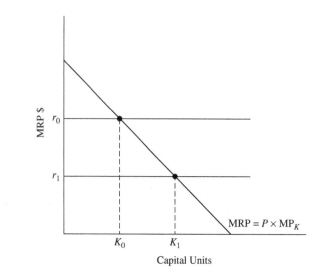

Figure 12-14 The demand for capital.

What can alter the demand for capital by a firm or an industry? If the demand for the firm's product increases, the product's price will increase in the short run and the marginal revenue product of capital will likewise increase. If firms change their technology such that the marginal product of capital increases, the demand for capital will increase. Finally, if the price of labor increases dramatically over time, firms will substitute capital for labor (see Chapter 8) and therefore the demand for capital can increase.

The reverse also holds. The demand for capital in a particular industry can decline if the demand for the industry's product declines or if the technology of the firms requires less capital and more labor.

Supply of Capital

Households supply capital. As mentioned above, households can choose to spend their disposable income on current consumption or they can save their money for future consumption. Because of inflation and individual preferences, most people would agree that consumption in the future is not as fulfilling as consumption today. The more impatient a household is to consume its disposable income, the greater the household's discount factor. The greater the discount factor, the more households must be paid to save their money for future consumption.

Firms want to borrow capital from households, but households want to use their disposable income for consumption. How can households be convinced to save some of their money? By providing a financial incentive called interest. The interest paid on savings is the price firms are willing to pay to borrow money for a specific amount of time. The greater the interest rate, the more households are willing to forego current-day consumption, save their money, and consume in the future. The lower the interest rate, the less households are willing to save, and more disposable income is spent on current-day consumption.

The supply of capital is thought to be upward sloping, as depicted in Figure 12-15.

Capital Market Equilibrium

The market for capital can be envisioned at different levels. There is the overall global market for capital in which suppliers and demanders of capital interact with each other across continents, national borders, and industries. Another way to model capital markets is at the industry level. In this approach, there is a demand for capital on the part of firms who are in a specific industry, say cellular phones. In the short run, there is a set supply of capital, that is, the supply of capital is perfectly vertical or perfectly inelastic. The interaction of the demand and short-run supply

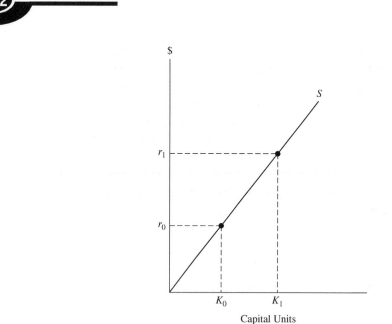

Figure 12-15   The supply of capital.

yields a short-run equilibrium interest rate and capital traded. However, there are other capital markets that represent industries where the demand and supply of capital yield different short-run equilibrium interest rates and capital traded.

For example, in a young, evolving industry the marginal revenue product of capital might be relatively high but the supply of capital will likely be relatively low. As a consequence, the short-run interest rate will tend to be relatively high. However, if capital markets are nearly competitive, then the high returns in the young, evolving industry will attract investors from other, perhaps older, industries where the interest rates are considerably lower. Such a situation is depicted in Figure 12-16.

In Figure 12-16, the older industry has a relatively high supply of capital S_0 and a relative low short-run interest rate. On the other hand, the young industry has a relatively small supply of capital S_0 and a relatively high short-run interest rate. When households recognize the difference in interest rate across the two industries, some households pull their capital out of the older industry and move their capital into the younger industry. The supply of capital in the old industry declines, from S_0 to S_1, which causes an increase in the interest rate paid in the older industry. Meanwhile, the supply of capital in the younger industry increases, say from S_0 to S_1, which causes a decrease in the interest rate in the younger industry. Over time, households continue to relocate their capital in pursuit of higher interest rates until

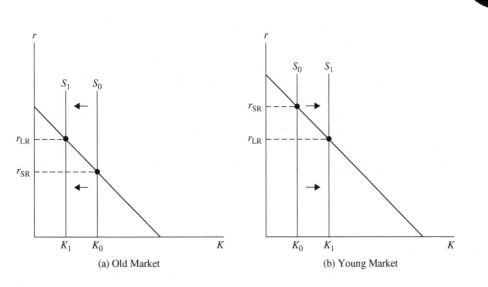

Figure 12-16 Interest rate convergence between young and old industries.

the interest rates paid in all industries are equal. However, in the short run there can be dramatic differences in the interest rates paid in different industries, which cause households to reallocate their capital to different industries.

The Professional Baseball Players Association

Major League Baseball has a long history in the United States. To many baseball fans, one of the sport's endearing qualities is the relative stability of the game. However, in August 1994, the Professional Baseball Players Association, which we can call the players' union, called a strike, thereby ending the season and canceling the World Series. The 1995 season opened late, and there was significant damage to the reputation of the team owners and the players alike. What was the strike in 1994 all about?

There are many different perspectives as to why the players' association called a strike, but the main concern centered on the new collective bargaining agreement that was under negotiation during the 1994 season. The team owners were seeking a salary cap, which would put a limit on the amount of money any particular team could pay its players in total. While a salary cap is not the same as a price ceiling, the team owners advocated a salary cap to stave off what they considered out-of-control player salaries. The players countered that they would rather go on strike than have a salary cap in place. While professional basketball and professional football both have salary caps in place, the experiences of players in these other leagues under the salary cap have been mixed. Many times, rookie players are paid more than veteran players; other times, veteran players with a lot of experience are paid more than younger players with better abilities. In essence, the baseball players' main resistance to the salary cap was a concern that it would put a limit on the ability of current and future players to freely negotiate their wages.

Who was in the right and who was in the wrong? In fact, both sides had legitimate causes. Team owners have been paying more for players, although the evidence does not suggest that they are paying more than players are worth. On the other hand, players have seen their salaries increase dramatically over the past two decades, and they naturally wanted to protect their rights to earning the highest wage for which they could negotiate rather than being artificially restricted in the amount they could earn by the salary cap.

The strike of 1994 was the latest in a relatively long series of work stoppages (both strikes in which the players refused to play and lockouts in which team owners refused to hire). The contentiousness of baseball's labor relations has been a problem in the past. Arguably, one of the main reasons for the historical distrust between players and team owners goes back to the nineteenth century, when professional baseball was in its infancy. In the early years of professional baseball, players were paid according to their abilities on the field and were able to negotiate with team owners for their annual salary. However, starting in the mid-1880s, the team owners argued that the salaries of professional baseball players were increasing too fast and were becoming too high to ensure (substantial) profitability. As a group, the team owners decided they should do something about the increase in player salaries. Rather than asking players if they would kindly take a lower wage for the next year (which most players would likely refuse), team owners began phasing in what was termed the "reserve clause."

The reserve clause was oftentimes the very last clause in a player's annual contract and stipulated that the team for which they played for that year held the perpetual rights to the player's baseball services. The player could choose not to play baseball, but if they did play baseball, they did so when and where the team said. The reserve clause shifted monopsony power to the team owners for approximately one hundred years, during which time some of the best players in the history of the game played for what were arguably below-market wages.

Starting in the early 1970s, players became more agitated about the reserve clause. Curt Flood of the St. Louis Cardinals sued Major League Baseball in federal court, arguing that the reserve clause was a violation of the 14th amendment which outlawed slavery or perpetual servitude, even if the worker voluntarily chose to enter an agreement that stipulated perpetual servitude. The U.S. Supreme Court eventually dismissed the Curt Flood case stating that, while the reserve clause was a clear restriction on the ability of a player to individually choose for which team they would play, it did not create a state of servitude because a baseball player could choose to work in another field or career.

While hardly satisfactory for the players' association, it is likely that the team owners understood that it was only a matter of time before the courts would find in favor of the players and rule the reserve clause illegal. In October 1975, the agent for Andy Messersmith, who was playing for the Los Angeles Dodgers that year, filed a lawsuit claiming that Messersmith had completed his obligations under his current contract (it had expired at the end of the season) and now qualified as a "free agent" and could sell his services to the highest bidder. The team owners did not respond favorably and eventually the issue went to an arbitration hearing. The arbitrator found in favor of Messersmith and co-claimer Dave McNally, making both of them free agents. The arbitration decision was eventually upheld by a federal court in February of 1976.

The immediate impact of free agency was not that dramatic. While the Atlanta Braves eventually paid Messersmith $1 million for a "lifetime contract" in 1976, Messersmith retired from baseball in 1979. Dave McNally had retired from baseball in June of 1975 and never returned to the game, despite being granted free agency. However, it didn't take long before baseball salaries began to increase. In 1980, the Houston Astros offered pitcher Nolan Ryan the first $1 million per year contract. By 2000, the highest salary in baseball was paid to shortstop Alex Rodriguez—$24.2 million per year.

How did salaries increase so much so fast? The ability for players to sell their services to the highest bidder after six years of major league experience transferred tremendous market power away from the team owners and to the players. Rather than team owners having monopsony power over the players, thereby paying below-market wages, free agency gave players monopoly power, thereby allowing them to dramatically increase their wages and extract rents from team owners.

Note that team owners are not paying players more than they are worth on average. A substantial amount of investigation suggests that while some players may get hurt or otherwise have an off year immediately after they sign a big contract, close statistical inspection suggests that this is not the case in general. Moreover, team owners are usually savvy businessmen who have accumulated hundreds, if not thousands, of millions of dollars in other business interests. It is hard to believe that team owners who are such good business people in various areas become, as a group, terrible business people when they buy a baseball team. This implies that team owners are unlikely to systematically pay players more than they are worth, that is, salaries are not higher than marginal revenue product.

Simultaneous with the increase in the highest salaries paid to baseball players, the average salaries in professional baseball have likewise been on the rise. This is a more compelling reason for why the great majority of baseball players supported the strike in 1994. By that time, the highest salaries were in the several millions of dollars, but the average salary was nearly $1.2 million per year. Rather than go on strike to protect the salaries of the highest paid players, it is likely that the majority of players supported the strike to protect their right to freely negotiate with the various teams to obtain the highest salary possible.

Figure 12-17 depicts the average salary in professional baseball from 1967 through 2005. As can be seen, average salaries were relatively low and stable until immediately after free agency. Starting in the mid to late 1980s, salaries start to escalate dramatically. After the 1994 strike was resolved, the increase in salaries was abated somewhat, but by the late 1990s and into the early 2000s, salaries continued to increase.

The agreement between the team owners and the players union, after the 1976 arbitration hearing established free agency, was to limit free agency to only those players with at least six years of major league experience. In the mid 1980s, players with three years of major league experience were allowed to file for final

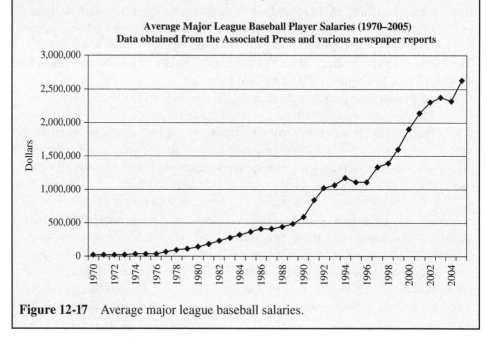

Average Major League Baseball Player Salaries (1970–2005)
Data obtained from the Associated Press and various newspaper reports

Figure 12-17 Average major league baseball salaries.

offer arbitration. Final offer arbitration entails the team owner and the player (usually through his agent) to each make a single salary proposal. Rather than take the average of the two values, which might motivate team owners to offer very small salaries and players to ask for outrageously high salaries, the arbitration panel chooses one offer or the offer. Final offer arbitration is intended to encourage more accurate arbitration offers, which it probably does. However, some economists and baseball experts blame arbitration as being the major cause of dramatic salary increases rather than free agency.

While those with six years and three years of major league experience have access to formal methods with which to negotiate for their wages, those who have less than three years experience work in the same reserve clause system that has existed since 1880s. Therefore, for players with less experience, the team owners still hold substantial monopsony power. Nevertheless, the players association does negotiate for a league-wide minimum wage. While players with less than 3 years experience can try to negotiate for a salary above the minimum wage, team owners are under no obligation to pay a higher wage because they face no competition from other teams.

Figure 12-18 depicts the minimum wage in major league baseball over the same time period, 1967 through 2005. As is readily seen, the minimum wage has increased over time but not as dramatically nor as high as the average salaries

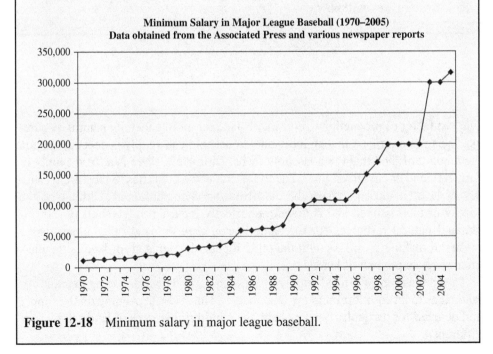

Figure 12-18 Minimum salary in major league baseball.

paid to more experienced players. This is expected because team owners have more monopsony power amongst players with less experience, and the players union will only negotiate for increases in the minimum wage when their collective bargaining agreement expires.

While the level of baseball player salaries and the salaries in the other three major sports leagues in North America often seem mind boggling to the average person, the experience in the professional baseball labor market is a valuable example of the power of monopsony. After free agency, and to a lesser extent, final offer arbitration, there was a dramatic shift in negotiating strength from the team owners to the players. This change in negotiating power has contributed to the dramatic increase in player salaries. However high salaries increase on average, it is unlikely the team owners would continuously pay players more than they are worth to the team.

While not proven here, it has been shown that while player salaries did increase after free agency, the movement of players from team to team did not dramatically increase after free agency. While it is true that some very famous players have left one team for another after free agency, there were just as many players moving from team to team before free agency. The difference between the two periods is who makes the decision of where a player plays. Before free agency, team owners decided where players went. After free agency, players decide where they will play.

Land

The last factor of production to consider is land, or more generally natural resources. The amount of land that an individual household can supply is dependent upon the amount of land that the household owns. Ultimately, there is a fixed supply of (private) land at any given time. Therefore, if a household tries to increase its supply of land, it must purchase the land from another household. Ultimately, the supply of land is fixed and is therefore perfectly inelastic in the short run. Firms demand natural resources for the same reason they demand other inputs—as a means of making profit. As with the other inputs, the demand for land is the marginal revenue product of land.

The interaction of a fixed supply of land and a downward sloping demand for land leads to an equilibrium in the land market. However, depending on the supply and demand for particular types of land, the equilibrium prices of land can be very different.

For example, the land in downtown Manhattan is very scarce. At the same time, land in Manhattan is extremely valuable in the sense that it provides a relatively high marginal revenue product. Therefore, the market for land in Manhattan combines relatively small supply with relatively large demand—the result is high prices of land in Manhattan, as depicted in Figure 12-19.

On the other hand, the land in West Texas is relatively abundant, that is, the supply is relatively large, and the marginal revenue product of land in West Texas is relatively low, especially when compared to Manhattan. The equilibrium price for land in West Texas is therefore considerably lower than it is in Manhattan, even if more land is utilized in West Texas, as depicted in Figure 12-20.

One interesting outcome of land markets is so-called urban sprawl. As cities become larger, land that was once only useful (and valuable) for farmland suddenly becomes valuable after an increase in the demand for homes, even if these homes are far from the city center. Eventually, large metropolitan areas become encircled with suburbs and exurbs built on land that once was quite cheap but is ultimately much more valuable after houses and amenities are built in the area.

Households often purchase land on the outskirts of metropolitan areas in anticipation of such increases in value. Such purchases are often speculative in nature because the household does not know whether or when the population movement will encompass the land they have purchased. Nevertheless, the steady progression of urban sprawl eventually makes land that was once valuable as farmland much

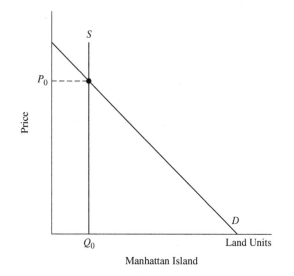

Figure 12-19   The supply and demand for land in Manhattan.

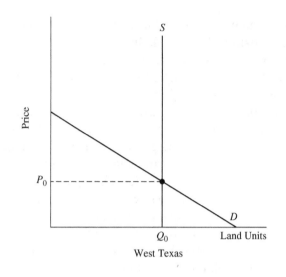

Figure 12-20 The supply and demand for land in West Texas.

more valuable as "house land." Farmers or other landowners are often motivated to sell to home developers because using the land as an operational farm might carry too high an opportunity cost for the individual farmer.

Many people are anxious about urban sprawl and associated economic and social problems, including pollution, driving congestion, and lack of green space. Some suggest that urban sprawl should be regulated or otherwise made illegal, or at least much more costly. Many times it is deemed necessary to turn to the government to address these concerns because simply asking the farmer to not sell his land to a developer is probably not the most effective means of combating urban sprawl.

When a farmer does what is in his own best interest, for example, selling his land to a house developer, without considering the impact of that decision on the others around him, economists claim there might be an externality or market failure. This concept is the focus of the next (and last) chapter.

Summary

This chapter describes the markets for the three major factors of production: labor, capital, and land. For the most part, these markets operate as other markets, except demand for factors comes from firms and the supply of factors comes from households. The market for labor was the first to be developed, focusing initially on the demand for labor. Firms demand labor (and other factors) according to the value of marginal product. In other words, the most firms are willing to pay workers is the amount of money the firm can earn from selling that workers' marginal product. Households supply labor, but households do not have to work. The minimum for which a household will work is called the reservation wage; each household has its own reservation wage. Further, there are two offsetting effects on the amount of labor supplied when wages increase. Households divide their time between labor and leisure. As wages increase, households shift time from leisure to labor to earn more money; this is the substitution effect. However, households spend most of their money during leisure time, that is, when they are not working. Therefore, as wages increase, the household is motivated to switch time from labor to leisure, known as the income effect. Depending on the relative strengths of these two offsetting effects, it is possible that a household would actually work less after an increase in wages.

The interaction of supply and demand determines the labor market equilibrium price and amount of labor hired in a particular market. If labor is paid the same wage, then all workers are paid the marginal revenue product of the last worker hired, which might be considerably less than the value of the first worker hired.

The market for capital was also developed. In industries where capital is highly productive, the demand for capital is relatively high; where it is not highly productive, demand is relatively low. Households supply capital to firms, but in doing so, they sacrifice current-day consumption for which they must be compensated. The interest paid by firms encourages households to trade current consumption for future consumption. In older industries where the supply of capital is relatively high, interest rates tend to be relatively low. In younger industries, where the supply of capital is relatively small, interest rates tend to be higher. As households discover the higher returns available in younger industries, households tend to shift their capital from older to younger industries. Therefore, the supply of capital in older industries tends to decline and interest rates in older industries tend to increase, and the supply of capital in younger industries tends to increase and interest rates in younger industries tend to decrease. In the process, interest rates tend to converge across industries over time.

The market for land is unique because the supply of land is fixed, that is, it is perfectly inelastic. Therefore, as the demand for land increases, the price of land can increase dramatically. This partly explains the dramatic difference in land prices between urban and rural settings. Land that is at a considerable distance from a major urban center tends to be in large supply, but the demand for such land is relatively low, therefore the price of rural land is low. However, as cities expand, the demand for the land on the edges of town increases although the supply doesn't change, hence the dramatic increase in the price of land on the edges of big cities.

Quiz

1. If the tenth and last employee hired by a firm increases the firm's output from 80 to 90 units per day and the firm can sell these units for $20 each, what is the highest wage the tenth employee can expect to be paid?

    a. $125 per day

    b. $150 per day

    c. $200 per day

    d. $20 per day

2. If high school teachers get paid very little even while society claims to value high school teachers highly, it might indicate that

    a. there is a small supply of teachers.

    b. teachers have a high marginal product.

    c. teachers have a bad contract.

    d. there is a large supply of teachers.

3. Urban sprawl is considered a problem by many environmentalists. What can explain the continuing expansion of major urban centers?

    a. The supply of land in the city center has declined.

    b. The price of land in the city center is considerably higher than on the edges of town.

    c. The demand for land in the city center is higher than on the edges of town.

    d. The supply of land at the edges of town is less than in the city center.

4. What can explain the fact that the only people playing golf on Tuesday afternoon are doctors and lawyers?

    a. Only doctors and lawyers play golf.

    b. The substitution effect dominates for doctors and lawyers.

    c. The income effect dominates for doctors and lawyers.

    d. Prices for golf are higher on Tuesdays.

5. If the minimum wage increases, which of the following will happen?

    a. The demand for minimum wage labor will increase.

    b. The demand for minimum wage labor will decrease.

    c. The quantity of minimum wage labor demanded will increase.

    d. The quantity of minimum wage labor demanded will decrease.

6. If the minimum wage increases, which of the following will happen?

   a. The supply of minimum wage labor will increase.

   b. The supply of minimum wage labor will decrease.

   c. The quantity of minimum wage labor supplied will increase.

   d. The quantity of minimum wage labor supplied will decrease.

7. If the government imposes a tax on capital gains from investing, what will happen to the supply of capital?

   a. It will increase.

   b. It will decrease.

   c. It will not change.

   d. It will only increase in older industries.

8. If a person receives a raise from $50,000 to $75,000 and decides to work six days a week instead of five, which of the following is likely true?

   a. The income effect dominates the substitution effect.

   b. The income effect just offsets the substitution effect.

   c. The income effect is $25,000.

   d. The income effect is dominated by the substitution effect.

9. Per-capita income has increased steadily in the United States since World War II. What is the most likely explanation?

   a. Minimum wage laws.

   b. The average savings rate in the United States is very low.

   c. U.S. labor is highly unionized.

   d. U.S. labor is highly productive and continues to get more productive.

10. If the interest rate in Industry A is 8% and the interest rate in Industry B is 4%, what would you expect to happen in the short-run?

   a. The demand for capital in Industry A will decrease as will the interest rate.

   b. The demand for capital in Industry B will increase as will the interest rate.

   c. The supply of capital in Industry B will decrease and the interest rate will increase.

   d. The supply of capital in Industry A will decrease and the interest rate will decrease.

11. A union that organizes labor in an industry with only two firms is likely

    a. a monopolistic seller of labor.

    b. a union that attempts to increase the demand for labor.

    c. a union that attempts to counter monopsony power.

    d. a union that restricts supply artificially.

12. Why would airline pilots have a union even while they are typically paid considerably more than the average worker?

    a. They have an upside-down contract zone.

    b. They have little ability to differentiate themselves and therefore have little negotiating power.

    c. They have considerable ability to differentiate themselves and therefore have little negotiating power.

    d. They do not have a union.

13. If a firm knows the worker's MRP is $250 per hour and the worker has a reservation wage of $100 per hour, which of the following is a possible outcome of one-on-one negotiations?

    a. $50 per hour

    b. $220 per hour

    c. $275 per hour

    d. None of the above

14. If a firm hires 10 units of capital and the marginal revenue product of labor is $15 per hour. What will happen to the marginal revenue product of labor if the firm hires an additional unit of capital?

    a. It will not change.

    b. It will decrease.

    c. It will only increase only if the capital is cheaper than labor.

    d. It will increase.

15. Assume that people in Christiania are paid $5 per hour to produce a product that sells for $2.50. What is the marginal product of the marginal worker in Christiania?

    a. 12.50 units per hour

    b. 250 units per hour

    c. 2 units per hour

    d. 5 units per hour

13

Market Failure and Government Intervention in Markets

Thus far, the focus has been on how agents interact through markets, including perfect competition, monopoly, oligopoly, and factor markets. Very little focus has been on the role of government in the market process. Other than protecting property rights and ensuring a stable set of rules with which agents can interact, there has been no other role for government in the models thus far developed. Nevertheless, economists have considered the practical implications of and reasons for government intervention in the free market process. These reasons are loosely grouped in what economists would call market failures.

There are two primary forms of market failure: public goods and externalities. Public goods are consumed jointly or communally with everyone else. It is difficult to determine exactly how much of a public good should be purchased and how much each person should contribute to the provision of the public good. Externalities arise when the production or consumption of a good causes third-party costs or benefits not accounted for in the original transaction.

The analysis of market failures necessitates a distinction between positive economics, or the study of what is, and normative economics, or the study of what should be. Most public policy intended to alleviate unemployment, poverty, or other social problems really target undesired outcomes of a market process. Before the efficacy of any particular policy can be determined, it is important to have a solid understanding of why the particular market outcome occurred and why it is undesirable. With this information, it is possible to determine whether a particular public policy would have a desired impact on the market outcome.

Therefore, economists initially establish the conditions of market failures (a positive result) and then analyze the possible effects of government action (also a positive result), but economists are not able to easily determine whether the government should or should not perform such actions (which is a normative question).

Public Goods

In Chapter 8, several reasons were offered for why the private firm is the preferred means of organizing production. However, the various levels of government offer many services, including national defense, police and fire protection, public schools, parks, libraries, and roads. It is true that private firms also offer many of these aforementioned items. Private security companies and bodyguards might replace the local police, and there are private schools and private roads.

However, there might be compelling reasons for why these goods are often offered by governments and financed through tax dollars collected from the citizenry of the government's jurisdiction. In other words, is there something special about national defense, relative to filling your gas tank or mowing your lawn, such that having the government provide the service is superior to providing it privately?

It is possible to characterize goods as private or public. A private good is characterized by both excludability and rivalry. A good is excludable when the person who purchases a unit of the good determines who actually gets to consume the good. For example, if you buy a loaf of bread, you can do what you want with it. You can feed it to the ducks, eat it yourself, or give it away. Regardless of what you ultimately do with the loaf of bread, it is your decision alone. A good is rivalrous if, when one person consumes a unit of the good, no one else can consume the same unit.

A public good is nonexcludable and is nonrivalrous. In other words, no one can be excluded from consuming a public good, and one person's consumption of a public good does not reduce the next person's ability to consume the same public good. An example of a public good is national defense. It is impossible to deny any single citizen the benefits of national defense and if one person enjoys the benefits of national defense it does not reduce the overall amount of national defense that can be enjoyed by anyone else.

A middle case is often called a mixed public good. Mixed public goods can contain a bit of either excludability or rivalry. For example, consider driving on an urban freeway. During rush hour, the consumption of the highway is nonexcludable, anyone with a car can get on the highway, but the freeway is rivalrous because the highway is congested during rush hour.

Governments often provide public goods, however this does not mean that the amount of the public good can be arbitrarily large. Public goods entail marginal costs, and therefore governments face many of the same constraints that firms face. One important difference between government production and private production is that governments are funded through taxes gathered from the citizenry of the government's jurisdiction. Because most citizens pay taxes, most citizens expect public goods to be provided at the level they personally feel is appropriate instead of the level that is socially efficient. This incentive for individuals to demand more public goods than they have adequately paid for is called the free rider problem.

A free rider is one who enjoys the benefits of consuming a good without bearing the full costs of purchasing the good. Free riding occurs in the case of public goods because it is difficult to accurately assess the true public marginal cost and marginal benefit of an additional unit of the public good. This is different than most private goods in which it is relatively easy to determine the marginal cost and benefit of an additional unit of production.

The challenge in providing public goods is not producing the good or service, after all, it is relatively simple for the government to collect taxes and pay for roads or schoolteachers. It is more challenging, and controversial, to accurately measure the marginal benefits and marginal costs of an additional road or school teacher. If the social marginal benefit of an additional teacher is less than the social marginal cost, economic theory suggests the money should be spent elsewhere, or perhaps rebated to the taxpayer. However, it is difficult for public officials to refuse to hire an additional schoolteacher based upon such logic because some will insist that the teacher is actually very valuable (at least to them) and not hiring the teacher puts children at risk of not learning. Such an allegation can be dangerous for the career of a professional politician. The study of public-good provision involves mitigating this free rider problem in order to ensure that the public good is provided in an efficient manner.

How does this work in practice? With a private good it is possible to derive a demand schedule that reflects the highest price consumers are willing to pay for each marginal unit sold (see Chapter 4). However, it is more difficult to do this with a public good because everyone consumes each marginal unit, whereas with a private good a single person consumes the marginal unit. To measure the total value of each unit of the public good, it is necessary to total the value of each unit to everyone.

Consider the question of how many teachers to hire for a public school in a small town of two people, Trisha and Dane. Table 13-1 lists the total and marginal benefit for the first four teachers for both Trisha and Dane.

Figure 13-1 depicts the total benefits to Trisha and Dane from hiring additional teachers. It is evident that Trisha does not value teachers as much as Dane. For each teacher that could be hired, the total benefit to society is the sum of the benefits to Trisha and Dane. The social marginal benefit for each teacher is the combined marginal benefit enjoyed by Trisha and Dane. Therefore, the social marginal benefit for the first teacher is $39,000 whereas for the second teacher the social marginal benefit is $26,000. The marginal benefit to Trisha and Dane for each teacher is depicted in Figure 13-2.

How many teachers should the town hire? A natural answer might be to hire five because more teachers are better. It is true that hiring five teachers would maximize the total social benefit, however teachers are not free—teachers have to be paid. Just like decisions made by firms and households, efficient decision making by governments entails equating marginal benefits with marginal costs. If Trisha and Dane have each accurately measured their own marginal benefit from additional teachers, then the sum of their marginal benefits is the social marginal benefit of each teacher.

Number of Teachers	Trisha		Dane	
	Total Benefit	Marginal Benefit	Total Benefit	Marginal Benefit
1	$17,000	$17,000	$22,000	$22,000
2	$25,000	$8,000	$40,000	$18,000
3	$28,500	$3,500	$50,000	$10,000
4	$29,500	$1,000	$54,000	$4,000
5	$30,000	$500	$55,000	$1,000

Table 13-1   The Benefits of Additional Teachers to Trisha and Dane

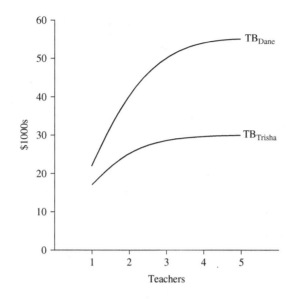

Figure 13-1   The total benefits of additional teachers to Trisha and Dane.

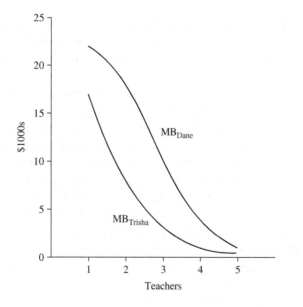

Figure 13-2   The marginal benefits of additional teachers to Trisha and Dane.

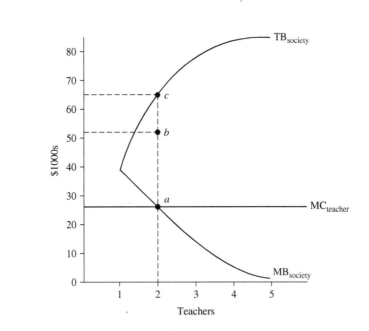

Figure 13-3 The total and marginal benefits of additional teachers to society.

Figure 13-3 depicts the total social benefit and the total social marginal benefit of each teacher. An efficient number of teachers is hired when the marginal cost of the last teacher is equal to the social marginal benefit of the last teacher.

For example, if a teacher's salary were $26,000 per year, then neither Dane nor Trisha would hire any teachers on their own because $26,000 is greater than Trisha's highest marginal value of a teacher ($17,000) and Dane's highest marginal value of a teacher ($22,000). However, after combining the marginal benefits of Dane and Trisha it is evident that the town will find it optimal to hire two teachers. At a marginal cost of $26,000 per teacher, the efficient number of teachers to be hired is determined by finding where the social marginal benefit is $26,000. In our example, and in Figure 13-3, that occurs at two teachers (Point a).

Hiring two teachers will cost the town $26,000 \times 2 = $52,000 (Point b in Figure 13-3), but the value of the two teachers to Trisha and Dane is actually $25,000 + $40,000 = $65,000 (Point c in Figure 13-3). The difference between the cost of the two teachers and the value society places on the two teachers is akin to consumer surplus (discussed in Chapter 6). Society would rather have more "consumer surplus" than less of it. However, often the actual amount of a public good is greater than the efficient level. This is because no single individual pays the full price for the public good.

How does the town actually hire the two teachers and pay them $26,000 each? The two teachers will cost a total of $52,000 and this money has to be raised through taxation of the citizens of the small town (?). How to distribute the burden of the taxes across Trisha and Dane? One possibility is to have Trisha and Dane split the tax burden equally, each contributes $26,000 to the hiring of teachers. However, Trisha values the two teachers at only $25,000, less than her equal share of the taxes necessary to hire the two teachers. From Table 13-1, it is clear that Dane values the teachers more than Trisha. An optimal policy would, therefore, tax Dane more than Trisha because Dane values teachers more than Trisha.

However, in some other good, say roads, Trisha might have higher total and marginal valuations than Dane. In this other good, Trisha should be taxed more than Dane. In the end, the overall optimal tax burden is difficult to determine because it is difficult to determine the actual marginal benefit for thousands of public goods being provided for millions of people. Often taxes are gathered through property, sales, and income taxes. The tax rates and contributions to the public treasury by different individuals can vary dramatically. The theory and practice of providing public goods are often very different.

Externalities

An externality is a third-party benefit or cost from an economic decision that is not included in either the benefits or the costs used to make the decision. Externalities can be positive, in the sense that outsiders receive benefit from an economic decision, or negative, in the sense that outsiders bear additional cost from an economic decision. Externalities can be thought of as a problem of missing markets. In other words, if an externality exists, then it is likely that a market to deal with the external benefits or costs does not exist.

A good example of a negative externality is pollution from a local power plant. The polluter chooses a level of output consistent with its private marginal benefit equaling its private marginal cost. In this case, private marginal cost does not include any costs borne by others for the pollution that is a result of power production, including potential health problems, dirty laundry drying outside, and so forth. These third-party costs are no less real than the costs of the power producer; however, they are not included in the decision of how much energy, and thus how much pollution, will be created. In the case of a negative externality, the social marginal cost (SMC) of a particular activity is greater than the private marginal cost (PMC), as depicted in Figure 13-4. For a given level of private marginal benefit, the privately determined level of output, and hence pollution, is greater than the socially optimal level, that is, $Q_P > Q_{SE}$.

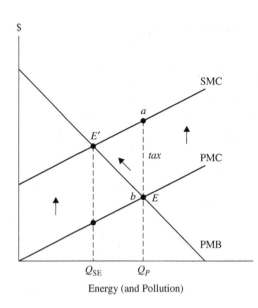

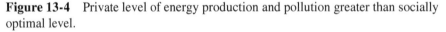

Figure 13-4 Private level of energy production and pollution greater than socially optimal level.

In Figure 13-4, the privately efficient level of energy output (and the accompanying pollution) is that which equates private marginal benefit (PMB) with private marginal cost (PMC). Therefore, the private equilibrium occurs at Point E, which corresponds with a level of energy production and pollution Q_P. However, if society could impose a tax on the polluter equal to the difference between social marginal cost (SMC) and private marginal cost (PMC), then the private marginal cost would equal the social marginal cost. In this case, the equilibrium would move to Point E'. At Point E', the socially efficient level of energy production and pollution is Q_{SE}.

An important lesson from Figure 13-4 is that the socially efficient level of energy production and pollution is not zero. At zero pollution, the private marginal benefit is greater than the socially marginal cost. This implies that a little bit of pollution-generating energy production yields a positive net benefit to society. How can this be? It is assumed that the pollution is a byproduct of an underlying productive activity, which in our example is energy production. Therefore, for low levels of pollution, the positive byproduct of the pollution more than outweighs the negative costs of the pollution itself. However, with more of the pollution-generating activity, eventually the costs of the pollution outweigh the benefits enjoyed from its byproduct.

If a negative externality has been identified, such as smoking or pollution, how does society reconcile the privately determined level of activity with the socially optimal level? One possibility is to pass a law that makes it illegal to pollute. However, as can be seen in Figure 13-4, this is not an optimal solution, regardless of how much certain individuals wish to make an activity illegal. The efficient alternative is to align private marginal cost with social marginal cost through a tax. The tax would be gathered by the government and ideally would be used to compensate the individuals who suffered the additional costs from the smoking, pollution, or other negative externality.

In Figure 13-4, the optimal tax is the difference between social marginal cost (SMC) and private marginal cost (PMC). Figure 13-4 is drawn assuming that the difference between SMC and PMC is the same regardless of how much pollution there is—this may or may not be a good assumption. In Figure 13-4, the optimal tax is the length of the line segment defined by Point a and Point b.

Externalities in the Air

There are considerable externalities in today's complicated economies. The obvious externalities, such as pollution, have been the focus of numerous public policy initiatives, not only in the developed countries such as the United States and Europe, but also in the lesser developed countries of the world. The improvement in the environment isn't always discussed on the local news, however in the United States considerable strides have been made in the past 30 to 40 years.

However, even as the obvious externalities are addressed, if not perfectly, by public policy, still other externalities seem destined to go little noticed. Still other externalities seem to be the unintended consequences of otherwise well-meaning public policy. An example of these types of externalities is the cell phone.

Cell phones have gone from the imagination of the movies to a commonplace in just under 20-year olds. Those under 30 have little comprehension of what life was like before cell phones became so ubiquitous, but even those who have grown up with the cell phone understand that the marvelous contraptions can cause tremendous negative externalities for others. The use of cell phones in church, restaurants, movie theaters, and, yes, even college and high school classrooms, has reached such proportions that public policy has begun to focus on their use.

In many states, there is pending legislation that would make it illegal to talk on a hand-held cell phone while driving a car. There is a growing body of scientific and statistical analysis focusing on the impact of cell phones on the quality of driving, although to many it would come as no surprise that the cell phone can significantly reduce driver concentration and safety.

The impact of cell phone use can therefore be very costly, as in the case of driving, or simply annoying, as in the case of a cell phone ringing in a nice restaurant. There are two ways that the use of cell phones in such situations could be reduced. The first is to increase the cost of using cell phones in inappropriate settings through social suasion. In other words, if the stigma of using the cell phone in a nice restaurant was sufficiently high, then individuals would turn their phones off, or at least set them to vibrate, rather than bear the cost of such scrutiny. Unfortunately (or fortunately, depending upon your point of view), the use of social stigma has generally fallen out of favor in the United States over the past fifty years. Therefore, it is unlikely that the distasteful stare will be enough to encourage people to voluntarily stop cell phone use in inappropriate settings.

The generally accepted alternative is to have laws that carry penalties, usually in the form of monetary fines, if cell phones are used in an inappropriate location. However, it is not clear if this alternative is necessarily more efficient because of the monetary and opportunity costs of enforcement. To date, cell phones have been banned on airplanes during flight, in certain hospital areas, and in two states and roughly 30 cities, it is illegal to talk on a hand-held cell phone while driving.

However, bans on hand-held cell phone use while driving are more common throughout the rest of the world. As of 2004, thirty nine countries (17%) had banned hand-held cell phones while driving; the majority of the countries are in Europe although several in Asia and the Middle East have also banned cell phone use, as can be seen in the accompanying atlas in Figure 13-5.

Why hasn't the United States also banned cell phone use while driving? Despite the high polling numbers in favor of banning the practice, it might prove politically challenging to effectively enforce a ban on cell phone usage. Furthermore, in many of the nations in Europe, a greater proportion of the population doesn't (or rarely) drive. In the United States, almost two-thirds of the population drives on a regular basis and therefore banning cell phones might be politically untenable.

Nevertheless, it is likely that there will be continuing pressure on the various states to ban the hand-held cell phone while driving because of the potential for negative externalities created through hazardous driving or accidents. Much like drunk driving is considered a crime because of the potential for negative externalities it creates, banning hand-held cell phones while driving would seek to address the negative externality problem. However, the success of cell phone

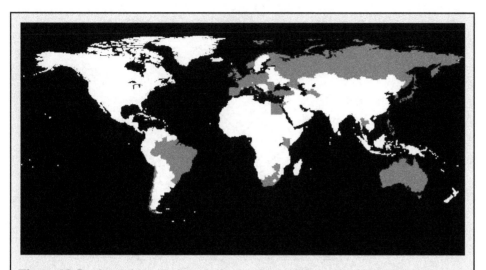

Figure 13-5   Countries with dark shades are those where hand-held cell phones are banned while driving. *(Data source: U.S. Department of Transportation)*

bans might be similar to drunken driving laws. While drunken driving accidents and fatalities are considerably lower than they once were, they are by no means equal to zero. It is likewise possible that habitual cell phone users might ignore the laws, thereby having little effect on their behavior.

Not all externalities are negative. An example of a positive externality is your neighbor planting a flower garden in his front yard or a young person getting a college education. In both cases, you receive some benefit from the private decision. Your neighbor or the young college student makes a private decision about how many flowers to plant or how many years of education to obtain by equating their private marginal benefit with their private marginal cost. However, the private decision does not include the additional marginal benefit you might receive from the flower garden or additional college education. Therefore, the social marginal benefit is greater than the private marginal cost, as depicted in Figure 13-6. For a given private marginal cost, the privately optimal level of the activity is less than the socially optimal level, that is, $Q_{SE} > Q_P$.

In Figure 13-6, the private marginal benefit of education and the private marginal cost of education are equated at Point E that represents the privately efficient equilibrium and corresponds to Q_P years of education. However, at the private equilibrium

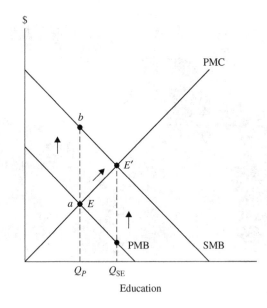

Figure 13-6 Private level of education less than socially optimal level.

level of education, the social benefit outweighs the private cost and therefore society would rather help the individual receive more education. In order to do this, society would subsidize the individual the difference between social marginal benefit (SMB) and private marginal benefit (PMB). The equilibrium would shift to Point E', which would correspond with more years of education at Q_{SE}.

The example above is known as a positive consumption externality, in which third-party benefits are generated when a person consumes more of a particular product, such as education or flowers. However, while less common, there do exist positive production externalities. Positive production externalities occur when producing one good generates undervalued, unrecognized or benefits to other firms. For example, orchards are often located near honey farms because bees are useful for pollinating fruit trees and fruit trees provide nectar that bees can use to create honey.

The dead weight losses created by positive and negative externalities can be reclaimed with accurate subsidies and taxes, respectively. Unfortunately, accurate subsidies and taxes require a considerable amount of information on the part of the government. The government must know the true social costs and benefits of an activity in order to impose or reward accurate taxes and subsidies. Often the information required for efficient taxes and subsides is not available. Moreover, it is difficult at times for the government to truly tax the behavior society might want less of, such as children born out of wedlock, and difficult to subsidize behavior society might want to encourage, for example providing a subsidy for maintaining a full time job.

An alternative to the daunting information requirements of taxes and subsidies is to create a market with well-defined property rights that individuals can trade. For example, in the case of pollution, a market for pollution can be created. This sounds weird to many people at first. Many people might suspect that the polluters will buy all of the pollution rights and the air and water will be dirtier than ever. However, this is unlikely to be the case. This is because those who hold the right to clean air do not have to sell the right to a polluter, and the polluter is not willing to pay arbitrarily high prices for the right to pollute.

The government could either create tradable property rights to clean air, perhaps by creating "chits" that are each worth one clean day. These property rights could be given to those who don't like pollution, in which case the demand for pollution is derived from firms that pollute and the supply of pollution comes from those who do not want pollution. As the price of pollution increases, polluters naturally wish to purchase fewer pollution rights, and those who have pollution rights to sell are motivated to supply more. Ultimately, the interaction of supply and demand will lead to an equilibrium level of pollution and an equilibrium price paid by polluters to those who do not like pollution, as depicted in Figure 13-7.

Just as in the case of the negative externality, the equilibrium in Figure 13-7 corresponds with a positive amount of pollution. However, unlike in the case of taxation where the government receives the payment from the polluter, in a private market

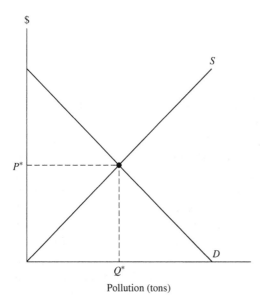

Figure 13-7   A market for pollution rights.

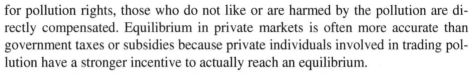

for pollution rights, those who do not like or are harmed by the pollution are directly compensated. Equilibrium in private markets is often more accurate than government taxes or subsidies because private individuals involved in trading pollution have a stronger incentive to actually reach an equilibrium.

It is possible to allocate the right to pollute to the polluter in which case the demand for clean air would come from those who do not like pollution and the supply of clean air would come from those who were initially granted the pollution rights. In the end, the same equilibrium price and quantity of pollution would be obtained. The only difference would be that those who do not like pollution would pay polluters *not to* pollute.

Consider an example. A steel factory and a laundry are located next door to each other. The factory produces smoke (pollution) that dirties the laundry's clean clothes, and thus the clothes have to be washed again. This is clearly a negative externality problem because the foundry's pollution increases the costs of the laundry. How can society rectify the problem?

Assume the cost of polluting is zero for the foundry, and the laundry has no property rights over which to sue. If the laundry were given the "ownership" or the right to clean air, then the factory would have to recognize that the laundry could sue to be compensated for any economic damages caused by the pollution.

Unfortunately, the right to sue is not guaranteed to solve the negative externality. If the foundry's options for pollution control cost more than the maximum damages it could expect to pay in a lawsuit, the factory will continue to pollute and simply pay the laundry any damages it wins from legal proceedings.

If the laundry were allowed to sell levels of pollution, then the factory could buy the rights to pollute at a socially efficient level of pollution. This is actually how the U.S. government deals with pollution. This method is much less demanding on the part of the government because the government is only involved at one point in the market, establishing the initial property rights. On the other hand, taxing or subsidizing externalities requires the government to be deeply and directly involved in the market at all times.

The normative question is whether government is better than individuals at determining social marginal cost and benefit. Many economists think the information required to *accurately* determine social marginal costs and benefits are so high that government taxes and subsidies are often inefficient, perhaps a cure worse than the disease. On the other hand, private markets require individuals to work things out on their own, and oftentimes the market outcome is not desirable to some. Thus, while the government might not implement perfectly efficient policies, many people might accept this reality because the free market outcome is so undesirable. However, these considerations are naturally normative in nature and move beyond the scope of positive economics.

Externalities in the Air Part II

Economists are quick to extol the virtues of markets and competition. While the theory of perfect competition described in Chapter 9 assumes no positive or negative externalities, it is often the case that markets with increased competition do have negative externalities. Whether any negative externalities are outweighed by the gains in efficiency, lower prices, and increased variety that market competition tends to promote is an empirical question.

For example, consider two different metropolitan areas—Atlanta, Georgia and New York City. Atlanta has only one major airport and New York has two major airports. The increased competition in the airline industry in New York (and other cities that have more than one airport) is expected to reduce airfares, increase the number of flights, and otherwise make it less expensive and more convenient to fly. Unfortunately, the additional competition does come with potential negative externalities.

There are two possible sources of negative externalities. The first type is borne by nonflyers. Those who live in the area of the multiple airports suffer potential externalities such as excessive noise and pollution. While it is likely that those who moved near an airport did so with the understanding that an airport was nearby, they may have anticipated a lower level of traffic.

A second type of negative externality is borne by those who fly. While multiple airports increases the competition for air travelers, decreasing price and usually increasing the number of flights offered, the local airspace is not always capable of handling the additional flights in a timely manner. This can lead to an increase in the number or percentage of flights that are delayed because of congestion in the air, on the runway, or at the gate.

What impact does a second airport *actually* have on the number or percentage of flights delayed? Using data from the U.S. Federal Aviation Administration it is possible to estimate the impact of the number of flights and the number of airports on the percentage of all flights to a particular airport that were delayed. In 1999, at the 52 U.S. airports in the sample used here, there were an average of 379,634 flights per year with approximately 6,507 flights per year characterized as delayed. Of the 52 airports in the sample, 23% were in cities with more than one airport, such as New York, Chicago, Dallas, and Los Angeles.

In 1999, the more the flights to a particular airport, that is, the busier the airport, the more the delayed flights experienced at that airport. However, having two or more airports in the city increased the percentage of flights delayed by 1.4 %.

Thus, air travelers in cities with more than one airport face a greater probability of being delayed.

The lesson is that while competition can reward consumers with lower prices, greater quantity, and greater variety, competition can also increase costs in areas that are not so obvious. In the case of air travel in the United States, the benefits of lower prices for air travel in cities with more than one airport are somewhat offset by the increased nonmonetary costs incurred by delays.

Airport	City	Flights in 1998	Delays in 1998	Percentage Delayed	Two Airports
ABQ	Albuquerque NM	228933	98	0.04281	N
ANC	Anchorage AK	310531	384	0.12366	N
ATL	Atlanta GA	909840	32737	3.59811	N
BDL	Hartford CT	180233	371	0.20584	N
BNA	Nashville TN	242370	155	0.06395	N
BOS	Boston MA	502822	14989	2.98098	N
BWI	Baltimore MD	303314	1573	0.5186	N
CLE	Cleveland OH	321420	3506	1.09078	N
CLT	Charlotte NC	444427	1277	0.28734	N
CVG	Cincinnati OH	396285	7333	1.85044	N
DAY	Dayton OH	151116	224	0.14823	N
DCA	Washington DC/NATIONAL	334768	2197	0.65628	Y
DEN	Denver CO	500605	1254	0.2505	N
DFW	Dallas/Ft.Worth TX	867338	16731	1.92901	Y
DTW	Detroit MI/METRO	559548	11522	2.05916	N
EWR	Newark NJ	463000	36553	7.89482	Y
FAI	Fairbanks AK	132320	7	0.00529	N
FLL	Ft. Lauderdale FL	280386	772	0.27533	N
HNL	Honolulu HI	346491	25	0.00722	N
HOU	Houston TX/HOBBY	259926	1150	0.44243	Y
HPN	Westchester County NY	222274	561	0.25239	Y
IAH	Houston TX/ INTERCONTINENTAL	463173	9516	2.05452	Y
IND	Indianapolis IN	252763	176	0.06963	N

Table 13-2 1999 Flights and Delays at 52 Select U.S. Airports
(Data source: Federal Aviation Administration)

Airport	City	Flights in 1998	Delays in 1998	Percentage Delayed	Two Airports
JFK	New York NY/KENNEDY	355677	13547	3.80879	Y
LAS	Las Vegas NV	544052	3870	0.71133	N
LAX	Los Angeles CA	778964	10646	1.36669	Y
LGA	New York NY/LA GUARDIA	368311	28474	7.73097	Y
MCI	Kansas City MO	219966	245	0.11138	N
MCO	Orlando FL	363694	2306	0.63405	N
MDW	Chicago IL/MIDWAY	297544	2874	0.96591	Y
MEM	Memphis TN	374599	305	0.08142	N
MIA	Miami FL	516504	4256	0.824	N
MSP	Minneapolis MN	510420	8801	1.72427	N
MSY	New Orleans LA	166972	185	0.1108	N
OGG	Maui HI	187942	5	0.00266	N
ONT	Ontario CA	157040	111	0.07068	Y
ORD	Chicago IL/O'HARE	897290	49202	5.4834	Y
PBI	West Palm Beach FL	199128	96	0.04821	N
PDX	Portland OR	322652	469	0.14536	N
PHL	Philadelphia PA	480279	14516	3.02241	N
PHX	Phoenix AZ	570788	11919	2.08817	N
PIT	Pittsburgh PA	438197	946	0.21588	N
RDU	Raleigh-Durham NC	291185	377	0.12947	N
SAN	San Diego CA	222458	840	0.3776	N
SAT	San Antonio TX	256148	309	0.12063	N
SEA	Seattle WA	433832	7982	1.83988	N
SFO	San Francisco CA	441606	21187	4.79772	N
SJC	San Jose CA	305501	676	0.22128	N
SJU	San Juan PR	223933	144	0.0643	N
SLC	Salt Lake City UT	368924	718	0.19462	N
STL	St. Louis MO	501484	9631	1.9205	N
TPA	Tampa FL	271998	612	0.225	N

Table 13-2 1999 Flights and Delays at 52 Select U.S. Airports *(Continued)*
(Data source: Federal Aviation Administration)

Summary

This chapter has outlined two major forms of market failures, or cases in which the free market might not obtain an efficient equilibrium and government intervention might make the market outcome more efficient. It is important to recognize that many economists are skeptical that government intervention in the free market is necessarily a solution to a problem. This is because households, many of which have their own agenda and goals that might not be compatible with an efficient market outcome, manage governments. All too often, government intervention is used to correct a market equilibrium that is efficient yet not desirable. For instance, government intervention such as price floors and price ceilings, described in Chapter 4, are often used to address market outcomes that are otherwise efficient.

However, there are some markets in which government intervention might be justified. The first is in the case of public goods, or goods that are consumed by all households simultaneously. Public goods, such as national defense or clean air and water, might be desirable to individuals but may prove too expensive for any individual to undertake. Governments, like individuals, should make decisions based upon the marginal benefit, marginal cost principle that we assume households and firms use. The marginal benefits of government intervention might be considerably high, but the marginal cost of the intervention might also be considerable. If the marginal cost of a public good is $100,000 and the marginal benefit of the public good is $1 for 100,000 different people, no single individual finds it in their best interest to purchase the public good—$1 is considerably less than the marginal cost of $100,000. However, if the government were able to collect $1 from every individual, society as a whole would be able to justify the expenditure on the public good.

The other type of market failure arises from negative and positive externalities, which involve third-party costs or benefits not accounted for in the original transaction. For example, a loud stereo system in a car might provide a negative externality to some in the neighborhood. When the owner of the car purchased the stereo system, she did not take into account the negative impact the stereo would have on her neighbors. This would be an example of a negative externality. The social costs are greater than the private costs. If the government can obtain sufficiently accurate information on the difference between the public and the private costs, an optimal tax can be levied on the externality generating activity that will reduce, but likely not eliminate, the activity. In the case of the stereo, additional speakers, amplifiers, and sub-woofers could be taxed in order to reduce the equilibrium number of speakers, amplifiers, and sub-woofers that would be installed.

A flower garden in your neighbor's yard might provide you a positive externality. Your neighbor incurs the costs of the flower garden, including seed, fertilizer, time and effort, and therefore plants the flower garden according to his private marginal benefit and marginal cost. Your neighbor does not consider your enjoyment of his flower garden when deciding how many flowers to plant. This makes sense because most of the time your neighbor is not going to put a fence around the flower garden but at the same time will have a hard time charging you a fee every time you look at his flowers. The positive benefits you receive from the flower garden indicate that the social marginal benefit of additional flowers is greater than the private marginal benefit. In this case, either you or the government could offer a subsidy to your neighbor—literally pay him additional money and this additional money would encourage your neighbor to plant more flowers.

Unfortunately, government involvement in subsidies and taxes requires a considerable amount of information. The government has to know, or estimate, the costs and benefits of all sorts of activities, many of which are difficult to assess. Some people do not like others smoking in restaurants during their meals, but it is difficult to accurately measure this dislike in dollars in order to know exactly how much to tax the cigarette smoker. Those who dislike smoking will claim a very high value on their clean air. But how many times have you seen a nonsmoker *pay* a smoker to put out their cigarette?

An alternative to taxes and subsidies is for the government to establish well-defined property rights and create a market where the rights can be traded between buyers and sellers. For example, those who sell their right to clean air would be compensated; akin to the cigarette smoker paying the nonsmoker for the right to smoke in a restaurant. The transaction between the smoker and the nonsmoker does not involve the government any more than establishing a tradable right to clean air. On the other hand, the government could establish the tradable right to smoke. In this case, the nonsmoker would pay the smoker not to smoke. The result is an equilibrium that is more efficient with less intervention by the government. These types of markets have been created by state and federal governments for logging or mining rights on public property, and for pollution in both the air and water. However, they remain one of the most controversial ways to deal with externality problems.

Quiz

1. National defense is an example of a

    a. private good.

    b. pure public good.

    c. mixed public good.

    d. economic rent.

2. Externalities involve

   a. a third party who receives benefits or costs.

   b. natural selection.

   c. fingers and toes.

   d. determining the cost of land rent.

3. A radio station provides a

   a. pure public good.

   b. a private good.

   c. a mixed good.

   d. public service good.

4. If a subsidy is offered to the voluntarily unemployed, what is expected to happen to the equilibrium number of voluntarily unemployed?

   a. It will not change.

   b. It will increase.

   c. It will decrease.

   d. Only the involuntarily unemployed will experience a change.

5. Why might some cities have recycling programs, whereas other cities do not?

   a. The citizens of some cities attribute high social cost to recycling programs.

   b. The citizens of some cities place high social benefit on recycling programs.

   c. Some cities are simply nicer than other cities.

   d. Different cities experience the same marginal benefits from recycling programs.

6. If a sports arena is built with public money rather than private money, which statement is most likely true?

   a. The team will perform better in a publicly built stadium.

   b. The team will perform worse in a publicly built stadium.

   c. A privately built stadium will tend to have fewer seats.

   d. A publicly built stadium will tend to have fewer seats.

7. Why are fireworks displays often paid for by local government?

    a. Because fireworks displays are excludable and rivalrous.

    b. Because fireworks displays are nonexcludable and nonrivalrous.

    c. Because fireworks displays are so expensive.

    d. Because of litigation concerns, cities cannot be sued.

8. The optimal tax on a negative externality

    a. aims to eliminate the externality.

    b. aims to completely eliminate the activity causing the externality.

    c. raises money for the government.

    d. aims to make firms or households consider the full costs of their decisions.

    e. none of the above.

9. What might explain the fact that state subsidies to public colleges have been declining over time?

    a. Fewer people are getting a college education.

    b. More people are getting a college education.

    c. The social marginal benefit is closer to the private marginal benefit than in the past.

    d. The social marginal cost is closer to the private marginal cost than it was in the past.

10. Why do some argue that immunization programs should be free to the patient but paid for out of public tax?

    a. Because immunizations are private goods.

    b. Because immunizations provide negative externalities.

    c. Because immunizations provide positive externalities.

    d. Because nationalized health care is cheaper.

11. If education provides a positive externality, then

    a. there will be too little education in a privately efficient equilibrium.

    b. there will be too much education in a privately efficient equilibrium.

    c. there will be an optimal amount of education in a privately efficient equilibrium.

    d. there will be too much education in a socially efficient equilibrium.

12. An efficient level of a public good is produced when

  a. The sum of all individual marginal benefits is equal to the sum of all individual marginal costs.

  b. The sum of all individual marginal benefits is equal to the public marginal cost.

  c. The sum of all individual marginal costs is equal to the public marginal benefit.

  d. The individual marginal benefit is equal to the individual marginal cost.

13. An idling engine is the least efficient and therefore generates the most pollution. Red lights cause engines to idle, and therefore red lights impose negative externalities.

  a. True, pollution affects all people.

  b. True, pollution only affects those who drive.

  c. False, pollution doesn't constitute an externality.

  d. False, the lights are generally not to blame for idling engines.

14. Traffic flow can be considerably disrupted if traffic lights are not used in highly congested areas. If red lights improve traffic flow and reduce congestion, then red lights provide

  a. A public bad, congestion is too great.

  b. A private good, congestion is too little.

  c. A mixed good, congestion is only reduced for a limited number of people.

  d. A public good, congestion is reduced for all drivers.

15. Given your answers to the previous two questions, what is the net effect of red lights?

  a. They provide a net public good if the positive externalities outweigh the negative externalities.

  b. They provide a net public bad if the positive externalities outweigh the negative externalities.

  c. They provide a net public bad, in both cases there are negative externalities involved.

  d. They provide a net public good, in both cases there are positive externalities involved.

Quiz Answers

Chapter 1

1. Answer d.

2. Answer b.

3. Answer a.

4. Answer c. Statements that contain the words "should," "could," or "would" tend to be normative statements.

5. Answer d. An economy facilitates each of the options.

6. Answer d. A $100 bill in itself is not a good or service used to produce another good or service. The bill might be considered financial capital, which can be used to purchase factors of production, such as a computer or an employee's time.

7. Answer d. In the United States, the government is actively involved in regulating, taxing, and manipulating many product markets. However, the factors of production are owned by private individuals, and the majority of production decisions are made by private firm owners.

8. Answer b. The profit motive is not necessary to the study of economic activity.

9. Answer a.

10. Answer c.

11. Answer b.

12. Answer c. Because the person prefers Green to Blue, $G > B$, and prefers Blue to Red, $B > R$, then it must be the case that the person prefers Green to Red, $G > R$. To see this differently, assign values to the various colors, say $G = 8$, $B = 5$, $R = 3$. It should be easy to see that $G > B$, or $8 > 5$, and $B > R$, or $5 > 3$, and therefore $G > R$ or $8 > 3$.

13. Answer b. The person who is not willing to pick up a quarter is signaling that he is satisfied up to the margin of $0.25.

14. Answer a. Even if the government produces automobiles, the government will have to operate within the construct of the market for automobiles.

15. Answer d. The individual is considered a firm because of her law practice, is considered a household because she purchases food, and is considered a government agent because she works for the local government as a councilwoman.

Chapter 2

1. Answer d.

2. Answer c.

3. Answer b. The equation $50 = 5X - 10Y$ can be rewritten as $10Y = 5X - 50$ or $Y = 1/2 X - 5$. The positive slope of $1/2$ indicates a positive relationship between X and Y.

4. Answer c. Isolate Y and divide both sides by 10.

5. Answer d.

6. Answer b.

7. Answer c. The value of Y is -6 when X is zero.

8. Answer b. Using two points on the line, say $X = 0$ and $Y = -6$, and $X = 7$ and $Y = 8$, the slope is calculated as $8 - (-6)/(7 - 0) = 14/7 = 2$.

9. Answer d.

10. Answer d. $Y = -6 + 2 \times 100 = 194$.

Chapter 3

1. Answer a.

2. Answer c. Unemployment would indicate that some inputs are not being used, and therefore, the country must not be able to produce on its production possibility frontier.

3. Answer d. It is not possible to produce outside of your production possibilities frontier, but you can trade with others according to comparative advantage in order to consume a combination of goods and services that falls outside of your production possibilities frontier.

4. Answer b. Country B's opportunity cost for a car is 20 bushels of corn, whereas Country A's opportunity cost for a car is one bushel of corn. Country B's opportunity cost for a bushel of corn is $1/20$ of a car, whereas for Country A the opportunity cost is one car for each bushel of corn. Country B has the lower opportunity cost for corn and therefore has a comparative advantage in that product.

5. Answer c. Labor is only one input to the production process. Improvements in technology might make it possible for fewer workers to produce the same amount of output as today.

6. Answer b. The slope of the PPF is the opportunity cost of the good on the horizontal axis. A steeper PPF implies a greater slope in absolute value and, therefore, a greater opportunity cost.

7. Answer a.

8. Answer c. Investment requires a sacrifice of current-day consumption goods' production possibilities.

9. Answer d. If the U.S. had to produce more of the oil it consumes, then it would have to move to another point on its PPF and therefore would likely have to produce less of one or more of other goods. The PPF itself would not change.

10. Answer a. Craig's opportunity cost for a widget is $2/3$ of a gadget, whereas Linda's opportunity cost for a widget is $1/2$ of a gadget. Linda's opportunity cost for a widget is less than Craig's, and therefore she has a comparative advantage in widgets.

11. Answer c.

12. Answer a.

13. Answer b.

14. Answer d.

15. Answer a. The price at which Gregoria and Daneland would trade would fall between the opportunity cost of oranges (in terms of clams) in the two countries. In this case, the price would fall between $8/5$ of a clam for every orange and $1/2$ of a clam for every orange.

Chapter 4

1. Answer d. A decrease in demand motivates equilibrium price and quantity to drop. A decrease in supply motivates equilibrium price to increase and equilibrium quantity to decrease. Both shifts motivate equilibrium quantity to decline, but the ambiguity lies in whether the decrease in price caused by the decrease in demand is offset by the increase in price caused by the decrease in supply.

2. Answer b.

3. Answer b.

4. Answer a.

5. Answer b. A freeze in Florida would reduce the supply of oranges and increase price.

6. Answer c. If consumers expect a Congressional ban on flip-flops to increase price in the future, then demand today will increase. On the other hand, if suppliers expect a Congressional ban to reduce the price they will receive in the future, then the supply of flip-flops today will increase.

7. Answer d. A greater population will increase demand, which motivates equilibrium price to increase and equilibrium quantity to increase. Fewer firms will decrease supply, which motivates equilibrium price to increase and equilibrium quantity to decrease. Therefore, price is guaranteed to increase, but it is uncertain whether equilibrium quantity will increase, decrease, or stay the same.

8. Answer a. A price floor keeps price from falling to its natural equilibrium level. Therefore, the quantity supplied is greater than the quantity demanded. Suppliers in a market typically support price floors to ensure a higher price received for the quantity that is sold.

9. Answer b. A price ceiling keeps price from rising to its natural equilibrium level. Therefore, the quantity demanded is greater than the quantity supplied, and consumers have to wait in lines for access to the good.

10. Answer b. The wage rate is the price of labor. Therefore, if binding, the minimum wage must be above the natural equilibrium price for minimum wage labor. This implies a price floor.

11. Answer d.

12. Answer c.

13. Answer d.

14. Answer a.

15. Answer c.

Chapter 5

1. Answer c.

2. Answer d. A one percent increase in population leads to a less than one percent increase in quantity demanded.

3. Answer d.

4. Answer c.

5. Answer b.

6. Answer c. A perfectly elastic supply curve is perfectly horizontal. Any change in demand will cause a change in equilibrium quantity but no change in equilibrium price.

7. Answer b. A perfectly inelastic demand curve is perfectly vertical. Any change in supply will cause a change in equilibrium price but no change in equilibrium quantity. The increase in supply corresponds to supply shifting to the right, which would correspond with a lower price.

8. Answer b.

9. Answer a. The elasticity can be calculated as

$$-\left(\frac{3500-4000}{250-200}\right)\left(\frac{250+200}{3500+4000}\right)=0.60$$

10. Answer b. The income elasticity can be calculated as

$$-\left(\frac{75-50}{12.50-10.00}\right)\left(\frac{12.50+10.00}{75+50}\right)=1.80$$

Chapter 6

1. Answer c. After demand increases, the equilibrium quantity and price increases. If supply doesn't change, the producer surplus will increase. Consumer surplus might increase, but this is not guaranteed.

2. Answer b. Consumer surplus will decline as price increases, and quantity decreases after supply declines.

3. Answer d. Both consumer and producer surplus increases as a good becomes more divisible.

4. Answer a. Willingness to pay is the most a consumer will pay for a product.

5. Answer b. Consumer surplus is defined as the difference between the value placed on a product and the price paid. In this case, consumer surplus equals $50 – $25 = $25.

6. Answer a. The original purchaser of the ticket is interested in maximizing her surplus. By attending the concert, she will receive $25 in surplus. If she can sell the ticket and receive more surplus, she will do so. If she can sell the ticket for $51, she would have $26 in surplus, which is more than if she attends the concert.

7. Answer c. The baseball fan wants to maximize her consumer surplus from attending the game. Package *a* yields negative surplus, Package *b* yields $50 in surplus, Package *c* yields $100 in surplus, and Package *d* yields negative surplus. Because Package *c* yields the greatest surplus, it is the most likely to be chosen.

8. Answer c. Producer surplus is the difference between price and the amount required to produce the product. In this case, producer surplus is $45.95 – $25.00 = $20.95.

9. Answer a. A price floor sets price above the equilibrium price and therefore reduces the quantity demanded. The consumer surplus with a price floor is lower than that which would occur without the price floor.

10. Answer e. The price increase could have occurred because demand increased with no change in supply, in which case consumer surplus would likely increase. On the other hand, the price increase could have occurred because supply declined, in which case producer surplus would likely decline.

11. Answer b.

12. Answer c.

13. Answer c. The tax revenue is calculated as ($6.4 – $2.4) × 27.5 × 1000 = $110,000.

14. Answer d. The dead weight loss is calculated as ½($6.4 – $2.4) × 10 × 1000 = $20,000.

15. Answer b. The consumer surplus is calculated as ½($10 – $6.4) × 27.5 × 1000 = $49,500.

Chapter 7

1. Answer b.

2. Answer b.

3. Answer c. Real income is defined as nominal income divided by the price of a good. Holding income constant, if the price of gasoline increases, then the household's real income must decline.

4. Answer d.

5. Answer c. The household's budget constraint will become steeper and the optimal mix of the two goods will likely entail purchasing more of Good Y, which is now cheaper, and less of Good X, which is now more expensive.

6. Answer d. Person A has set his marginal rate of substitution equal to the price ratio and is therefore maximizing utility. Person B, however, should consume more of Good X and less of Good Y to reduce his marginal rate of substitution from 8 to 4, which is the relative price of Good X to Good Y.

7. Answer a. As all prices increase, the income constraint will shift to the left, thereby reducing the combinations of goods that are affordable.

8. Answer b.

9. Answer a. Kevin's utility would be $(5 \times 4) + (10 \times 6) + 0.5(4 + 10) = 20 + 60 + 7 = 87$.

10. Answer d. The relative price of widgets to gadgets is determined as $5 per widget divided by $10 per gadget, or half of a widget for every gadget or one widget costs two gadgets.

Chapter 8

1. Answer c. Firm's hire inputs where the marginal rate of transformation is equal to the relative input price, that is, the slope of the isocost and the isoquant are equal.

2. Answer b.

3. Answer b. If an input price declines, for a given cost the firm can purchase more inputs and therefore produce more output.

4. Answer e. Average costs are affected by technology and factor prices but are not connected to consumer preferences.

5. Answer c.

6. Answer b.

7. Answer c.

8. Answer c. As the price of one or more factors of production increases, the marginal cost curve shifts up, and the profit maximizing output declines. This is true for all firms that hire the input whose price has increased, and therefore the supply of the product shifts left.

9. Answer d.

10. Answer b. Firm A should increase it's usage of capital and reduce its usage of labor, reducing the marginal rate of technical substitution from 8 to 0.5, the relative price of capital to labor. Firm B should actually hire less capital and more labor to increase its marginal rate of technical substitution from 0.25 to 0.50.

11. Answer b.

12. Answer a.

13. Answer e.

14. Answer c.

15. Answer e.

Chapter 9

1. Answer b. If the firm can cover average variable cost, the firm is better off producing, paying its variable cost, and dedicating the remainder to its fixed cost. If the firm cannot cover average variable cost, then it is better to shut down and simply lose the fixed cost.

2. Answer c. In this case, marginal revenue is greater than marginal cost, and the firm should increase output.

3. Answer c. Both marginal costs and average costs are influenced by factor prices.

4. Answer e. Profit can be calculated as $(P - ATC) \times q$.

5. Answer a. Positive profits will encourage entry, an increase in supply, and a decrease in price.

6. Answer b. All competitive firms charge the same market price.

7. Answer c. Perfectly competitive firms cannot unilaterally alter price.

8. Answer b. A corporation fee would affect fixed costs but not marginal costs. Only marginal costs and marginal revenues affect the profit maximizing quantity.

9. Answer c. A corporation fee would increase total cost and, *ceteris paribus*, would reduce profits.

10. Answer b. As prices fall, consumers can afford to purchase more, and they enjoy greater consumer surplus. However, the profitability of the firms in the market will decline, making firms worse off.

11. Answer a.

12. Answer b.

13. Answer c.

14. Answer a.

15. Answer d.

Chapter 10

1. Answer d.

2. Answer c.

3. Answer d. Monopolists are not guaranteed positive profits in the long run.

4. Answer d. Marginal revenue is less than price.

5. Answer b. Positive profits will encourage entry and decrease the demand for all firms already in the industry.

6. Answer d.

7. Answer b.

8. Answer d.

9. Answer c. Price is determined after the monopolist chooses its profit maximizing quantity, which is determined by the interaction of marginal revenue (derived from demand) and marginal cost (derived from technology and factor prices).

10. Answer a.

11. Answer c.

12. Answer c.

13. Answer e.

14. Answer c.

15. Answer a.

Chapter 11

1. Answer b. Residual or excess demand is the difference between the quantity demanded and the quantity supplied by the other firms in the market.

2. Answer c.

3. Answer c. Relative to perfect competition, monopolistic competition does produce less and charge a higher price.

4. Answer c. Price is greater than average cost. P = $3.00, ATC = $3.50, and marginal cost is same as marginal revenue.

5. Answer a. Negative profits will encourage exit and increase the demand for all firms that remain in the industry.

6. Answer a.

7. Answer a. Negative profits will promote free exit and the resultant reduction in product selection will increase the demand facing all remaining firms.

8. Answer d. Both types of firms have some market power.

9. Answer d. The firm's demand will be inelastic below the current price.

10. Answer b. Oligopolies are characterized by few firms producing very similar products; strategic interaction is the key difference in these models.

11. Answer b.

12. Answer d.

13. Answer c.

14. Answer b.

15. Answer d.

Chapter 12

1. Answer c. The worker's marginal revenue product is $90 - 80 = 10$ units $\times$ $20 per unit = $200 per day. The worker could not expect to be paid more than this.

2. Answer d. If there is a large supply of teachers, the equilibrium wage for teachers will be low even while those who demand teachers, that is, parents, claim to value the teachers highly.

3. Answer b. Land is cheaper at the edge of town because it is not as productive, before it is developed, as the land in the city center. The lower price and plentiful land at the edges of town motivates development to the suburbs.

4. Answer c. The doctors and lawyers are substituting out of labor and into leisure.

5. Answer d. The minimum wage is the price for lower-skilled workers. Therefore, an increase in price will only affect the quantity demanded for this type of labor.

6. Answer c. The minimum wage is the price for lower-skilled workers. Therefore, an increase in price will only affect the quantity supplied of this type of labor.

7. Answer b. Because at each increase in tax on capital gains, the net return is lower, households will find alternative uses for their capital, perhaps in international markets or in purchasing other assets such as land, where they will not be taxed as much.

8. Answer d. Because the individual works more after wages increased, the person substitutes away from leisure and into labor.

9. Answer d. Labor productivity is the major source of increased wages in the United States.

10. Answer c. Households will relocate their capital from Industry B to Industry A, increasing the supply of capital in Industry A and reducing interest rates in that market, and decreasing the supply of capital in Industry B and increasing interest rates in that market.

11. Answer c.

12. Answer b.

13. Answer b.

14. Answer b.

15. Answer c.

Chapter 13

1. Answer b. National defense is neither excludable nor rivalrous.

2. Answer a. Externalities can be positive or negative.

3. Answer c. A radio broadcast is excludable but not rivalrous.

4. Answer b. The subsidy will increase the benefit of voluntary unemployment.

5. Answer b. If the citizens of a city do not value recycling at least at the cost of the program, recycling will not be implemented.

6. Answer c. A privately built stadium will not necessarily consider the positive externalities generated by the stadium and will therefore be smaller than a publicly built stadium.

7. Answer b. Fireworks displays are neither rivalrous nor excludable.

8. Answer d. Completely eliminating the externality generating activity is rarely efficient.

9. Answer c. The benefits of education may be more internal and less external than in the past, which would justify reducing the public subsidy to higher education.

10. Answer c. Immunizations reduce the transmission of diseases and provide positive externalities.

11. Answer a.

12. Answer b.

13. Answer a.

14. Answer c.

15. Answer a.

Final Exam

1. The increase in crude oil prices after the U.S. invasion of Iraq in 2003 was likely due to

   a. legal considerations with the United Nations.

   b. the fear that demand might decline.

   c. the fear that supply might decline.

   d. the fear that supply had increased.

2. Externalities involve

   a. a third party who receives benefits or costs but wasn't involved in the original transaction.

   b. natural selection.

   c. fingers and toes.

   d. the cost of land rent.

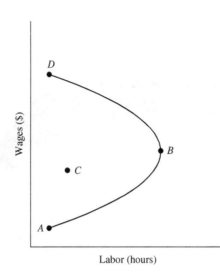

Figure B-1   Household labor supply.

Use Figure B-1 for the next two questions:

3. At which point(s) is the reservation wage?

    a. *A*

    b. *B*

    c. *C*

    d. *D*

4. At which point(s) is the substitution effect equal to the income effect?

    a. *A*

    b. *B*

    c. *C*

    d. *D*

5. Diminishing marginal utility

    a. does not fully explain upward sloping supply curves.

    b. fully explains upward sloping supply curves.

    c. does not exist; the theory was disproven in the 1970s.

    d. does not fully explain downward sloping demand curves.

6. The marginal rate of substitution is defined as

   a. the change in utility gained after losing a unit of a good.

   b. the amount of a good needed to maintain a given level of utility when a unit of another good is taken away.

   c. the amount of a good needed to obtain a higher level of utility when a unit of another good is taken away.

   d. the amount of a substitute good consumed with complementary goods.

Use Figure B-2 for the next three questions:

7. Figure B-2 illustrates a(n)

   a. inefficient competitive market.

   b. positive externality.

   c. grounds for direct government intervention.

   d. all of the above.

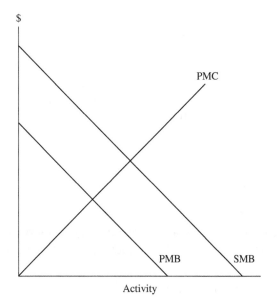

Figure B-2

8. In Figure B-2, the market has an efficient private equilibrium.

   a. True

   b. False

   c. Don't know

9. In Figure B-2, the market has an efficient social equilibrium

   a. only if the correct tax is used.

   b. only if the correct subsidy is used.

   c. only if there is a free rider problem.

   d. none of the above.

10. Pure public goods often suffer from the

   a. free rider problem.

   b. overbearing demands of the consumer.

   c. competition of private firms.

   d. competition of oligopolistic firms.

11. A radio station would be providing a

   a. pure public good.

   b. pure private good.

   c. mixed public good.

   d. monopolistic good.

12. The benefit or satisfaction that a person receives from the consumption of goods and services is called

   a. marginal utility.

   b. utility.

   c. consumer demand.

   d. consumer equilibrium.

13. Suppose we observe a decrease in the quantity of Sport Utility Vehicles (SUVs) sold in the United States. Which of the following is a possible cause?

   a. A decrease in the price of gasoline

   b. A decrease in the insurance premiums on SUVs

   c. An increase in the price of steel

   d. An increase in the price of minivans

14. The change in total revenue resulting from employing an additional unit of labor is the

    a. marginal product of labor.

    b. marginal revenue of labor.

    c. marginal revenue cost of labor.

    d. marginal revenue product (MRP) of labor.

15. The typical way in which unions and professional associations increase wages is by

    a. increasing the marginal (physical) product of labor.

    b. increasing the MRP of labor.

    c. increasing the demand for labor.

    d. decreasing the supply for labor.

16. "Banks should lower the interest rate," is an example of what kind of statement?

    a. Normative

    b. Positive

    c. Normal

    d. Kind

17. Economists are typically more worried about

    a. normative statements.

    b. money.

    c. positive statements.

    d. trying to find a good job.

18. Firms might move to another country if

    a. they are unpatriotic.

    b. they don't care about their workers.

    c. the MRP of labor is less than the minimum wage.

    d. the Marginal Product of labor is less than the minimum wage.

19. Ronald Coase suggested _____ would correct for negative externalities.

    a. having a big round-table discussion

    b. asking nicely

    c. properly defining property rights

    d. coercing courts to hand down large damages

20. Increasing returns to scale occur when

    a. cost per unit of output increases as production decreases.

    b. cost per unit of output decreases as production increases.

    c. cost per unit of output does not change as production increases.

    d. none of the above.

21. The Postal Service is an example of

    a. a competitive firm.

    b. a natural monopoly.

    c. a legal monopoly.

    d. a public good.

22. Baseball teams shut down in the winter because

    a. they cannot cover their average variable costs.

    b. they cannot cover their average total costs.

    c. they are mean and do not want to give the people what they want.

    d. it is too cold to play baseball.

    e. they cannot cover their average fixed costs.

23. If Cynthia has a price elasticity of –3.2 and Dennis has a price elasticity of –1.8, which person would be charged a higher price in third degree price discrimination?

    a. Cynthia

    b. Dennis

    c. Both Cynthia and Dennis

    d. Neither Cynthia nor Dennis

24. If an increase in price causes a decrease in total revenue, then demand is

    a. unitary elastic.

    b. constant returns to scale.

    c. relatively elastic.

    d. relatively inelastic.

25. An equilibrium is defined as

    a. a position that once obtained cannot be maintained.

    b. a position that once obtained tends to be maintained.

   c. a position that is better than an optimum.

   d. a waste of time because we never see an equilibrium.

26. The United States is best characterized as a

   a. mixed economy.

   b. command economy.

   c. barter economy.

   d. monopoly economy.

27. Scarcity in production can be displayed through all of the following, except

   a. the supply curve.

   b. the production possibilities frontier (PPF).

   c. the firm's demand schedule.

   d. none of the above.

28. Trade, coupled with comparative advantage, allows a country to

   a. produce outside its PPF.

   b. produce within its PPF.

   c. not worry about its PPF.

   d. consume outside its PPF.

29. Paying less for an airline ticket by purchasing one month in advance, is an example of

   a. first degree price discrimination.

   b. second degree price discrimination.

   c. third degree price discrimination.

   d. price gouging.

30. If Congress debates a gun-control legislation that is aired on television, what would one expect to see happening?

   a. An increase in the demand and an increase in the supply of debated guns

   b. An increase in the demand and a decrease in the supply of debated guns

   c. A decrease in the demand and an increase in the supply of debated guns

   d. A decrease in the demand and an decrease in the supply of debated guns

   e. None of the above

31. The more divisible a good becomes, the supply and demand model yields
    a. more Consumer Surplus.
    b. more Producer Surplus.
    c. less Consumer Surplus.
    d. less Producer Surplus.
    e. more Consumer Surplus and Producer Surplus.

32. If Good X is preferred to Good Y and Good Y is preferred to Good Z, then it must be true that
    a. Good A is preferred to Good X.
    b. Good X is preferred to Good Z.
    c. Good Y is preferred to Good X.
    d. Consumers do not care about Good X in relation to Good Z.
    e. None of the above

33. The difference between fixed costs and variable costs is that
    a. fixed costs vary with quantity produced.
    b. there is no difference; they are exactly the same.
    c. variable costs depend upon the quantity produced.
    d. variable costs are included in profit maximization while fixed costs are not.
    e. none of the above

34. A firm's cost constraint can shift outward due to which of the following:
    a. An increase in the price of any factor of production
    b. A decrease in the price of any factor of production
    c. An increase in the marginal productivity of labor
    d. A decrease in the total cost the firm is willing to spend
    e. None of the above

35. The Average Total Cost curve can shift due to all of the following, except
    a. improvements in technology.
    b. shifts in the product's supply curve.
    c. shifts in the supply curve of a factor of production.
    d. shifts in the preference structure of the households.
    e. Both (b) and (d)

36. The long-run equilibrium in a monopolistic market is characterized by

    a. a positive profit, guaranteed.

    b. a negative profit, guaranteed.

    c. a zero profit, guaranteed.

    d. a positive or zero profit.

    e. guaranteed positive dead weight loss.

37. A per-unit tax is guaranteed to

    a. increase producer prices.

    b. cause an increase in producer surplus.

    c. cause an increase in total welfare.

    d. impose a dead weight loss in the market.

38. A monopolist is different from a competitive firm in that

    a. the competitive firm always has marginal revenue greater than price.

    b. the monopolistic firm always has marginal revenue greater than price.

    c. the monopolistic firm always has a lower quantity than a competitive firm.

    d. the monopolistic firm always has marginal revenue less than price.

    e. the competitive firm always has marginal revenue less than price.

Use Figure B-3 for the next three questions:

39. Which point indicates firm's equilibrium?

    a. *A*

    b. *B*

    c. *C*

    d. *D*

40. Which point is not affordable to the firm?

    a. *A*

    b. *B*

    c. *C*

    d. *D*

    e. None of the above

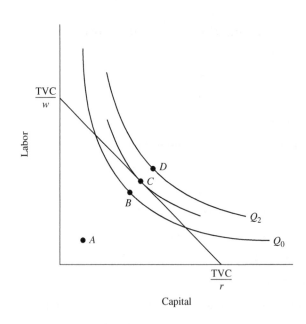

$\dfrac{\text{TVC}}{w}$

Labor

D

C

B

A

Q_2

Q_0

$\dfrac{\text{TVC}}{r}$

Capital

Figure B-3 A monopolistically competitive firm.

41. At the point of equilibrium for the firm, which of the following is true?

 a. The amount of capital and labor hired is necessarily the same.

 b. The price of capital and labor are the same.

 c. The slope of the isocost is equal to the slope of the isoquant curve.

 d. The slope of the isocost is less than the slope of the isoquant curve.

42. The price of DVDs falls from an average of $22 to $16. As a result, sales increase from 50,000 units per year to 85,000 units. Calculate the price elasticity (of demand).

 a. −3.25

 b. −1.64

 c. −1.00

 d. −2.43

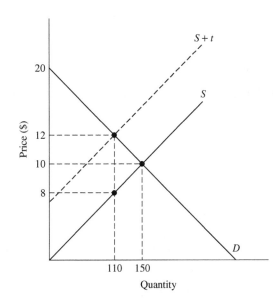

Figure B-4   A market with a per unit sales tax.

Use Figure B-4 for the next four questions:

43. In the market depicted in Figure B-4, what is the per-unit sales tax?

    a. $4.00

    b. $2.00

    c. $2.50

    d. Impossible to tell

44. In the market depicted in Figure B-4, what is the tax revenue generated?

    a. $800

    b. $4000

    c. $345

    d. $440

45. In the market depicted in Figure B-4, what is the consumer surplus after the tax?

    a. $880

    b. $1200

   c. $100

   d. $440

   e. None of the above

46. In the market depicted in Figure B-4, what is the dead weight loss caused by the tax?

   a. $160

   b. $80

   c. $40

   d. $400

   e. None of the above

47. Total cost curves indicate

   a. all costs incurred by any firm.

   b. all costs incurred by a typical firm.

   c. all costs incurred by a single firm working at efficiency.

   d. all costs incurred by a single firm regardless of efficiency.

48. If Bill mows the grass for a neighbor and is paid at an hourly rate, this is

   a. a market activity.

   b. a nonmarket activity.

   c. considered part of household leisure time.

   d. the income effect.

   e. none of the above.

49. The supply curve for the monopolist

   a. is upward sloping.

   b. is downward sloping.

   c. is perfectly horizontal.

   d. none of the above.

50. Which of the following is a characteristic of monopolistic competition?

   a. One buyer and many firms

   b. Several sellers with differentiated products

   c. Barriers to entry do exist

   d. They are always harmful to consumers

51. Normative statements

    a. concern the average American citizen.

    b. are true statements.

    c. are statements of what should be.

    d. are those used least often by the general populace.

52. Economics is the study of

    a. how to allocate scarce resources to unlimited wants.

    b. how to read the Wall Street Journal.

    c. how to allocate unlimited resources to limited wants.

    d. the back of my eyelids.

53. If Courtney can produce 3 widgets for every 2 gadgets, and Tino can produce 8 widgets for every 7 gadgets, then Tino has a comparative advantage in widgets.

    a. True

    b. False

    c. Can't tell with the information at hand

54. If demand decreases and supply decreases, then in the short-run

    a. both equilibrium price and quantity increase.

    b. both equilibrium price and quantity decrease.

    c. equilibrium price increases and equilibrium quantity decreases.

    d. equilibrium quantity decreases and equilibrium price can either increase or decrease.

    e. the equilibrium price and quantity will not change.

Use Figure B-5 for the next six questions:

55. Which point indicates monopoly quantity?

    a. *O*

    b. *A*

    c. *G*

    d. *B*

    e. None of the above

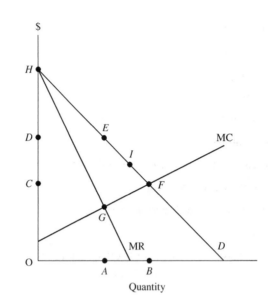

Figure B-5   Monopolistic market structure.

56. Which point indicates price if the market was perfectly competitive?

   a. H

   b. D

   c. C

   d. O

   e. None of the above

57. Which area represents dead weight loss due to the monopoly?

   a. Area *DCEF*

   b. Area *EFG*

   c. Area *ABGF*

   d. Area *HGE*

   e. None of the above

58. Which area represents the consumer surplus under monopoly?

   a. Area *HDE*

   b. Area *AED*

   c. Area *EFG*

   d. None of the above

59. At which point is the demand curve unitary elastic?

    a. *H*

    b. *E*

    c. *I*

    d. *F*

    e. None of the above

60. Is this monopoly a 'good' or 'bad' monopoly?

    a. Good

    b. Bad

    c. Both

    d. Cannot tell with the information at hand

61. If supply decreases and a downward sloping demand curve stays constant, what happens to consumer surplus?

    a. It increases.

    b. It decreases.

    c. It does not change.

    d. None of the above.

62. Typically a monopoly will have an equilibrium in which

    a. price and quantity are higher than competition would obtain.

    b. price and quantity are lower than competition would obtain.

    c. price is higher and quantity is lower than competition would obtain.

    d. quantity is higher and price is lower than competition would obtain.

63. People often speed because

    a. the marginal cost of getting caught is low.

    b. the overall cost of getting caught is low.

    c. the opportunity cost of getting caught is low.

    d. the opportunity cost of not speeding is considered high.

64. If the income elasticity of demand for a good is –0.04, then the response of demand to a change in income is

    a. perfectly elastic.

    b. perfectly inelastic.

c. relatively inelastic.

    d. unitary elastic.

65. If the cross price elasticity of demand for a good is 3.16, then the goods are

    a. relatively inelastic complements.

    b. relatively elastic substitutes.

    c. perfectly elastic substitutes.

    d. perfectly inelastic complements.

66. If Mr. Beatty can increase production of Good X without decreasing the production of any other good, then Mr. Beatty

    a. is producing on his production possibility frontier.

    b. is producing outside his production possibility frontier.

    c. is producing inside his production possibility frontier.

    d. must prefer Good X to any other good.

67. If Christian can use his resources to produce either Good A or Good B, then Good A and Good B are

    a. substitutes in production.

    b. complements in production.

    c. substitutes in consumption.

    d. complements in consumption.

68. Suppose we observe an increase in the number of oranges sold. Which of the following is *not* a possible cause?

    a. An increase in the price of apples

    b. A freeze in Florida

    c. A report that says that oranges cure the common cold

    d. An increase in the price of furniture made from orange trees

69. The demand for an input is

    a. dictated by national standards.

    b. is constrained by certification processes.

    c. identical to the value of marginal product for the factor.

    d. identical to the marginal product for the factor.

70. Online retailers often charge lower prices than brick-and-mortar retailers. Which of the following is the most likely reason?

    a. Online retailers have lower marginal costs.

    b. Online retailers have greater demand.

    c. Brick-and-mortar retailers have higher fixed costs.

    d. Brick-and-mortar retailers have lower demand.

71. The long-run effect of an increase in market demand in a perfectly competitive industry is

    a. the exit of sellers and an increase in price.

    b. the entry of new sellers and an increase in price.

    c. the entry of new sellers and economic profits revert to zero.

    d. the exit of sellers and an increase in economic profits.

72. The major problem with people who run red lights is?

    a. They only pay when they are caught.

    b. They impose positive externalities on other drivers.

    c. They impose negative externalities on other drivers.

    d. They negate the use of stop signs.

73. In a Cournot duopoly, the total quantity produced is

    a. greater than in monopoly, less than in competition.

    b. greater than in competition, less than in monopoly.

    c. greater than in monopolistic competition.

    d. more than in perfect competition.

74. In perfect price discrimination, the dead weight loss is

    a. maximized.

    b. nonexistent.

    c. less than in perfect competition.

    d. infinite.

75. A magazine subscription is an example of

    a. first degree price discrimination.

    b. second degree price discrimination.

    c. third degree price discrimination.

    d. price gouging.

76. In a market with a dominant firm,

    a. price is greater than in monopoly.

    b. quantity is greater than in competition.

    c. price is greater than in Cournot duopoly.

    d. price is less than monopoly but greater than competition.

77. Assume the corn industry is perfectly competitive. If a bushel of corn sells for $6 and the cost of a bushel of corn is $3.50, corn farmers should

    a. not grow any more corn.

    b. grow more corn.

    c. maybe grow more corn, depending on the marginal revenue.

    d. maybe grow more corn, depending on the marginal cost.

78. Production is

    a. necessary.

    b. the process of converting factors of production into goods and services.

    c. three-fifths energy and two-fifths brain power.

    d. the process of converting goods and services into factors of production.

79. Individuals trade because of

    a. different opportunity costs.

    b. the law says that they have to.

    c. it is the only way to get something.

    d. they want to be nice to each other.

    e. none of the above.

80. Diminishing returns claim that

    a. the more the effort spent on one process, the greater the change in returns.

    b. the more the effort spent on one process, the lesser the change in returns.

    c. the lesser the effort spent on one process, the lesser the change in returns.

    d. none of the above.

81. Growth in an economy

    a. is easy, just pass a few laws and economic growth occurs.

    b. requires the sacrifice of current day consumption.

c. requires the sacrifice of future consumption.

d. has not occurred in the last 50 years.

82. An economy facilitates which of the following?

    a. What is produced

    b. How much is produced

    c. Who will get what

    d. All of the above

    e. None of the above

83. Preference and local nonsatiation imply that agents produce

    a. within their PPF.

    b. outside their PPF.

    c. on their PPF.

    d. regardless of their production possibilities frontier.

84. Economic profit

    a. equals $TR - TC - OC$.

    b. is profit reported to share-holders.

    c. is approximated by nominal profit regardless of efficiency.

    d. none of the above.

85. If price is equal to the average cost of production, then the firm's nominal profits will

    a. be greater than zero.

    b. be less than zero.

    c. be equal to zero.

    d. not enough information to answer the question.

Use Figure B-6 for the next four questions:

86. Which point(s) indicate profit maximization?

    a. *A*

    b. *B*

    c. *C* and *D*

    d. *D*

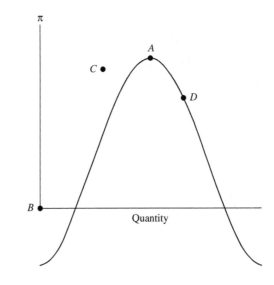

Figure B-6 Profit curve.

87. Which point(s) indicate technological and allocative efficiency?

    a. *A* and *B*

    b. *B* and *C*

    c. *A* and *D*

    d. *D* and *B*

    e. None of the above

88. Is the above firm making a positive, zero or negative profit?

    a. Positive

    b. Negative

    c. Zero

    d. Not enough information to answer the question

89. If the firm in the graph is perfectly competitive, it can expect to see

    a. its profits decline in the future, but its price will increase.

    b. its profits decline in the future, and its price will decrease.

    c. its profit not change in the future, although it will have to raise its price.

    d. its profit drop in the future, although it will have to raise its price.

    e. none of the above.

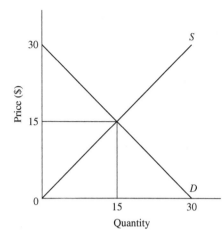

Figure B-7   A demand-supply graph.

90. In Figure B-7, if the good is infinitely divisible, then the total consumer surplus is

    a. $12.

    b. $112.50.

    c. $250.

    d. $350.

91. In Figure B-7, if the good is infinitely divisible, then the total producer surplus is

    a. 300.

    b. 250.

    c. 120.

    d. 112.50.

92. If the population becomes wealthier and the number of firms increases what would happen to the equilibrium price and quantity in or competitive market?

    a. Quantity increases and price decreases

    b. Price increases and quantity change is ambiguous

    c. Price decreases and quantity change is ambiguous

    d. Quantity increases and price change is ambiguous

    e. None of the above

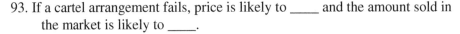

93. If a cartel arrangement fails, price is likely to _____ and the amount sold in the market is likely to _____.

    a. rise; increase

    b. not change; decrease

    c. fall; increase

    d. fall; decrease

94. Price floors are typically favored by

    a. producers.

    b. consumers.

    c. the government.

    d. none of the above.

95. Price ceilings are typically favored by

    a. producers.

    b. consumers.

    c. the government.

    d. none of the above.

96. Which of the following is not a result of a binding price floor?

    a. Excess supply

    b. Long lines for consumers

    c. The cost of removing excess supply

    d. Some consumers are priced out of the market

    e. The cost of shifting resources away from their comparative advantage

97. Through which method do markets most often equilibrate?

    a. Threats of sanction

    b. Debate in price

    c. Government legislation

    d. A method that is totally unknown and open to future research

98. Firms wish to maximize profits. They do so by producing where

    a. total revenue equals total costs.

    b. marginal revenue equals marginal costs.

    c. marginal revenue is greater than marginal cost.

    d. marginal revenue is less than marginal cost.

    e. total revenue is greater than total cost.

99. The value of studying the model of perfect competition is that

    a. it is the most common market structure in the United States.

    b. it provides a framework for comparison with other market structures.

    c. the main goal of purely competitive firms is profit maximization.

    d. all of the above.

100. If a perfectly competitive firm realizes negative economic profits, it can expect to see its profit maximizing quantity

    a. rise.

    b. fall.

    c. stay the same.

    d. not enough information to answer the question.

101. Which of the following is *not* a characteristic of perfect competition?

    a. Freedom of entry and exit in the industry

    b. Perfect information on the part of all agents

    c. Differentiated products

    d. Short-run profits can be positive, negative, or zero

102. The demand curve facing a monopolist is

    a. horizontal as in a competitive market.

    b. vertical since demand is perfectly inelastic.

    c. downward sloping as it faces the market demand.

    d. none of the above.

103. The price elasticity of demand for a competitive firm is

    a. equal to infinity.

    b. greater than the price elasticity of demand for the market.

    c. the same for all of the other firms in the market.

    d. all of the above.

104. Price in a monopoly is determined by

    a. supply only.

    b. the monopolist, unilaterally.

c. demand, technology, and factor prices.

d. the government.

e. technology only.

105. Normal profits are defined as

    a. the average profits in an industry.

    b. the most profit a firm can make, determined by law.

    c. a normative level of profit that no one can guess.

    d. the profit level required to keep the owners of a firm "interested."

    e. none of the above.

106. Scarcity necessitates

    a. utility.

    b. efficiency.

    c. inefficiency.

    d. choice.

    e. government regulation.

107. Allocative efficiency implies

    a. that the firm is producing a given output at the lowest possible cost.

    b. that the firm is producing as much as it wants with given input levels.

    c. that the household is always filling the dishwasher before starting it.

    d. that the firm is producing as much as possible with given inputs.

    e. none of the above.

108. $3 + 3 = 7$. This is a _____ expression.

    a. normative

    b. positive

    c. normal

    d. casual

109. The supply of capital in young industries tends to be

    a. about as much as in older industries.

    b. much more and offers the same return as in old industries.

    c. much less and offers a lower return than in old industries.

    d. much less and offers a higher return as in old industries.

110. Consumer surplus measures

    a. extra cans of dry goods on household shelves.

    b. value above and beyond that paid by suppliers.

    c. value received by consumers above and beyond that paid for goods.

    d. none of the above.

111. A fireworks display is an example of a

    a. pure public good.

    b. pure private good.

    c. mixed public good.

    d. monopolistic good.

Use the following information for the next three questions:

Price	Quantity	Total Cost
20	50	100

112. The overall profit level of this firm is

    a. 300.

    b. 900.

    c. 90.

    d. −1000.

    e. Not enough information to answer the question.

113. If the above firm is a monopoly, what would you expect to see happen to price?

    a. It would increase.

    b. It would decrease.

    c. It would not change.

    d. Not enough information.

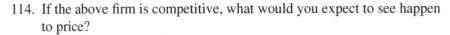
114. If the above firm is competitive, what would you expect to see happen to price?

    a. It would increase.

    b. It would decrease.

    c. It would not change.

    d. Not enough information.

115. College students often skip class because

    a. they view the explicit cost of class as too high.

    b. they view the opportunity cost of attending class as high.

    c. they view the dollar cost of class as too high.

    d. they view the opportunity cost of attending class as low.

116. Product differentiation is an attempt by firms to

    a. make their demand curves more elastic.

    b. avoid government regulation.

    c. to strengthen their residual demand.

    d. to take advantage of the unsuspecting consumer.

    e. none of the above.

117. A market

    a. is a mechanism that allows agents to allocate scarce resources.

    b. can have households, firms, or governments.

    c. can have an equilibrium that is not an optimum.

    d. requires both suppliers and demanders.

    e. all of the above.

118. A teacher being paid $35,000 and a professional athlete being paid $3.5 million is consistent with

    a. the degradation of Western culture.

    b. the continuing in-your-face attitude that society has towards teachers.

    c. teachers having a lower MRP than athletes.

    d. teachers having a lower marginal product than athletes.

    e. teachers having a higher marginal product than athletes.

119. The relationship between price and marginal cost is?

     a. Marginal cost is the highest that the price can be.

     b. Marginal cost is the highest that the demand can be.

     c. Marginal revenue is lower than marginal price.

     d. Marginal cost is the lowest that the price can be.

120. Which of the following is *not* a factor of production?

     a. Garden tractors

     b. The Mississippi River

     c. Economics professors

     d. A $100 bill

121. Land in Dallas is more expensive than land in West Texas because

     a. the demand for land in Dallas is greater.

     b. the supply of land is less in Dallas.

     c. the value of marginal product of land in Dallas is greater.

     d. all of the above.

122. If a firm has a production function of $Q = 2 \times K \times L$, and hires 10 machines and 20 workers, how much output will the firm produce if it is efficient?

     a. 200

     b. 2000

     c. 400

     d. 4000

123. If the firm's management decides to replace workers with machines, it is likely that

     a. machines are relatively more expensive than workers.

     b. machines are more productive than workers.

     c. workers are relatively more expensive than machines.

     d. the government decreased the Social Security Tax.

124. If a price decrease causes the quantity demanded to drop, then

     a. the substitution effect dominates the income effect.

     b. the substitution effect equals the income effect.

     c. the substitution effect does not exist.

d. the income effect dominates the substitution effect.

e. none of the above.

Use Figure B-8 for the next three questions:

125. Of the prices listed on the vertical axis, which is most likely to be a price ceiling?

    a. 5

    b. 10

    c. 15

    d. 12

    e. None of the above

126. If the most likely price ceiling is implemented, there is

    a. a shortage of 60 units.

    b. a surplus of 60 units.

    c. a shortage of 30 units.

    d. a surplus of 50 units.

    e. none of the above.

127. Of the prices listed on the vertical axis, if the most likely price floor is imposed, what is consumer surplus?

    a. $250

    b. $400

    c. $125

    d. $1000

    e. None of the above

128. A professional athlete might choose not to sign a $10 million contract if

    a. his MRP is greater than $10 million.

    b. his MRP is less than $10 million.

    c. his reservation wage is less than $10 million.

    d. his reservation wage is greater than $10 million.

    e. there is no evidence that this has ever happened.

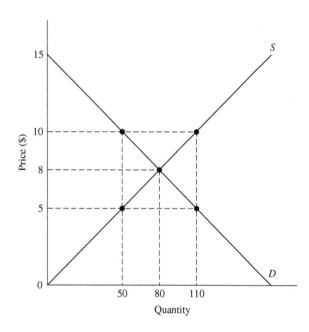

Figure B-8 A demand-supply graph.

129. The household's supply for labor is backward bending when

    a. the substitution effect outweighs the income effect.

    b. the income effect outweighs the substitution effect.

    c. the income effect equals the substitution effect.

    d. the household is lazy.

    e. the household has a limited education.

130. If a monopoly exhibits increasing returns to scale at large quantities, it might

    a. price lower and produce more than competition.

    b. price lower and produce less than competition.

    c. price higher and produce less than competition.

    d. price higher and produce more than competition.

131. One reason firms hire labor is because

    a. firms desire to be nice.

    b. labor has a comparative advantage in many things.

    c. firms are forced by laws to hire labor.

    d. labor ought to be hired.

132. Firms engaged in monopolistic competition

    a. have positive long-run profit, guaranteed.

    b. have zero long-run profits.

    c. have negative long-run profits, guaranteed.

    d. face market-level demand curves.

    e. none of the above.

133. The study of economics would become irrelevant if

    a. there was no scarcity.

    b. the government gave everyone $100,000 when they were born.

    c. the choices of individuals were reduced in number.

    d. there was world peace.

134. Dead weight loss is a measure of

    a. inefficiency in the market.

    b. efficiency in the market.

    c. why government is necessary to intervene in markets.

    d. why firms pose positive externalities on other agents.

    e. all of the above.

135. Why would sports leagues limit entry into cities where they already have a franchise?

    a. Entry makes demand more elastic, resulting in higher prices and lower profits.

    b. Entry makes demand less elastic, resulting in lower prices and lower profits.

    c. Entry makes demand less elastic, resulting in higher prices and lower profits.

    d. Entry makes demand more elastic, resulting in lower prices and lower profits.

Final Exam Answers

1. Answer c. Chapter 4.
2. Answer a. Chapter 13.
3. Answer a. Chapter 12.
4. Answer b. Chapter 12.
5. Answer d. Chapter 7.
6. Answer b. Chapter 7.
7. Answer d. Chapter 13.
8. Answer b. Chapter 13.
9. Answer b. Chapter 13.
10. Answer a. Chapter 13.
11. Answer c. Chapter 13.
12. Answer b. Chapter 7.
13. Answer c. Chapter 4.
14. Answer d. Chapter 12.
15. Answer d. Chapter 12.
16. Answer a. Chapter 1.
17. Answer c. Chapter 1.
18. Answer c. Chapters 12 and 8.
19. Answer c. Chapter 8.
20. Answer b. Chapter 8.
21. Answer c. Chapter 10.
22. Answer a. Chapter 9.
23. Answer b. Chapter 10.
24. Answer c. Chapter 5.
25. Answer b. Chapter 4.
26. Answer a. Chapter 1.
27. Answer c. Chapter 4.
28. Answer d. Chapter 2.
29. Answer c. Chapter 10.
30. Answer a. Chapter 4.
31. Answer e. Chapter 6.
32. Answer b. Chapter 7.
33. Answer c. Chapter 8.
34. Answer b. Chapter 8.
35. Answer e. Chapter 8.
36. Answer d. Chapter 10.
37. Answer d. Chapter 6.
38. Answer d. Chapter 10.
39. Answer c. Chapter 8.
40. Answer d. Chapter 8.
41. Answer c. Chapter 8.
42. Answer b. Chapter 5.
43. Answer a. Chapter 4.
44. Answer d. Chapters 4 and 6.
45. Answer d. Chapter 4.
46. Answer b. Chapter 6.
47. Answer c. Chapter 8.
48. Answer a. Chapter 8.
49. Answer d. Chapter 10.
50. Answer b. Chapter 11.
51. Answer c. Chapter 1.
52. Answer a. Chapter 1.
53. Answer b. Chapter 3.
54. Answer d. Chapter 4.
55. Answer b. Chapter 10.
56. Answer c. Chapter 10.

57. Answer b. Chapter 10.
58. Answer a. Chapter 10.
59. Answer c. Chapter 10.
60. Answer b. Chapter 10.
61. Answer b. Chapter 6.
62. Answer c. Chapter 10.
63. Answer d. Chapter 1.
64. Answer c. Chapter 5.
65. Answer b. Chapter 5.
66. Answer c. Chapter 3.
67. Answer a. Chapter 4.
68. Answer b. Chapter 4.
69. Answer c. Chapter 12.
70. Answer a. Chapter 8.
71. Answer c. Chapter 9.
72. Answer c. Chapter 13.
73. Answer a. Chapter 11.
74. Answer b. Chapter 10.
75. Answer b. Chapter 10.
76. Answer d. Chapter 11.
77. Answer b. Chapters 8 and 9.
78. Answer b. Chapter 3.
79. Answer a. Chapter 3.
80. Answer b. Chapter 12.
81. Answer b. Chapter 3.
82. Answer d. Chapter 1.
83. Answer c. Chapter 3.
84. Answer a. Chapter 8.
85. Answer c. Chapter 8.
86. Answer a. Chapter 8.
87. Answer c. Chapter 8.

88. Answer a. Chapter 8.
89. Answer b. Chapter 9.
90. Answer b. Chapter 6.
91. Answer d. Chapter 6.
92. Answer b. Chapter 4.
93. Answer c. Chapter 10.
94. Answer a. Chapter 4.
95. Answer b. Chapter 4.
96. Answer b. Chapter 4.
97. Answer b. Chapter 4.
98. Answer b. Chapters 8 and 9.
99. Answer b. Chapters 9 and 10.
100. Answer a. Chapter 9.
101. Answer c. Chapter 9.
102. Answer c. Chapter 10.
103. Answer d. Chapters 5 and 9.
104. Answer c. Chapter 10.
105. Answer d. Chapter 9.
106. Answer d. Chapter 1.
107. Answer a. Chapter 8.
108. Answer b. Chapter 1.
109. Answer d. Chapter 12.
110. Answer c. Chapter 6.
111. Answer a. Chapter 13.
112. Answer b. Chapters 8 and 9.
113. Answer c. Chapter 10.
114. Answer b. Chapter 9.
115. Answer b. Chapter 1.
116. Answer c. Chapter 11.
117. Answer e. Chapter 1.
118. Answer c. Chapter 12.

119. Answer d. Chapter 9.

120. Answer d. Chapters 1 and 8.

121. Answer d. Chapter 12.

122. Answer c. Chapter 8.

123. Answer c. Chapter 8.

124. Answer d. Chapter 7.

125. Answer a. Chapter 4.

126. Answer a. Chapter 4.

127. Answer c. Chapter 6.

128. Answer d. Chapter 12.

129. Answer b. Chapter 12.

130. Answer a. Chapter 10.

131. Answer b. Chapters 3 and 12.

132. Answer b. Chapter 11.

133. Answer a. Chapter 6.

134. Answer a. Chapters 9 and 11.

135. Answer d. Chapters 9 and 11.

INDEX

Page numbers followed by italic *f* indicate figures.

CPSIA information can be obtained
at www.ICGtesting.com
Printed in the USA
BVHW011529110722
641546BV00004BA/29

9 780071 459112